SEABED HORRO...

Apollo faced the shark, presenting the
Megalodon with the smallest possible target. The
huge jaws opened again and the Megalodon set
himself an angled attack course, swimming up
and over the whale to bring his teeth to bear in a
raking slash across the widest part of Apollo's
body.

The Megalodon turned again towards the
target. This time, he had the ceiling and he swept
down on Apollo in a long dive that allowed him
to sense the whale no matter which way it
moved. He opened his glistening jaws again and
inclined his head in preparation for the ripping
bite that must follow.

The whale realized quickly that it had made a
bad mistake allowing the shark to get above it. It
jerked left and right and dived but it could feel
the gathering vibrations as the shark stayed on
its tail and the distance between them closed ...

Shark!

ROBIN BROWN

SPHERE BOOKS LIMITED
30–32 Gray's Inn Road, London WC1X 8JL

First published in Great Britain by
Michael Joseph Ltd 1981 under the title of *Megalodon*
Copyright © Robin Brown 1981
Published by Sphere Books Ltd 1983

Printed and bound in Great Britain by
Cox & Wyman Ltd, Reading

For Tiffany
Lisa
Victoria

1

Nine thousand feet beneath the shifting pewter surface of the Pacific Ocean, responsibility aboard the Ohio-class ballistic missile submarine *Jules Verne* had just shifted to the Green Watch and the direct command of the captain, James Tessler.

Tessler considered himself some inches too tall for the submarine service and he had a love of running that was out of context. But he commanded with tangible confidence, projecting the impression that to disobey his carefully enunciated orders would be more a case of stupidity than insubordination. It was generally agreed among the crew that they all felt safer with Tessler on the Green Watch, especially under present circumstances.

The *Jules Verne* was hard aground and, apart from the rattle and suck of her air scrubbers, blowers and filters, she was as silent as a corpse.

She squatted like a huge matt-black sea cucumber on a shelf of rock just wide enough for her considerable girth. Thirty feet of her bow protruded over an abyss that went down in shades of purple and midnight blue to an aching thirty thousand feet of high-pressure emptiness; the great undersea trench known as the Molokai Fracture Zone, three hundred and eight miles due southeast of the Hawaiian island group.

She had been squatting thus for nearly two weeks and it was driving Tessler quietly out of his mind. In that same time, he had discovered why he loved the submarine service. Its tensions, the demand for fast, complex decisions and the admittedly masochistic thrill of commanding the most sophisticated and lethal weapon ever built by man, were the stimulants of his metabolism.

Inanimate sea slugs pulsing laser beams that set your teeth on edge were somebody else's ball game. He stared stonily at the chart table and the static tracer arm of the Inertial Navigation System. He reviewed the banks of dials crowding the ship's System State board, but not a needle flickered. He ran his eyes hopefully along the lines of telltales monitoring the state of the pressure hull, the ballast tanks, master gyros, main motors, turbo generators, hydraulic power plants, missile compartments, boilers and, most important, the reactor.

All shone cheerfully green.

A buzzer sounded and he lifted the stubby in-ship phone eagerly. 'Galley, Captain. We have either steak or chicken tonight. And do you want a TV dinner or shall we set the ward room?'

Tessler sighed. 'I'll call down later, for a sandwich and coffee.' He hung up and sat at the chart table until he realized he was drumming his fingers and that he was being observed, with some compassion, by the helmsman.

'Steady as she goes, chief,' Tessler said sourly.

'Steady as she goes, sir ... as steady as a rock'. He paused. 'What have they got down there, skipper, that needs a fancy nuke to babysit it?'

'None of your business, chief.'

An electronic gong sounded once.

Tessler turned accurately towards the sound, a steel desk where Sonar Technician Williams sat before a large circular screen displaying shifting strobes of neon light.

'Contact,' said Williams without emotion. 'Zone Seven, range three miles. No sound signature ...' There was an appreciable pause. 'No sound at all.'

'What?' Tessler snapped. 'No engine? Check your phones.'

'Hydrophones fully functional,' Williams sang out, tapping his earphones. 'I'm getting everything else. Contact closing. Range two-and-a-half miles. Still no sound signature.'

'Say again!' Tessler barked. 'There has to be sound. And you say Zone Seven—that's virtually straight down! You have equipment malfunction.'

'Contact closing fast,' Williams continued irritably. 'No malfunctions indicated. I confirm Zone Seven ... Range now two miles.'

'How fast is fast, Williams?' Tessler cried, aware that his voice was rising. 'Hit him with the IFF.'

A radio operator touched a button and the International Friend or Foe Challenge was transmitted.

'Fast is thirty knots,' replied Williams, turning to look at Tessler for the first time. 'Range one-and-a-half miles and closing. Computer confirms we are the projected rendezvous.'

'Like hell we are,' Tessler snapped. 'The slightest vibration could nudge us off of here! Hello, *Eros*. Hello, *Eros*. Are you copying this?'

A tired voice came through the bridge speakers. 'Hello, Searcher. I'm copying your IFF and domestic transmissions but there's nothing on our sonar, over.'

'What the hell is that thing?' Tessler yelled. 'No engines, no sonar image topside ...!'

'We're between it and Zone Seven, skipper. They won't see it yet,' Hoskins said tersely. 'Shall I activate the visual monitors?'

'If you have enough light. Engine room stand by. Weapon systems, arm all chemical torpedos and evacuate the forward tubes.' Tessler turned to the large TV screen over the sonar desk. 'Where is it?'

'It's only three-quarters of a mile away, Skipper. But we just don't have enough light.'

Tessler glanced at his watch. Incredibly, less than three minutes had passed since first contact. He activated his command microphone a second time. '*Eros*, I'm declaring a Yellow State emergency. Incidentally, who am I talking to?'

'Hello, Searcher. Suskin, commander, signals. I acknowledge your declaration. But we still do not copy your contact.'

'You're up late, Eugene. Look, I need a pattern of quartz-iodide flares dropped as soon as you can arrange it, and that may be less than thirty seconds—confirm!'

'Confirmed, Searcher. Wait.'

'I can't wait long, sir. We need that light fast!'

Ten seconds passed, slow as drops of lead falling from a heated cauldron. Williams started calling the approach of the contact in thousands of yards.

'Searcher ... Suskin. Flares firing in ten ... now nine, eight, seven ...' Tessler and every other head on the bridge of the *Jules Verne* turned to the big television screen above the sonar console. It filled from the centre with light. In that silvery halo a projectile appeared, hurtling towards them.

'A ball?' Tessler queried. 'Like a fireball!'

'It's the flares,' Williams explained. 'They give a very brilliant image for just a few seconds. Unfortunately, they've exploded behind it ... but look, it's lengthening, probably turning. Skipper, it's big!'

'What's that?' Tessler rapped. 'That big central projection. Like a fin ... Has anyone put together a sub with a conning tower coming to a point? The hell with it, Williams. Range?'

'Eleven hundred yards, sir.'

'*Eros.* Copy. Condition Red. Permission to fire my forward tubes, confirming, conventional, I say again, conventional warheads.'

But the request came too late. The silver eye in the orb of electric brilliance winked. Suddenly the contact was gone. A moment's silence settled on the *Jules Verne* and then that silence was exploded as the contact, lifting out of the dark abyss, struck savagely at the submarine's bow.

In the chaotic thirty-six hours that followed, postmortems of every kind were conducted aboard the huge converted tanker *Eros*, mother ship to the *Jules Verne*. These examinations revealed, with one grand exception, everything that was required for official record and for the telegrams to next of kin.

The exception was a total dearth of information as to what had attacked the *Jules Verne*.

For the naval officers of middle rank aboard the *Eros* like the communications commander, Eugene Suskin, this period also provided them with their first real perspective as to the importance of the project with which they were involved.

In spite of the fact that the cause of the accident, or perhaps the shape of the enemy, remained unknown, Suskin found himself transmitting a coded message to Naval HQ, Pearl Harbor, requesting an urgent replacement for the *Jules Verne*. Suskin wondered how much Ohio-class nuclear submarines cost.

Suskin also transmitted, coded and this time scrambled, a further long signal to an office in the Pentagon which said in essence, 'Get us every kind of submarine detection facility that exists and to hell with the cost.'

In the Pentagon, the *Eros* signal was programmed into a

computer which, with virtually no human involvement, caused a number of anonymous oldish-youngish government men to board flights for destinations around the world.

The one who joined the midmorning Qantas flight, New York-Los Angeles-Honolulu, opened a bulky file as soon as he was airborne and started to read with no great interest.

Within minutes, his eyes were bulging with incredulity. When, some twelve hours later, he climbed into a battered truck labelled *'Institute of Marine Studies, Hawaii'* alongside a smiling round man of middle height and middle years with a shock of curly white hair and very red, rosebud lips, he was openly suspicious of the contents of the file, much of which related to this English academic.

'You are a most welcome person,' the garden gnome gushed. 'Whom do I have the pleasure of addressing?'

'James Vance, sir. Are you Professor Asquith?'

'Indeed, I am. Yes, you are most welcome. A little official recognition is just what we need.'

'I must say, sir, that I've read about the work of the Institute on the way down here and find some of it hard to believe.'

'A lot of people have that reaction, Mr. Vance. Never mind, it will all come right when you meet Doris. Now, we must get on, mustn't we? The call I received indicated that this was very urgent.'

'Very urgent,' Vance confirmed.

'The problem is,' Asquith said sadly. 'I've lost the ignition key.'

Vance reached under the dashboard, finding the necessary wires without difficulty. He turned to check that the gears were in neutral and caught Asquith studying him with a quizzical half smile. A key was dangling from his right hand.

'No bother. I've found them. Where did they teach you to do that, Mr. Vance?'

Vance, momentarily disconcerted, did not answer.

'And what exactly, Mr. Vance, would you like to see at the Institute?'

Thus the agent, Vance, did not meet Doris. Nor, somehow did he get to see anything of any importance at the Asquith Institute. He was relieved of his request, given a light lunch in a pleasant room overlooking a beach fringed with coconut trees, and driven by Asquith to the airport in time to catch the Pan Am flight back to L.A.

Harry Asquith went immediately to Number Four Lab, where Doctors Frank Acreman and Barbara Monday were swapping adjectives with Doris, and ordered Acreman to his office.

'You look like a cat that's just had a bath in cream,' Acreman observed with open suspicion. He was a tall, loose-limbed thirty-two-year-old. He looked healthy, kept his hair short and had to wear glasses. His most distinctive features were his eyes, a very light, clear blue and Barbara Monday thought it was a pity about the glasses. He had a Ph.D. in marine biology from Berkeley, backed up with a scholarship year at the Max Planck Institute, specializing in animal communication. He thought Harry Asquith was probably a genius and *knew* he was slightly irrational.

'Go and pack an overnight bag, Frank. I'll explain why on the way.'

Acreman grinned and sat down.

'You'll explain first. Then I might, just might, listen a little longer.'

'We've made it,' Asquith announced, savouring the words with a rotary movement of his little red lips.

'That's the name of a planet in a science fiction book I just read. Otherwise, as usual, what you've just said is meaningless.'

'The government urgently needs our help. They sent a man down all the way from Washington. There's a helicopter from Hopkins landing here in half an hour. We've made it.'

'You're getting warm, Harry.' Acreman nodded. 'That almost verged on coherence. What do they need our help for?'

'They've lost something. They need Doris.'

'They can't have Doris. What have they lost?'

Asquith beamed with triumph.

'A nuclear submarine.'

'Jesus,' said Acreman.

'Go pack your bag,' his boss instructed, no longer smiling.

'Right,' said Acreman.

The Navy helicopter took less than two hours to ship the pair of them from the Institute's backyard to the *Eros*. As they came in to land on the huge tanker, Acreman, an experienced diver, noted with wonder the almost black slick of water, denoting great depth, in which the ship was moored. He also noted the matt-black shape of the Ohio-class nuclear submarine tied alongside the tanker.

They were bustled without ceremony along a number of wide steel passages and down several steep flights of steps to a room occupied by about a dozen people, all of whom looked either irritated or uneasy.

Acreman was reminded of a hospital waiting room and was a little guilty when their names were called a few minutes later. He felt as if he were jumping a queue.

In an adjoining room, six men sat behind a long table cluttered with papers and large books. Four of these were in Navy uniform, amply endowed with gold braid. There was also a woman stenographer in Navy uniform. Acreman thought that the dark stockings were doing wonders for her legs and, from the way she had them crossed, she knew it.

The head of the group told them he was an admiral and that his name was Whitting. Having made this announcement, he looked at his watch.

'After the accident,' Whitting said wearily, 'we issued a non-specific request for aid from any relevant government-funded agency. We should, I confess, have been more specific. The purpose of this board is to assess the value of those who have responded to our appeal.'

'To sort out the wheat from the chaff,' Asquith suggested.

Whitting nodded.

I hope we're chaff, Acreman thought.

'I've been given some detail about the accident,' Asquith said. 'But your representative was unable to tell me anything about what caused it.'

Whitting frowned. 'If we knew that, Professor, we wouldn't need you. We've experienced a submarine collision involving one of our ships. We have to find the other object. You, apparently, have been receiving funds for the development of what are described here as original submarine search techniques.'

Asquith looked guiltily at Acreman.

'You mean Doris,' he said.

Acreman, who was watching Whitting's face, wished himself elsewhere. And to think that in certain circles, Harry Asquith had a formidable reputation as a political lobbyist and fund-raiser.

'Is that some kind of code name for your work?' Whitting asked.

'No, that's her real name. Her given name.'

He's enjoying himself, Acreman realized suddenly.

Whitting's voice dropped to a harsh whisper.

'Some of the people in the outside room have been here all day ...' He drew a deep breath. 'To the point, Professor. Who is Doris, and how can she help us?'

'Ah,' Asquith said. 'For that, I have to hand you over to Dr. Acreman.'

Acreman looked at the silent members of the panel and knew the despair of a condemned prisoner asked if he had any last word to say.

'Doris,' he said loudly and clearly, 'is a dolphin.' His clinical tone made no difference. With a sick sense of *déjà vu,* he watched the faces before him shift to that familiar mask of disbelief that had bedevilled his early career and had since forced him to accept the dangerous patronage of Harry Asquith. In his whole life, he had met only two people who had not worn the mask. One was a very old person, Dr. John Cunningham Lilly, the other was Professor Harry Asquith.

It was Lilly, a sometime guru to a small elite of the 60s, who had believed that the dolphin had a brain sophisticated enough for speech.

What the hell, Acreman decided. *Why should Harry have all the fun?*

'Doris is our *talking* dolphin,' he said with some pride, staring defiantly at Asquith. To his considerable surprise, his boss grinned approvingly; a grin very similar to the one he had given Acreman an hour or so after their first meeting. Acreman remembered that day very vividly ...

No dolphin had ever talked properly to John Lilly but, in a series of inspired books, he wrote of why he believed they eventually would, and what another intelligent, coherent animal on earth would do to and for the status of man, the naked ape.

Acreman had discovered the Lilly books during a period when he doubted whether he could qualify. From the start of his master's course, he had been aware that there was something radically wrong with the way man studied animals;

more simply, that these studies were largely designed to denigrate animals and so justify the excesses man allowed himself because of his so-called superiority.

Lilly presented the dolphin as a symbol. He proposed that this earthbound alien, famous for its grace, gentleness and intelligence, presented the human race with an evolutionary alternative. Man's elevated position in the natural kingdom was not dependent on superior power and aggression. An intelligent animal existed in the sea which had attained a similar high status by a totally different route.

It had also been on earth for fifty million years compared to man's meagre three.

Acreman revelled in the Lilly theory but realized eventually, as had Lilly in his time, that it would require more than a silent symbol to steer man away from his apparently inexorable imperatives. For the human race to accept the dolphin alternative, the animal would have to match man in the one area that man deemed himself unique.

The human race would listen, if the dolphins could speak.

Lilly had tried with limited success. Acreman studied his experiments and found fault only with the technology.

He heard of the Institute of Marine Studies—under the direction of the eccentric English academic, Professor Harry Asquith—during his year at the Max Planck Institute. One paper in particular—about how the electric fish of the Amazon basin communicate by varying their fields—had been drawn to his attention by those dour Austrian researchers. And Acreman fancied Hawaii.

When the time came for Acreman to return to the States, he bullied a programmer at the Delft Communication Theory Laboratory into producing a computer model of an electronic translator that could handle the full range of dolphin whistles and vocode them out as an ersatz humanoid voice. He labelled the machine 'Janus Major' in honor of John Lilly's original devices, and posted the proposal to Asquith.

Asquith's reply had come by cable. 'Intrigued by your gizmo. Come immediately.'

There was no mention of salary or travelling expenses. Acreman sold a much-loved guitar and left for Honolulu the following morning.

Harry Asquith met him at the airport or, more accurately,

Acreman found him after a good deal of searching, asleep in the airport parking lot behind the wheel of a cream vintage Bentley that Acreman calculated to be worth almost as much as the rickety charter he'd taken from Los Angeles.

On the way to the Institute, Acreman outlined his feelings about dolphins.

Asquith nodded with interest. 'We have some here, you know.' He turned the large car off the road. 'Would you like a bite to eat?' Asquith pulled into a burger drive-in. 'They have roller-skating waitresses here with huge tits.'

'I beg your pardon!'

'I've always wondered why they don't talk. Here she comes … will you look at that! So what's your answer?'

'I hate hamburgers.'

Asquith cast him a worried look and ordered six Big Macs and four milkshakes. Acreman wondered what the hell he had got himself into.

'Not that question,' Asquith said. 'It's really *better* if she's really loaded down. My assistants like hamburgers. I don't pay them much. They think working with marine mammals is … "significant". Why don't they speak?' he said looking at the waitress.

Acreman's head was buzzing but he took a deep breath and gave Harry an emotive answer because, the way the conversation was going, he didn't think he had much to lose. He regretted selling the guitar.

'Because we've been asking them to speak dinosaur. Just suppose that the natural dolphin language—dolphinese, if you like—is infinitely more sophisticated than ours. We know they transmit clicks that bounce off everything and can make very accurate readings of the echoes. We think they can read each other's echo messages. They may be exchanging three-dimensional messages like the bubbles in a comic strip. And, on top of that, they also whistle. We think the whistles are for emotional exchanges, if all you really need to know has already come back in an echo message. The whistles would be equivalent of us saying, "Good morning," or "Have a nice day." '

'But I still don't understand your reference to dinosaurs,' Asquith said, tearing his eyes reluctantly off the waitress weaving towards the car.

'I mean,' said Acreman quickly, aware that he had about a minute before he lost Asquith's attention altogether, 'that you can't expect an animal that already uses two information systems to revert to using something as simple as human speech. It would be as difficult as us trying to use the grunts of dinosaurs.'

'I like it,' Asquith said. 'Absolute rubbish probably, but original rubbish. You're hired.'

From then it had been, if not plain sailing, a kind of wind-surfing experience during which Acreman had come to like hamburgers, big-breasted waitresses, and Professor Harry Asquith.

He had accepted a file that very afternoon entitled 'Intersubmarine Communication Between Responsive Cetaceans.' It contained about twenty sheets of paper giving budget costs, addresses for copies of reports, chains of command, conditions of service and a page labelled 'Terms of Reference'. Summarized, this said that Acreman would—'Investigate the prospect of using dolphins with submarines as a cost-effective alternative to existing radio communication methods.'

Harry had stood proudly over Acreman while he glanced through the file and read the 'Terms of Reference'.

When Acreman went red and said, 'But that's absolute bullshit,' Harry looked extremely pained.

'I thought it was one of my better ones,' he said with obvious disappointment.

'Dolphins couldn't do it,' Acreman expostulated.

'Um,' said Harry. 'You've missed the point.'

'This is all nonsense,' Acreman went on, waving the file.

'Now you've got it!' Harry beamed delightedly. 'Make sure you memorize it! And at least once a month, lie in your bath and come up with half an hour's worth of severe problems. Our lords and masters will bother us about that often. Your lab is Number Seven. I've got a queue of assistants wanting to work with you. You seem especially significant. There's only one of them who's any good ... Miss Monday, even though she is rather a mean person.'

Acreman never worked out what Harry meant by Barbara Monday being a mean person. Barbara told him it was because she'd once told Harry to piss off when he had asked her for her personal measurements. But with her considerable help, and in spite of Harry's almost inexorable interference, Acreman had built the first primitive Janus machine in two months. He spent more money in that time than he had ever thought existed in science.

The Janus Major, then and now, was simply a translator.

It was not, however, a simple translator. Into the memory banks of the Institute's very large and very expensive computer, Acreman had programmed the ten miles of dolphin-sound tapes he had spent every minute since his college days compiling.

Harry had produced another three miles of tape, which were also inserted. When Acreman, having established the extraordinary quality of the tapes, asked where they came from, Harry had replied that he had picked them up somewhere. One of the tapes had an introduction in a foreign language. Acreman had asked what it was and Harry had replied, 'Russian.'

Equipped with this programme, the computer began to listen to the six dolphins living in a huge complex of pools on the seaward side of the Institute. Underwater cameras watched the dolphins day and night while the computer listened. Silicon chips opened and closed their invisible circuits and electronic ears and eyes compared notes. When a certain *action* could be allied with a certain *sound*, the computer allied it. After six weeks, a small green light lit up on Acreman's panel and, with a spasm of almost excruciating excitement, he pressed a key marked *'Hold'* and went running to find Barbara and, as an afterthought, Harry.

Above the control panel, there was a large television screen, and alongside, a speaker. Acreman pressed a button marked *'Replay'* and held his breath.

In slow motion, they played back a taped picture of the tank activity of the previous few moments, which included a recording of the sounds made by the dolphins. They watched a pair move in on a fish, squeal disdainfully and swerve away.

'That must be it,' Acreman said. 'Those sounds lock in with the green light we got from the computer. Okay, everyone cross your fingers. Barbara, let's have that sound tape through the vocoder.'

The sophisticated vocoder was the piece of equipment that had not been available to earlier researchers like Lilly. More properly named a 'voice decoder', it could turn alien sound signals into an electronic voice. The Janus computer had indicated with a green light that it could recognize the sounds the dolphins had made—that they could be matched to the English alphabet.

'Ready,' Barbara said.

Acreman nodded. 'Run it.'

The green light flashed on the Janus control. The vocoder spoke two words:

'Bad fish.'

Barbara grabbed Acreman and kissed him jubilantly. Acreman stared through the view port at the circling dolphins and said, 'Welcome.'

Harry Asquith asked: 'How on earth do they know?'

Acreman, filled now with a hot, almost sexual flow of fulfilment, commanded everyone to be silent. 'We have it one way. Let's see now if we can reach them from our end.' He called into the microphone.

'Tank Four—who's on watch up there?'

'It's me, Frank. Dave Spurling.'

'Dave, there's a rejected butterfish in the top end of your tank. Fish it out for me, please.'

'I think it's contaminated, Frank. I noticed they won't touch it.'

'Get it, Dave. Be careful.' The underwater camera showed a long-handled net descending into Tank Four.

'I have it.' Dave Spurling's voice betrayed his concern. 'I'm sorry, Frank. There's no real way of telling if they are bad.'

'Nobody's blaming you, Dave. Now listen carefully. Go to Tank Three ... that's Doris and Macho, right? When I tell you, dump that fish in there.'

'It's definitely bad, Frank. I just smelled it.'

'We're studying their reaction, Dave. Just do as I tell you.'

Acreman switched cameras to Tank Three, where the young male, Macho, and an older female, Doris, both *Tursiops truncatus* bottlenoses, were moving rapidly around their tank. These two were the most active and noisy in the Institute.

'I'm ready, Frank.'

Acreman punched the computer to '*Record*', the tape circuit to '*Standby Hold*', and his transmitter circuit to the point on the tape that had given him the green light.

'Let it go, Dave.'

The contaminated butterfish hit the water. The two dolphins reacted instantly to the foreign body entering their tank. They turned to investigate. Acreman stabbed his finger down on the '*Play*' button and the Janus machine demonstrated its other skill. '*Bad fish*' was converted into a thin, only slightly punctuated whistle which entered Tank Three by an underwater hydrophone.

The two dolphins stopped dead in their tracks and turned in bewilderment to the source of the sound.

Acreman's hand stabbed down again. A second time the dolphins reacted as if touched by a hot poker. They screamed with excitement and rushed madly round the tank, then slowed and approached the fish again. There was a thin scream from the loudspeaker. Acreman looked down at his control panel. The green light was on.

He turned to Harry with a glow of contentment.

'We've cracked it, Harry. They understand.'

'Um,' said Harry. 'Well ... I suppose congratulations are in order. Bottle of champagne in my office, I think.'

'Am I included in that?' Barbara demanded gleefully.

Harry looked at her T-shirt, which was heaving with uncontrolled excitement. 'Of course, my dear.'

As they left the lab, he added, 'I still don't understand how they can tell it's bad.'

'Does it matter?' Acreman demanded. 'You've just heard the first language exchange between man and dolphins. What's the matter with you, Harry?'

'I have an insatiable curiosity.' Harry sounded worried. 'It's often more irritating than my piles.'

From that time on it had not been easy, but progress was extraordinarily rapid. In the weeks that followed, the green light flashed continuously as the computer isolated an ever-expanding vocabulary of dolphin action/sounds.

The dolphins learned to expect confirmation from the computer.

After six months, Acreman and Barbara, working sixteen hours a day in two shifts, began to instruct Doris and Macho in the complexities of syntax and grammar. They used symbols linked to artificially manufactured sounds to teach interrogatives, negatives and positives. They stuck to the '*bad fish*' line as though it were the Rosetta Stone; wrapping it in questions and embroidering it with secondary meanings. '*Bad fish*' became 'It is bad fish', to 'Is it bad fish?' to 'It is not a bad fish.' They synthesized 'good' as a whistle and the Janus machine played games with dead butterfish. 'This is good fish.' 'This is a bad fish.' 'Find' had been one of the earliest natural sounds spotted by the computer, so 'Find the good/bad fish' became the first command sequence. Within a year, the dolphins had joyfully played themselves up to a language-under-standing employing a vocabulary in excess of six hundred words.

Acreman spent more and more time with the dolphins, mostly alone, often working deep into the night. Although their vocabularies were now extensive, there remained complex problems of understanding. Human examples were often totally useless and it took a long time for Acreman to adjust his thinking and his questions to matters which were not based on a specific human precedent. In the early hours of the morning, he sometimes approached a kind of meditative state in which he could conceive of the absolute size of the dolphin world and the freedoms that went with it. A listener would have found these exchanges strangely ethereal. Once Acreman had been found at dawn slumped in the dolphin control room after a nine-hour session which had explored the various meanings of just one word—'Space'.

'Dr. Acreman!'

Acreman returned from his reverie reluctantly. He was being addressed by one of the Navy people, the officer who had been introduced as Suskin, of communications.

'Dr. Acreman. We're all a bit stunned with what you've just said. I'm sure it's very significant. But there's an aspect of this that could be of more immediate importance. Don't the dolphins have a very effective sonar detection system?'

'Yes.'

The expression on Admiral Whitting's face altered fraction-ally.

'How effective?'

'They can get a clear impression of almost anything in the sea up to a mile away. We also have an *Orca*—a killer whale—who may be even better, but he's a very young animal and not up to describing that well what sonar images he's getting.' Acreman looked across the table. Several mouths were hanging open.

'Acreman ... would you seriously have us believe that you have dolphins and a whale that can give you detailed information?' Whitting spoke with exasperation. 'When you first referred to a talking animal, I naturally assumed you meant sounds of the type made by, say, parrots!'

'That's mimicry, not language. No, our animals can express themselves quite well.' Acreman allowed himself a slight smile. 'Especially Doris.'

'Okay,' Suskin broke in excitedly. 'Let's say one of these Dorises spots a metal object underwater at a mile distance. How much could it tell you about it?'

'*She,*' said Acreman with emphasis, 'could tell you its exact size to within one-millionth of an inch. She could tell you how fast it was moving through water. And reading variations of sonar echo one-thirtieth of a millionth of a second apart, she could tell you what kind of metal the object was made of, whether it was hollow or solid, or both.'

'Bravo,' said Harry Asquith.

'Holy shit,' said Suskin. He stared at Whitting. 'Admiral!'

'Would you two gentlemen mind waiting outside while we confer?' Whitting said uneasily.

They were called back less than ten minutes later.

'We'd like you to prepare an appropriate number of animals for shipment here,' Whitting said. 'What sort of facilities will you need?'

'Some form of on-board holding pool of sufficient size,' Harry Asquith said immediately. 'If you were to flood one of the tanks here, it would be ideal. Otherwise, it's a matter of simple provisioning, very easily arranged.'

Whitting nodded. 'I think I'd best be on record as having severe reservations about all this, Professor. But our communications officer is impressed with the detection abilities you claim for your animals, so we will give you a try.' He paused. 'That puts you in a different security category and out of my hands. Do you have any good reason for not being able to proceed directly from this vessel to our Project administration office in Washington? We'll arrange transport.'

Asquith smiled. 'Not so long as you're footing the bill, Admiral.'

'So be it. Dr. Acreman, we have a helicopter shuttle going back up the islands in a little over two hours. And now, if you'll excuse me, I have a submarine to inspect.'

Acreman could never remember afterwards what caused him to make the request.

'Is that the submarine that was hit?' Whitting nodded over the papers he was collecting together.

'Could I take a look at the damage?'

'What purpose would that serve?'

'I might be able to tell you what hit it and give my animals some indication of what to look for. The sea's a very big place, with a lot of things in it.'

Whitting cocked an eyebrow.

'But how could you do that?'

'There must be some traces from a collision of that force. Organic, or more likely inorganic, traces. Certain crustacea only exist in certain parts of the world. A submarine based in Pearl would have a very different accretion to one based, say, in the Baltic.'

'It wasn't another submarine,' Whitting said dryly. 'That much I can assure you. But your suggestion has merit so long as you confine your interest to the exterior of the hull and remember, in any event, that you are now bound by the most stringent security regulations.'

Acreman and the Navy inspection team were lowered on to the hull of the *Jules Verne* by helicopter. The sea was a surging, angry grey and even the black metal deck seemed a very insubstantial platform as they hovered over it. Wearing a safety harness, Acreman dropped four feet onto the slippery, wet surface, where he was grabbed by two sailors who immediately clipped his line to a rail running down the centre of the deck. When the three members of the Navy team had been similarly deposited, they followed an officer in oilskins down the long length of pitching HY-80 steel, past twenty-four Trident One missile tube caps, to the damaged bow section.

At first glance, Acreman thought it was an optical illusion. The *Jules Verne*'s bow appeared to have been bent slightly sideways. Where this apparent deviation began, there was a series of shiny impressions in the hard metal. Some of these were more like deep scratches, but others in the deck were definite puncture marks. They marched across the metal, down out of sight on the port side, like an indented necklace.

Several of the indentations had sharp edges that had caught strands of green and brown seaweed. Acreman was down on his knees near the curve of the port side collecting a weed sample when a flash of white in a hole just over the edge caught his eye.

'Loosen my line and hold on,' he instructed one of the sailors. 'I have to reach out here.'

With the blade of his penknife, he picked at the object which filled quite a large hole until suddenly it came loose and he just managed to catch it. Conditions were too hazardous for an immediate examination, so he put it in a plastic sample bag and continued his inspection of the rest of the bow. But apart from the necklace of indentations and the fact that the forward thirty feet of the submarine was definitely out of line, he found nothing else of interest.

Back on the *Eros*, he sought out Suskin, who had seemed the most sympathetic character around and asked whether there was anywhere he could examine his samples. Suskin told him that the ship had been converted for marine research and there was a biology laboratory on the bridge deck.

'I don't think the lab's manned though,' Suskin said. 'I never did see anybody in there on this trip. You've been booked on the shuttle in an hour. Your boss has already left. He said to tell you that he'd be in touch and that you should start getting your animals ready.'

Acreman found the bridge and eventually the laboratory, which looked as though it had not been used for months. He examined the weed samples under a low-power microscope and found they were all local. He turned to the object in the plastic bag. It was larger than he remembered, about four inches across the base, rising to a blunted triangle about three inches high. Acreman stared at it a long time, studied the base under the microscope lamp, sniffed it, then laid it down carefully on a cork pad. He went to the bookshelves and began to go through several thick zoological references. When he found what he was seeking he took the book across to the bench and compared a photograph with the white shard. Then he measured the shard very carefully, using a micrometer, and compared these measurements with a table in the book.

When a young officer of Suskin's team came to tell him to

make his way to the helicopter pad, Acreman was seated at the bench, breathing deeply and looking pale.

'Are you all right, sir?'

'Yes ... yes, I'm fine. Perhaps I shouldn't take the shuttle right away. Could I get a few words with Commander Suskin?'

'I am afraid you can't at the moment, sir. He just flew off to Pearl to supervise delivery of a new bank of sonar transmitters they're shipping out here.'

Acreman got to his feet, carefully picking up the shard which he had returned to its packet, and made his way thoughtfully up to the helicopter deck. He sat in silence throughout the flight home and could only manage a distracted ''Lo, Dave,' for the assistant who came for him in the truck.

When they arrived, he said, 'Will you find Barbara for me and ask her to come see me in our lab?'

'It's after nine o'clock, Frank.'

'Tell her it's really important, please.'

Barbara Monday arrived in a long dressing-gown some fifteen minutes later, her hair rolled in a towel. She was carrying a plate of fruit, cheese and a half-empty bottle of white wine.

She walked over to Acreman and kissed him on the cheek.

'Dave says you might have had a hard day.'

'More than that.'

'Harry been chewing on you?'

'Worse maybe even than that.' She shook her head sympathetically, pouring wine into a big glass. 'Drink.' Acreman did as he was told. She leaned over the desk to hand him the food, aware that the action allowed the gown to open and reveal the pale orbs of her small high breasts.

He smiled at her and reached forward lightly to stroke the soft down on her tanned face. 'Concentrate. I have to call Harry urgently. Before I do, I need a second opinion.'

She made a face and settled into a chair, pulling the gown together at the neck.

'Yes, Doctor.'

Acreman showed her the white shard. Barbara's qualifications as a biologist were more academic than his own and, in addition, she had a degree in chemistry. He also handed her a small glass dish of white powder.

'I just ground it,' he explained. 'Ahead of a proper analysis, can you give me a first impression? More important, is it live material, as opposed to fossilized?'

She looked at the shard carefully, holding it against the bright desk lamp, then dipped a finger in the powder and tasted it.

'Yuk!'

'Live?'

'Yes, it is certainly not a fossil.'

'Have you any idea what it is?'

'Oh, come on, Frank, it's much too late for guessing games. If you want that kind of an opinion, I'll have to work on it. At first glance, if that's what you're after, I'd say it was a broken shark's tooth, but that's ridiculous.'

'Why?'

She stared at him incredulously. 'Because of the size!'

He pushed an open copy of Commander Richard Perry's *The Unknown Ocean* across the desk to her. 'Read that.'

'Aloud?'

Acreman nodded.

Barbara cast him a questioning glance but proceeded to read the reference he had marked.

' "Photographs of a fish, possibly a shark, between twenty and thirty feet in length, have been taken at a depth of more than six thousand feet in Southern California and there must be numbers of unknown species of sharks in the deeps ..." '

'That's right,' Acreman broke in. 'A Portuguese shark was found trapped in weed in nine thousand feet and the crew of the bathyspere *FRNS-3* saw sharks at thirteen thousand feet off Dakar in 1954. I just double-checked.'

'So what, Frank? What's this got to do..?'

'Read on a while.'

Again she stared at him, then set her lips and complied. ' "There is no reason why the giant shark, *Carchardon Megalodon*, may not still survive. Indeed, it may be a more likely survivor than the living-fossil fish, *Coelacanth* ..." '

'They've found several of those off South Africa,' Acreman broke in again. 'Go on to the bit about fossil shark teeth.'

'Frank,' she protested weakly.

'Please! I have to memorize this for Harry.'

'Okay. "*Carchardon Megalodon*—the manganese deposits on the teeth of this shark, dredged up from the red clay bottom at depths approaching fifteen thousand feet in the South Pacific, suggest that their owners may still have been in existence after the last Ice Age. Megalodon probably belonged, or belongs, to the same genus as the Great White Shark, which still survives in warmer seas throughout the world and is itself a fearsome creature, reaching lengths of more than thirty-six feet. Armed with appalling serrated and triangular teeth two-and-a-half inches high, the latter can chop up an animal as large as a sea lion. Since the Megalodon teeth recovered were more than twice that size, it has been asserted that this monster must have been at least ninety feet long … " ' She stopped reading abruptly.

'That's it, Frank,' she said irritably. 'That's enough. You know I don't subscribe to that "fearsome, appalling, monster" stuff!'

'Neither do I, but apart from the adjectives, the biology is accurate. He goes on to point out that because sharks have skeletons of gristle or cartilage instead of bone, we don't find fossil bodies, and that the only way we'll prove that the Megalodon still lives is by coming across a beached carcass.'

Barbara said dryly, 'Or unless someone comes up with a living tooth.'

'Right.'

'Oh, come on, Frank,' she cried. 'What's happening to you? You don't normally go in for wild speculation!'

Acreman shook his head slowly. 'Nor would I on this occasion, were it not for the fact that, at this moment, Harry is committing us to take Doris, and Macho and probably Morgan, out there to look for whatever it is.'

Her eyes blazed and the colour went out of her cheeks. She stared down at the white shard.

'What are you waiting for, Frank? Stop him!'

2

Harry Asquith sat in an office deep inside the Pentagon. The walls were a drab grey colour. A reproduction of President Reagan's portrait hung near the entrance. A secretary in a long floral print dress with a high neckline, her hair in two puffy plaits, was seated behind a pristine IBM golfball typewriter. She had been smiling fondly at Harry for a good thirty seconds when she said abruptly, 'It won't be long now.'

Harry, who had been wondering whether the homely appearance belied hidden sexual potential, flushed with embarrassment until he realized the reference was not to himself. He looked hurriedly away at the portrait of Reagan.

The girl, noting his interest, said confidentially, 'He is handsome, isn't he? He's a real hero of Hopi's. They used to play golf together in California.'

'Hopi?' Harry queried tentatively, wondering whether the U.S. War Room could finally have fallen to that once magnificent tribe of Indians.

'General Hope Ward, Professor. He'll be taking your interview.' The phone rang. She listened, frowned and held out the receiver. 'It seems it's for you, Professor.'

Harry took the phone rather reluctantly. The girl said, 'You'd better answer it.'

Harry put it to his ear, recognized Frank Acreman's voice and listened in silent relief. For a while.

'Say that *all* again, Frank ... slowly!'

A few minutes later, he added, 'Yes, of course I'm taking you seriously, but what more can I say? I have to think about it. Here's what I want you to do. Photograph it, go to the all-night post office on Waihine Street and telex them to me here. To the office of General Hope Ward. The animals? I think you should go ahead with your essential travel arrangements. We

28

are under starter's orders, old chap. What? Fine, I'm fine ... they keep very late hours here.'

He handed back the phone.

'What time is it, Miss?'

'Six p.m., Professor.'

'Good Lord, it's nearly nine o'clock where I come from.'

The door to the inner office opened. A vast form in hairy tweed jacket, baggy cords and thick mountain boots filled the gap.

'You're General Hope Ward,' Harry said confidently.

'You're Asquith,' said Hope Ward as though he had just discovered a new species of Arthropod. 'Come in, Professor. Okay, Mandy, you finally get to make that tea you've been hoarding.'

The inner office was as spartan as a basketball court. Hope Ward's huge desk filled one wall. Behind it hung a tattered Old Glory on a brass pole. On the facing wall, Harry saw a map of the Pacific with the Molokai Fracture Zone ringed in red pins.

'By the way, Professor. You don't call me "General". I'm on civilian allocation.'

'But the project is military? I was not aware of that.'

'Not really. We're State and the Department of the Interior, if anybody asks. But because of the project's security status, we're based here and we have a substantive military complement. It's necessary.'

Mandy swept in with a tray containing two small cups in which brown sachets lay torpid. Hope Ward took a swig.

'I'll be damned, Professor, if I know how you drink that stuff. I'm a coffee addict myself!'

'Actually,' said Harry to the girl's retreating back 'I'm also ...'

'You drink the damn tea, Professor,' Hope Ward interrupted. 'Otherwise, I'm going to have to.'

When the girl returned with the coffee, she also carried a set of telex photographs. Harry took them eagerly and examined them with great care.

'Are you still with me, Professor?'

'Sorry.' Harry looked up.

'Trouble?'

'I don't know. Shall we do our business first?' Hope Ward nodded and pressed an intercom switch. Vance came into the office, moving directly across the room to take a seat. Harry watched him closely, drawing on his considerable abilities as an anthropologist. The smile was too fixed, the Ivy-league blazer and slacks too neat. They did not properly disguise a face that was thin and latently tense, tiny crow feet showing as white lines in the suntan around the eyes, or the way the hair was combed carefully forward to hide a receding hairline. Least of all Harry liked the empty blue eyes. He had an almost irresistible urge to snap his fingers in front of Vance's face to see whether the grin or the eyes would shift.

'You know James Vance, Professor. He'll be looking after security out on the *Eros* now that things have gotten a little messy there.'

Harry started to feel very uneasy, but nodded.

'We called you up here, Professor, because yours is a civilian outfit that's about to get involved with a project under military supervision. You have to have a security clearance and, as Vance is heading your way and you know each other, I thought we could kill two birds with one stone.'

'What birds?' asked Harry weakly.

'He has to give your place a look over and take a quick peep at your personnel files.'

Vance smiled and nodded. Harry was reminded of a nodding dog car mascot. 'Just routine, Professor.'

Harry made a quick calculation of the Institute's assets and next year's cash flow forecast. Neither required more than a few seconds' consideration. He sighed.

You are probably well aware, Harry thought, *that I can't foot the bill and that every political instinct in me is screaming 'pay dirt'.* The photographs caught his eye. He succumbed.

'I accept your conditions,' he croaked. 'What exactly is the *Eros* doing that is causing you to go to such trouble?'

'And expense, Professor. Isn't that what you mean?' Hope Ward grinned knowingly. 'It's a mining survey.'

Harry blinked. 'In the deepest marine trench in that part of the world? That's ridiculous!'

'You obviously know your geography, Professor, but not your geology, I suspect. That's my field when I am wearing my other hat ... Corps of Engineers. And I'm surprised to hear you, an Englishman, make that kind of judgment.'

'What's being English got to do with it?'

'Didn't they say that about North Sea oil—that it was difficult to get at?'

'You've found oil out there? Even so, it's ten times deeper than the North Sea.'

Hope Ward nodded. 'So whatever it is that's down there has got to be ten times more valuable than oil. You're getting warm.'

Harry threw up his hands. 'Gold ... uranium?'

'Very good, Professor. Both. Go on like that and you'll get Mr. Vance here real worried.'

Harry looked again at the photographs. Reluctantly, he said, 'It might be more difficult to get at than you think.'

Hope Ward shook his head. 'You haven't realized the implications of what's down there. We think we have the equivalent of the Witwatersrand basin in South Africa; massive quantities of andesitic and rhyolithic volcanic quartz with the gold in quartz-pebble conglomerates and, as they have on the Rand, pebble-grain uranite. That's the uranium. We found that first, or really, it found us. One of our geophysical survey vessels reported a wide band of radioactivity along the length of the Molokai Fracture.'

Harry found the courage to pick up one of the photographs. 'Even so ...'

But Hope Ward had been caught by gold fever.

'The Witwatersrand deposits are ten kilometres thick and they produce up to thirty-one grams of gold to the ton, not counting the uranium. Up to now they've produced three-quarters of all the gold that the world has ever seen, and there's probably as much more to come!

'We think there's as much as that and more down that hole in the sea, but we don't know for sure yet. That's what the sub's for. It has laser equipment that will map the lodes and the depth of the ore bed. We already know it's very rich, but we have to know how rich if we're to consider mining it.'

'And only a submarine can do your survey,' Harry said.

'How do you know that?'

'Deduction,' said Harry.

'You're right. The equipment has a limited range. Nobody ever saw the need to build anything that would work down through forty thousand feet of sea and rock. The sub is just a sunken work platform for the gear.'

'But essential,' said Harry.

'Sure.'

Harry handed Hope Ward a photograph.

'I'm sorry to do this to you, General, but you have more of a problem than you realize.'

'What is this?'

'It was removed from the bow section of the *Jules Verne* by my assistant, Dr. Acreman. He telexed these photographs at my request.'

'What the hell is it?'

'A section of living dontal material.'

'Dontal—you mean dental … a tooth?'

'A somewhat large tooth, I think you might agree.'

'Okay … so?'

'Dr. Acreman thinks it may be the tooth of an extinct species of shark, the *Carchardon Megalodon*.'

'I still don't get your point, Professor.'

'It would be a very large shark, sir.'

Hope Ward took the other photographs and examined them carefully.

'Professor, am I missing something here, or do you have a purpose I don't know of for being cryptic?'

'It may have attacked the *Jules Verne!*'

Hope Ward leaned back in his chair and grinned.

'Oh, really!'

'Yes, really,' Harry said crossly. 'I know it may seem fantastic, and I accept that the evidence is speculative. But I felt it was my duty to …'

Hope Ward leaned forward and said reassuringly, 'Come on, Professor. Calm down. I can only say I'm delighted!'

'What! You believe … ?'

'Oh, I don't know whether I believe you. You're going to have to come up with a little more evidence than these snapshots. But if you're right—hell, that's fantastic. I can't tell you the relief that brings me. I've been sitting in this office wondering whether it was a Soviet vessel, or maybe Chinese and that they had made some incredible breakthrough that allowed them to run completely silently and were invisible to sonar. Can't you see what a frightening prospect that could be?'

'This animal could be one hundred feet long—and lethal!'

'Great! *I'm* talking about the power balance of the Western world, Professor. Do you not know the firepower of the Ohio-class subs? They could handle a shark that stretched all the way from here to Peking.'

'You won't listen.'

'Hell, I'm all ears, Professor. I'll back you right down the line. If you can prove to the satisfaction of me and my superior that this was a shark attack, I'll see your Institute doesn't have to worry about funding for the rest of the century. That's a promise.'

Harry got shakily to his feet. 'I'm not altogether sure I can persuade my colleagues to expose our cetaceans to such a risk.'

'Then it could get hungry down your way. You'll understand I don't have time to be diplomatic. And there's another thing, Professor. I don't want any of your bleeding-heart liberals jumping on the ecology bandwagon. We don't want frogs taking priority over dams like happened at Athabaska, if you take my point. That could be dangerous. The ecology lobby has a lot of pull. Sharks I can handle. Just make sure they don't get turned into heroes at your end. Right?'

Harry said nothing. He felt peculiarly angry and nauseous, not least with himself. 'Anyway,' said Hope Ward. 'You'll have Vance to help you.'

In the first light of dawn, Acreman began to thrash about in a way that brought sleepy protests from his companion. He slipped from the bed and went out onto a beach that was tinting coral pink, peach and gold.

The coconut trees cut neat silhouettes in a strawberry and vanilla sky. The wind off the sea was distinctly musical.

Every morning Acreman took an early swim and the special beauty and tranquillity of the dawn had never failed to calm him. This morning it seemed to contain an echo of menace. *Is this how Adam felt*, Acreman thought, *when he first noticed there was a snake in the tree?*

He heard footsteps and turned to watch Barbara coming down the beach, her thin cotton wrap reduced to a shifting pastel veil by the wind and the rapidly changing light. Acreman held out his hand and she took it silently. They walked towards the sea until Acreman stopped and pointed.

'What is it, Frank?'

'I thought I saw … No, maybe not. A trick of the light.'

'A shark?'

'No.'

She gripped his hand.

'I think you should keep away from the sea today. Go and talk to Doris. She won't stand any of this nonsense.'

Acreman grinned. 'Right. But let me know the moment Harry gets back.'

He watched her leave and then walked the subterranean corridors to the big open pool where Doris and Macho and a group of young initiates were working.

'Good morning,' said Doris as he entered.

They had replaced the television monitors with two huge, four-inch-thick glass portals and Acreman suffered a moment of disorientation. It was difficult to rid himself of the impression that *he* was in a tank, rather than the dolphins: even harder to accept that they both were.

'Morning, Doris,' he mumbled.

'Morning. Are you angry?' asked Doris casually through the vocoder, sliding up to the window.

'What?'

'Did you hear me?'

'Sure, I heard you. How do you know, I feel ... angry?'

Doris waggled her silver head. Acreman knew her well enough to know that this was her communicating the nonverbal signal, 'I'm thinking.' He waited.

'There are two ways of knowing,' the dolphin announced eventually. 'One is easy, the other I have just learned.'

'I do not even understand the easy one,' said Acreman. Doris and Macho, the two most advanced dolphins, could just about handle English short-forms like "I've" or "Don't" but they tended to avoid them and Acreman tried to keep his speech formal. He suspected their natural communication was much more mathematical and precise than English. But it still made their exchanges sound stilted.

'The easy one,' Doris said, 'is that a *happy* Acreman says, "Good morning, Doris." The angry—possibly, unhappy— Acreman says "Morning." A different phrase, yes?'

'Neat,' said Acreman.

'No, "Morning",' Doris corrected. 'What's *"neat"?*'

'It is a compliment.'

'Thank you.'

'You said there were two ways of telling I was angry. What is the other?'

'*Happy*, you look at me and wave a hand. *Unhappy*, not.'

'Very neat.'

'Very?'

'A bigger compliment.'

'Examples, please?'

Acreman shook his head ruefully.

'Hey, Doris, did you have your breakfast yet? My head hurts.'

'No. The people are all still asleep. Are you ill?'

'No. I am worried.'

'You have an unhappy brain.'

Acreman grinned. 'That's very good, too, Doris. Yes, I have an unhappy brain.'

'Take a small white pill.'

'I will. Say, Doris, do dolphins get unhappy brains—get worried?'

'Yes. A lot.'

'Examples, please?'

'You said your head hurts.'

'It is getting better. What things worry you?'

'Not things, Acreman. No things.'

'I don't understand.'

'Emptiness. No others. Nothing days.'

'Loneliness? Being on your own?'

'Yes,' said Doris. 'Also emptiness.'

'I don't understand.'

'Emptiness of the head.'

'I understand,' said Acreman. 'We call the first loneliness; the second, boredom.'

'Is that why you have an unhappy brain?'

'No,' Acreman paused. 'I have that thing you cannot understand.'

Doris waggled her head for a moment.

'Fear?'

'Yes.'

'Acreman, why do we not understand fear?'

'I think it is because of the way you have grown,' Acreman said carefully. 'We humans grew another way. We had to kill other apes to find space to live. Sometimes one group killed

35

and lived, sometimes they were killed. It was never sure. Not to be sure that you will go on living makes fear. You have all the sea, which is seven times larger than the land. You have always had much room. You have never killed for room or lived with others who will kill you. You did not grow fear. I think that is it. Do you understand?'

'Much,' said Doris. 'Not all. I have no fear, so it is hard to understand your fear. Like water, remember?'

Acreman grinned. He recalled the morning Barbara had tried to describe to the dolphins that they lived in a heavy viscous substance that was lethal to man. The dolphins had looked around their tank in amazement and asked as a group: 'Where?'

'You may get to know fear by being with us,' Acreman said. 'Doris, I must go and have my breakfast. It will help my head.'

'I have to work anyway,' said Doris.

'What are you doing today?'

'Inspecting aircraft engines for faults in the metal castings.'

'That's a very good sentence, Doris!'

A line of bubble lifted out of the dolphin's blow hole. *Laughter?* Acreman wondered.

'It is not mine. It is what Dave *said* I was doing. *I* am looking through these things for spaces.'

Acreman smiled.

'Did you find any spaces yet, Doris?'

'They all have spaces.'

Acreman's eyebrows lifted.

'I understood they were all new engines!'

Again the bubbles as the dolphin waggled her head. Acreman knew a lot about the immense sophistication of dolphin sonar pulses. Forty years ago, Dr. Woods had proved they could easily tell the difference between various metals. But it was also accepted that no human knew exactly how sophisticated that sonar could be. The best pointer had been a Dutch experiment in which it was revealed that dolphins could read a secondary sonar echo off a hollow sphere which was returning one-thirtieth of a millionth of a second slower than the echo from a solid sphere of identical size. When Doris spoke of 'spaces', meaning cracks, no human could tell how fine they might be. Acreman wondered, however, how

36

the aircraft manufacturers who were paying for this piece of work would react to the suggestion that all their brand-new engines were full of 'spaces' in dolphin terms.

'Did Dave tell you what size of "space" we are interested in?'

'Those that your instruments could see.'

'How many of those have you found?'

'None.'

Acreman paused. He was intrigued. He knew that their progress with language had been rapid but was constantly aware that getting proper information from the dolphins was increasingly not just a question of language.

They were entering a ghostly area where the dolphins were trying to describe things of which man had no knowledge.

'Example, Doris? Can you tell me what you see? What do the spaces look like?'

Doris paused for a long time.

'When Dave cleans the pool, if things that are wrong fall in, he uses a net. Your fishing people use nets. Understand?'

'I understand.'

'It is like a net. But very small. And not so well made.'

'You see a metal engine casting like a fine, broken net!' Acreman cried, astonished.

'Yes, Acreman.'

Acreman thought about it. 'Don't tell Dave that, Doris. Stick to the spaces we can see with our equipment.'

'Why, Acreman?'

'You might bring world aviation to a standstill,' Acreman grinned.

'Aviation … ? Standstill … ?'

The phone rang.

'Excuse me, Doris,' Acreman said reluctantly.

'Frank, it's me. You're not going to believe this!' Acreman grinned. 'After the conversations I've just been having, you could be wrong.'

'Harry's back! He's just sitting in his office. From the looks of it, I would say he's been there since the early morning.'

Acreman breathed deeply for several seconds.

'When Harry gets devious, it's trouble. Can you come and take over here?'

'Yes … and, Frank, be careful. There's a foreign body in the administration office going through the personnel records with Frederickson. Fred looks frightened as a rabbit.'

Acreman grinned. 'Maybe it's time you came and talked to Doris.'

'Gladly. Tell her I'm on my way.'

Acreman found Asquith ostensibly asleep behind his ornate desk, a creaky New Orleans copy of a Louis XIV secretaire; his white track shoes resting on its leather inlay. It was the position of the plimsolls on that treasured surface that convinced Acreman that Harry was playing possum.

'Oh, come on,' he snapped.

Harry opened one eye, glanced at his wall clock and straightened reluctantly.

'Must have nodded off. Been burning the midnight oil here, Frank. What are you doing up so early? I hope you haven't turned into one of those lunatic jogger people. Have you ever studied their faces? Roving epilepsy.'

'Harry, what's going on! Did you tell them?'

Asquith sighed.

'I told them you'd found a giant shark, if that's what you mean.'

'And.'

'And I must say they took it very well.'

'Took it … you mean they accepted the prognosis?'

'Hook, line and sinker,' Harry grinned.

'So they're pulling their ships out. We can stand down.'

'I am afraid not.'

'What! Don't they appreciate the possible danger?'

'Nope.'

'Do you?'

'I pass.'

'I don't believe this … '

'Then let me put it another way,' said Asquith. 'Firstly, sit down. You just exceeded the amount of shouting you're allowed to do in my office. You have *not* found a Megalodon shark. Is that specific enough?'

Acreman sat down. He felt sick and empty.

'You just told me the ship people accepted the finding, Harry!'

'They're still accepting the Domino Theory. Listen, Frank. I don't believe you can build the largest organism in the history of the world out of a shard of dental material, any more than I would allow you to build Eve out of Adam's rib. How is Miss Monday, by the way?'

'Fine. Will you stick to the point?'

'The point is, Frank, that you … we … have been presented with a heaven-sent chance to investigate the possibility that a unique and fascinating species, erstwhile considered extinct, may still exist. We will have every facility this great nation can provide, no expense spared. Your surface support will be the luxury of a giant tanker and your investigation will be staged from a nuclear submarine …'

'But …'

'No buts, Frank. Couple all that with the fact that you have developed a marine search facility the like of which the world has never seen before and I think one is forced to conclude that fate …'

Acreman held up a limp hand, palm out.

'Okay, Winston, I get the message. We fight them on the beaches, right?'

'The helicopter that brought me here is waiting on the lawn. There's another on its way for the animals.'

Acreman nodded. 'Just do me one favour, Harry. If Barbara should ever talk to you about this interview, tell her I argued real hard.'

Asquith allowed himself a few moments of warm self-congratulation after Acreman left, then he remembered that the visit had interrupted an important chore. He picked up the microphone of his dictation machine. The red light still glowed.

He reflected on the use of the malapropism as an important tool of politics, then resumed his dictation.

' … and so, George, I give advance notice, before being expressly forbidden by the dead hand of officialdom, that my Institute may find itself a reluctant party to a rare-species tragedy. On the basis of our long personal friendship, I hope the National Ecology Trust will accept the role of my ace in the hole … no, strike that, Miss Watson … of being my ethical insurance.'

Harry grinned and wondered whether Hope Ward played poker. It was not Harry's game. But as a whist player, he had been famous for his prescience and he still believed that he rarely missed a trick.

He dialled Mrs. Smith's. It was the only whorehouse on the island open at this hour. 'Do you think Betty might fancy a few early-morning push-ups, Mrs. S.? Breakfast? Good Lord, what a splendid idea! Eggs Florentine with melba toast, lox and a bottle of Moet '75.'

Then, on his way out, he stepped into his library and checked 'Witwatersrand' in an English/Afrikaans dictionary, finding, as he suspected, that it translated as 'Race of white water'. Harry smiled contentedly. He read the *I Ching* most days and found consolation in omens.

3

Acreman found Barbara Monday and explained the situation to her. She insisted Acreman eat breakfast and told him the weather forecast was terrible.

'I don't think it's a good day to go.'

Acreman told her he did not think he could stand being around Harry Asquith in his present mood; that if they didn't go today he might decide not to go at all and, generally, that he suspected their involvement in the business going on around the *Eros* was a mistake.

'So why are you going on with it?'

He thought while listlessly munching a slightly burned English muffin, then admitted that he wanted to establish the truth about the Megalodon.

Barbara, growing impatient, said he sounded like Captain Ahab. 'It's not Moby Dick, you know. It hasn't actually done anything to you!'

Acreman hadn't thought about that aspect of it. He had his own considerable reservations about man's inexorable inquisitiveness. Eventually he admitted to himself that, right or wrong, he couldn't leave things as they were.

'Quite apart from our interest,' he concluded, 'we can't let them send any more vessels down until our animals have looked the place over. That could be suicidal.'

Barbara shrugged and went off without further comment. Acreman went upstairs to see two Navy helicopters from Hopkins Field murdering the Institute's palm thicket on the front lawn. The wind was blowing like a knife and he ducked inside and phoned the Seismic Sea Wave Warning Station in Honolulu.

'I want to fly two dolphins and an orca out to the Molokai Fracture Zone today. We have a wind that seems to be trying

41

to become a hurricane. Will we make it?' He was told that the wind was westerly and that provided they flew east of the islands they would be all right. Sea conditions were rugged in the Zone but not impossible.

'How long is it likely to last?'

'If you need to go, go now. We're forecasting a three-day blow and there's a lot of rain to come. It's going to get a lot worse before it gets any better.'

Acreman gave himself a moment to consider the state of his head if he had to spend four days worrying about what the Megalodon might be up to, then set out for the dolphin pools at a run. Halfway across the lawns, he saw the wide doors to the pool entrance swing open and the spiderlike structure of the boat-lift crawl out towards the helicopters. The lift had been adapted for this purpose and he saw the two dolphins in slings hanging between the lift's ten-foot-high wheeled legs. Barbara emerged behind the lift with a wide-gauge hose gushing water. She walked alongside the lift, spraying the animals continuously.

'I knew you'd go,' she said. 'I think you should be careful, Frank. Harry knows what strings to pull.' She told him that she'd packed a suitcase of clothes for the two of them. Acreman went to collect it and by the time he got back, both dolphins along with the orca, Morgan, were resting in their slings in the big chopper's cargo bay. The pilot was a regular who'd flown animals for them before.

'How long is this going to take?'

'About three hours. I'll hug the east coast as far as the Alenuiha Channel. Then we'll head out. We'll hit a westerly head wind which won't be nice, but we can handle it.'

After an hour, Acreman was bitterly regretting the decision to fly. Warm thermals from the active Mauna Loa volcano were being torn apart by the screaming cold westerlies and the helicopter bucked like a quarter horse. Behind him, Acreman heard the dolphins communicating in a high-pitched whistle sequence. Barbara had covered them with two blankets which she kept soaked from a big bucket of sea water. He noted that she had also coated the skin around their blow holes with lanolin cream to prevent chapping.

Conditions improved somewhat as they turned out to sea but the westerly wind was now on their quarter and it seemed to catch the chopper under its wide body, causing a series of sickening lurches. Acreman was very nearly sick when the pilot made an emergency dive to avoid a huge flock of gulls seeking sanctuary from the wind on tiny Laysan Island.

Heavy rain started when they were an hour out from the *Eros*.

'Don't worry, our instruments could just about land us on their own,' the pilot reassured them. Acreman didn't believe him and went aft to help Barbara with the animals. When he returned to the cockpit, the chopper was creeping slowly down toward the raised platform on the *Eros*' stern.

'There might be a bit of a bump,' the pilot said. 'Stand by … we're going in.'

Freezing cold in spite of his polar anorak, Acreman looked across the cargo bay as he felt the wheels strike and saw Barbara leaning anxiously over Doris's eight-foot canvas sling. Alongside, Macho, in a similar sling, raised his head in protest and whistled shrilly. The portable Janus translator, served by a tiny computer, was much slower than its parent at the Institute and it was almost five seconds before it could manage a staccato translation.

'You *choose* to travel like this?'

Acreman smiled and shook his head at Macho.

'I don't choose to be here at all, Macho. It will be better soon. How is Doris?' Again there was a long delay while the Janus turned this into a whistle sequence.

'Bad, Acreman. Her heart is weak and her muscles have almost had enough. You understand … with no water … we have to use energy all the time to support our bodies.'

'I know, friend,' said Acreman gently. 'You will be in water in a few minutes. Please tell Doris she must not stop living.'

'I have been telling her that all the way. But her last word was "Why?"'

Acreman looked at Barbara in alarm. But she had heard and was already applying a stethoscope to Doris's gleaming flank.

'Macho,' she said urgently. 'Tell Doris to wake up. Her left side is asleep.'

'You know we can sleep one-half of our bodies while the other is awake. Is her other side asleep?'

Barbara quickly moved the stethoscope. She looked up with relief. 'Okay that side … but I don't like the heartbeat, Frank!'

'Macho, I'm going to give Doris an injection. To make her heart go quicker for a little while until we can get her into the tank. Do you understand?'

'Yes. Do it.'

Barbara had the syringe filled and in operation within seconds. As the stimulant took hold, Doris stirred and opened both eyes.

'Macho, tell Doris to hold on for ten minutes. We are there. She must not stop living. Talk to her all the time. The Janus is not quick enough for conversation.'

Without reply, a thin stream of whistles and clicks began to stream from the rapidly fluctuating blow hole of the male dolphin. Acreman jumped down and yelled at the handling crew fighting to wheel a mobile crane under the lowered blades of the helicopter.

'Move it! I've got an animal about to go out on me!'

'Fuck your animals, mister,' an anonymous voice complained. 'In this sea, we're all in danger of going over the side.'

But eventually the crane was in place and lifted the sling, inching slowly across the slippery deck to the rolled-back hatch which covered part of the tanker's original tank space. Filled with two million gallons of salt water, it was the largest and deepest dolphin pool in the world.

Doris was still moving as she went over the edge. In fact Acreman noted an increase of activity as she felt the cold touch of the flying rain. He shone a powerful light into the pool and saw the pointed black head of the orca lifting from the water as Doris's sling came down towards him.

He stepped back to supervise Macho's safe removal from the aircraft, knowing that Morgan would look after Doris once she was out of the sling and would hold her close to the surface air, if she had any further difficulties.

Macho was still whistling busily as he was slung across the deck. As he disappeared out of sight, Acreman heard a faint translation from the Janus which Barbara was still operating from the chopper.

'Doris is swimming now. She will not stop living.'

Barbara stepped wearily down from the chopper and put her arm through Acreman's.

'That was just too close.'

He nodded, pulling her through the rain to the welcoming

44

light of an open steel door, where a junior officer was waiting to take them to their quarters.

Dave Spurling met them in a cabin in the stern of the ship that had been set aside for their use as an office. Spurling was watching the animals in the big tank through a television monitor and was patently very glad to see them.

'How are they, Dave?' Acreman asked. And then, with some embarrassment, 'How are you?'

Spurling, who had not missed Acreman's priorities, said, 'Doris is still a bit limp. But she'll do. At the moment, she's using Morgan as a life raft, rather more than she needs, I reckon. Macho's monitoring her breathing and keeping us posted.'

Spurling looked up, his face portraying concern and confusion. 'Can you tell me what this is all about, Frank? Louise has been pestering me all the way out. Then when we saw those two huge submarines out on the port side ... she's up there looking at them still.'

Acreman broke in abruptly. 'Two submarines!'

'There's two all right,' Spurling insisted. 'I asked one of the Naval people what was going on and he said they were readying one of the subs for a dive. Something about transferring equipment ... '

'They're out of their minds!' Acreman swore. He looked at Barbara. 'Get Louise down here. I don't want her wandering about on her own. I'll be back.'

Spurling looked nervously at Barbara.

'Boss looks strung out. We got trouble?'

'No,' Barbara said shortly. 'You just mind the animals.'

'Yes'm,' Spurling touched his forelock with mock servility. 'You'd better move your ass if you want somewhere to sleep. Course there's always my bunk, if you can't find nothing better.'

'Where would you sleep?' Barbara said caustically.

Acreman, feeling tired and out of his depth, made his way to the control room on the bridge deck.

He found it crowded with Navy people, most of them still in full uniform, and government administration types in their uniforms of tight grey trousers, New York shoes and short-sleeved shirts over T-shirts.

Acreman saw Suşkin, the communications controller, and

tried to catch his eye. Suskin saw Acreman and tried to look away, but Acreman moved quickly through the mêlée and caught Suskin's arm.

'What's this about a new sub?'

'Not now, Doctor. We've got real problems.'

'What problems?'

'The weather, man! There's a billion dollars' worth of hardware banging itself against our side right now. The Navy say they can't get her down on station in this storm and I'm trying to tell them that she can't stay where she is if they want her in one piece.'

'Good.'

'You think that's good!'

'It's good that she hasn't gone down.'

'I don't have time to debate that. And, with respect, it's not your field. I reckon she'd be much safer down there where she's designed to be.'

'No,' Acreman said harshly. 'She wouldn't be safer.'

Suskin sighed. 'Look, sir, unless you've got some specific information that I should have, will you get the hell out of here and let me do my job the best way I know how? I hear you got your animals on board okay.'

'The animals are fine. Don't let that sub go down until we've had a chance to discuss it.'

'You know that's not my decision. She goes down when the Navy says she can go down. Now, sir, please … !'

'Who's in charge of the Navy side of this?'

'For now, the skipper of the sub, Captain O'Halloran. He's on board. You shouldn't be bothering him though.'

'I won't. But before any decision is taken to position that sub, I want a conference with him. Will you note that?'

Suskin stared at him. 'The best I can do is to pass on your request. That's the best I can do.'

Acreman stared back. 'You tell him I have information that could bear on the lives of anyone who goes down in that craft.'

But Suskin had already turned to answer an urgent summons from another quarter.

Acreman had one last try.

'Listen,' he said urgently, grabbing Suskin's arm again. 'Have your communications people been keeping tapes of the sonar sweeps? All of them?'

'Jesus, Doctor! That's a detail. The way this operation is being run, I'm sure we keep everything!'

'Don't let that sub go down!'

'Sir!'

'I'll have evidence by the morning.'

But Suskin had turned away again and was shouting instructions. 'Then use mattresses. String them on ropes or something. We're just not fitted for this!'

Acreman left him to the chaos. He dropped down two decks to the large cabin where the radar and sonar monitors were housed. In a cubicle at the rear of the cabin, he found a very young Navy lieutenant reading a *Superman* comic.

'Lieutenant, I'm Dr. Acreman, in charge of the Cetacean Search Team.'

'Intriguing animals, Dr. Acreman,' the lieutenant said brightly.

'Yes. Lieutenant, I want to run the tapes of the sonar sweep of the night of November seventeenth.'

'I'd need authorization for that, Dr. Acreman. And some time. We have several miles of tapes in the vault.'

'It shouldn't be too difficult, Lieutenant. That was the night of the *Jules Verne* alert.'

'I recall the night, Doctor. Would you object to my calling my superior officer?'

'I'd object to the waste of time. Suppose we agree that you stay alongside me while I examine those tapes. And I'll sign your log.'

Still looking doubtful, the lieutenant eventually nodded. 'If you sign the log, I'll go find them.'

An hour later, Barbara found Acreman. He had discovered that the communications room kept a continuous log of its sonar recordings and there had been no difficulty finding the two-inch tapes containing the sweeps made on the night of the *Jules Verne* disaster. There were time markings on the tape and Acreman was jumping it forward to find the start of the sequence that had put the *Jules Verne* and the *Eros* on the alert.

'This could take all night,' he told Barbara.

'We have a cabin.'

'*A* cabin?'

'Mmm. Ship's stuffed with bodies.'

Acreman winced. He was not at all sure he wanted Barbara moving in with him. He wasn't at all certain he was ready for that. He did know for sure that his nerves were short and that for the next few days he was going to be on edge. And Barbara was demanding. But this new worry was suddenly shelved as he spotted a small series of white lines etching the viewing screen.

'Stop it there,' he snapped.

The lieutenant looked at Acreman.

'That's nothing to do with the alert. We're too early.'

Acreman rewound the tape and let the sequence play through. The *Eros*' sonar system was the most sophisticated in existence. Based on sound reflections, it had an intermediate stage controlled by a computer. The computer took the returning sound reflections, milked them of their information and converted this into an electronic picture of considerable detail. Thus a school of fish was seen as a series of white dots on the screen rather than a carillon of 'pings' that only a trained operator could translate.

On the screen before them was a white dish-shape; a half moon cutting the bottom third of the screen.

'So what the hell is *that*?'

'I'll check the log, sir.'

Eventually, the lieutenant looked up and smiled nervously.

'You should know what this is, sir—a whale.'

Acreman stared at him angrily until the young officer looked away.

'That's what it says here, sir. There's also a second opinion—rockfall near the trench bottom.'

'Really,' Acreman said scornfully. 'Barbara, come over here.'

He replayed the tape, studying the images more carefully. The flat disc was in fact more of a triangle spreading slowly up from the base of the screen. As it grew, the image flattened and thinned, moved towards the middle of the screen and blanked out a third of the *Jules Verne*. Then there was a lot of white misting before the triangle separated and fell towards the bottom of the screen, where it vanished into a white veil of particles.

The sequence took no more than ten seconds.

Acreman's hands were sweating and his mouth dry. He played the tape back until the image was masking the maximum amount of submarine, then held it. Both images were very clear and white, which meant they were both solid.

'And you think that's a whale, do you?' he demanded fiercely.

'It's not my report, sir. I wasn't on duty that night.'

'Well, you're on duty now. I want you to call another alert!'

'Good God, sir. I can't do that!'

'Then call somebody who can.'

The lieutenant cast Acreman a frightened glance, noted the line of his mouth and fled.

Barbara came over and stood close to Acreman.

'Frank, be careful. Don't make a fool of yourself. You're tired. Is there anything here that can't be left to the Executive Briefing in the morning? All the top brass will be there.'

He shook his head and turned her slowly to look at the fixed image on the screen.

'Firstly, it's definitely not a whale and they should have spotted that because these sonar sets were developed for submarine use and the technicians trained to use them are familiar with whale outlines. They even have reference books of known images.

'But even if that was missed—and I don't think it was—you can't possibly mistake that for a whale. Look at the way the image flattens—the image from a whale is more or less the same no matter which way it turns.'

Barbara's nails dug into his hand.

'You think it's a fish—the top view flattening as it turns!'

'You know what I think it is!'

She started to say something, then her voice faltered. 'But ... Oh, God, Frank. That would make it immense ... almost half the size of the submarine ... almost a hundred feet!'

'Yup,' said Acreman, sitting down slowly.

Barbara sat down abruptly on the steel console, her voice urgent and appealing.

'It could be a rock, Frank, like the report says! Anyway, we should think about it, sleep on it. Nobody's going to believe you. You're used to sonar images, an expert. All they'll see is funny white shapes!'

He stared at her with disbelief.

'But they're getting ready to do it again, love! Tonight probably. The new sub's here and waiting. They have to believe me. Anyway, that's not the worst of it.' He reached forward and ran the tapes on a few feet.

'This is a view taken about twenty seconds after the *Jules Verne* ran into trouble. The operator followed "the whale" before deciding he was losing his focus—or his marbles—because, as you can see, it blanks out the whole of the top of the screen.'

'And you think you know what that is?'

'I do know what it is! It's the bottom curve of the Megalodon. We can't even see the top of it, that's why it seems to be just a line. And the only way this system could pick up an image like that is if the thing was relatively close to the sound emitter. I've always assumed, because we've never come across one of these before, that it had to be a creature of very deep water. That would give us a chance. But that's wrong. This thing can come up. When this scan was on, it couldn't have been more than a thousand feet under the *Eros*. This ship, Barbara!'

There was a noisy commotion behind them.

The lieutenant hurried in, followed more sedately by a Navy officer in full dress uniform, whose face betrayed a mixture of humour and anger.

'Commander Philbert, Duty Officer. Seems you've frightened the shit out of my lieutenant, Doctor. The man's gibbering about a Yellow Alert. As you may have heard, we have important business topside.'

Acreman drew a deep breath.

'I have to tell you, Commander, that we have evidence that there are potentially lethal marine predators active in the vicinity of this ship. I insist the new submarine stay on the surface until whoever is in charge here has been apprised of this.'

'You insist? Now, sir, you have to give me more information than that. The only lethal marine predator I know is the shark.'

'Yes,' said Acreman hopelessly.

'Sharks.' Philbert's smile tightened. 'You want me to hold the dive of a fully operational nuclear submarine because there are a few sharks in these seas?'

'The creature I'm talking about is … '

But Acreman was not allowed to finish.

'I have respect for your work, Dr. Acreman,' Philbert said.

'I've been told what your dolphins can do. But I can honestly assure you that our subs are … shark-proof.' He smiled. 'I know you had a hard time coming in tonight. Don't you think you should get some sleep?'

'But … !'

'Frank,' said Barbara sharply. 'Leave it.'

Acreman felt his spirit collapse. He was swept by a wave of tiredness that was almost tangible.

'All right,' he conceded. 'Perhaps I'm going off half-cocked. But there is evidence the Project should hear, Commander. That much I do insist on.'

Philbert nodded, pleased that a scene had been avoided. 'There's the Day Briefing at 0900. You have a right to attend.'

'We'll be there,' Barbara said hurriedly. She lifted the copy tape off the machine. 'Frank, come on now!'

She watched him with great compassion as he listlessly unpacked his kitbag. He fumbled awkwardly with the buttons of his thick anorak and she came forward to help him. He stood with his hands at his sides, letting her do it.

'Come on, Frank,' she insisted. 'Let's take a shower. It'll warm you up.'

He smiled at her wryly as she went on undressing him. The shower compartment was tiny, too small for the two of them. Barbara soaped him gently, then with increasing purpose. He took her in his arms and held her for a long time, his eyes tightly shut, the hot water welding their bodies together in a pastiche of the heat of love.

Acreman felt himself lift, the physical echoing the mental, and he kissed her wet face. She moaned softly and moved her breasts across the wet hair of his chest.

He stepped back out of the shower, bringing her with him. He felt the sexual urge rising in him like anger, a crying need to vent his emotions and frustrations in some simple, powerful act.

She turned from him and lay on the narrow bunk, her legs spread wide, her head turning urgently on the pillow.

Acreman, normally a concerned, gentle lover, fell on her with avid aggression, lifted her knees and thrust into her, all in the same movement. There was no control. He was aware he was using her. When he came, it was like an explosion, too quick for love, too individual for any bond. But Barbara's eyes

51

opened wide, a fierce smile of elation melted her mouth and she gripped him tightly and used him cleverly to build her own, different, orgasm.

She reached to the floor and gently arranged the discarded blankets over their locked bodies. She stared at the grey-painted bulkhead above her head and gently played with the short hairs at the back of Acreman's neck. In a very short time, she felt his heavy breathing and realized he had gone to sleep.

Barbara smiled a small smile of satisfaction. It had not been their finest lovemaking. But, for the first time, she felt she had given him something genuine and she lay in the moving darkness wondering how she, who had never dared approach the phenomenon before, would cope with this thing that others had described as love.

Moments before she fell asleep she heard the faint sounds of increased activity on deck. The *Eros'* siren sounded ghostly through the several layers of decks and there followed a throb of marine engines.

She sat up carefully, unwilling to disturb her partner, and peered through the cabin's tiny porthole. She was able to detect the shifting silhouette of a long black shape low in the waves, a hundred yards from the *Eros*. A line of lights was strung from a raised projection amidships and two very bright lights were on a level with the waves, fore and aft. As she watched, the front light vanished, then the midships display slid slowly into the blackness of the sea.

The *Jules Verne*'s replacement, the US Ohio-class nuclear submarine *Aquanaut*, had started her slow descent to the stygian reaches of the Molokai Fracture Zone.

Barbara turned slowly to look at Acreman. He was deeply asleep. She let her hand fall gently across the side of his head, covering his ear, and then she lay down and went to sleep herself.

On its three-hourly pass over the huge US military dockyard at Pearl Harbor, a Soviet spy satellite routinely counts Naval units and makes simple comparative calculations. It can recognize hull shapes and it had recorded the U.S.S. *Aquanaut* on the surface, moving out to the Molokai Fracture Zone. Days earlier, it had routinely reported a large tanker and the U.S.S. *Jules Verne* in the same area.

No part of this had disturbed the Soviet strategists assessing the satellite's daily returns; in their eyes, a submarine alongside a tanker was as normal as a mother feeding her child. That assessment changed dramatcally when the two U.S. submarines were detected alongside the *Eros*. Strategically, there is never a need for two Ohio-class ballistic missile submarines ever to be together. Other, that is, than when one is in trouble or both are considering making trouble of a kind that even Soviet military strategists would prefer not to contemplate.

Almost as automatically as the silicon relays in the satellite, they sought out their own nearest compatible unit and instructed it to steer slowly, and with great caution, on a certain southerly course.

The following morning, Barbara told Acreman that she had heard the sub go down and felt oddly pleased with herself when he accepted the news equably.

'There wasn't much we could do about it. I finally realized last night that they weren't going to believe me. The briefing is going to be very difficult.'

'They haven't seen the tapes or the tooth shard.'

Acreman shrugged.

'I doubt even they will be enough. Even Harry is hedging his bets about the shard. And what are the tapes exactly, especially to untrained eyes—spots on a TV screen.'

From the doorway a voice spoke: 'Be of good cheer, children. Your fairy godfather has arrived!'

Asquith, his rotund figure, tentlike in a dripping ochre-yellow cyclist's cape, stood smiling in the doorway.

'Jesus, Harry!' Barbara cried. 'Don't do that!'

'At least you're both dressed.' He looked hard at Barbara. 'Well, on the outside at least. And in good health. Now where does a shipwrecked waif find coffee in this labyrinth?'

'What are you doing here?' Acreman demanded.

Harry looked over his shoulder, holding a finger to his lips. 'Outside ... positively lurking ... is a man whose presence I will have to explain to you innocents. But first—I must eat!'

The mess deck of the *Eros* was the size of a floor of Woolworths, crowded with sailors drawing plates piled high with eggs, bacon, sausage links and large china mugs of coffee.

The whole place was wreathed in steam and condensation and had a vague smell of urine, but Harry's eyes sparkled as he rushed off to take his place in line. The tall, silent man who had followed them down the corridor moved forward to take the next tray.

'What the hell's going on, Frank?' Barbara whispered.

'I don't know. But the fact that Harry's here at all makes it ominous. The fellow acting like a bodyguard is called Vance. Harry mentioned him briefly in his office. Something to do with the accounts and security now that we're getting funds from a government agency.'

'It's the man who was quizzing Fredrickson,' she said. 'He doesn't look at all like an accountant.'

'That's all Harry told me. Look, he's been served. If you get some food for us, I might get the chance for a few words before Vance sits in.'

Barbara nodded and headed for the food queue. Acreman grinned. She had grabbed a tray and, with a slight wiggle of her neat hips, ingratiated herself in front of the government man to give Acreman a few extra minutes. Harry was already seated, wolfing his food.

'Bulk protein,' he grinned at Acreman through a full mouth of scrambled egg. 'Just what I need.'

'That guy will be with us in a moment, Harry. Do you want to take the opportunity to tell me what this is all about?'

'No need to concern yourself with Vance, Frank. He knows about our little problems.'

'Even so, I have a few little problems I'd like to discuss with you privately.'

'Right-ho,' Harry said cheerfully. He looked up. Vance was coming towards them.

'Mr. Vance,' Harry cried. 'Would you mind pissing off?'

Acreman felt himself flush with embarrassment.

'What!'

'I have to discuss something personal with my assistant.'

'You know my orders, Asquith.'

'Are they intended to encompass the private sexual problems of my staff?'

Vance stopped short in his tracks. He looked around, and without further comment, moved up the room to a table near the door.

Harry waved and beamed at Vance then turned back to his breakfast, his eyes on Acreman.

'This has nothing to do with my private life, Harry,' Acreman said shortly.

'Oh.'

'You know what I want to talk about.'

Harry looked thoughtful. 'Vance is a little like a dog I once had. He was a bloody nuisance but just couldn't help himself reacting to strong commands. I wonder what Vance would do if I lost my temper and ordered him to jump over the side.'

'Harry!'

Asquith heaved a resigned sigh.

'I'm *here,* Frank, because last night, just as I was about to start into something that is no concern of yours whatsoever, a cretin called Philbert phoned me to say you were having hysterics!'

Acreman flushed again.

'That's a gross exaggeration ...'

'It doesn't matter what it actually was,' Harry said severely. 'You had the man in a right old tizzy. Something about you wanting to stop a submarine diving to its station, because the sea was full of sharks. Did you say that, Frank?'

'I ...' he stopped. Barbara had arrived at the table. She thumped down the loaded tray and looked accusingly at Harry.

'That's exactly what he said, Harry,' she growled. 'And you know damned well why!'

Acreman broke in. 'Did you know they had planned to replace the *Jules Verne?*'

'I knew they wanted to. I had no knowledge of when it would happen. I didn't expect a government department to move this fast.'

'It went down last night,' Acreman said.

A flicker of doubt touched Harry's face.

'Nutty Philbert,' he said slowly, watching Acreman closely, 'also said that you planned to gatecrash the Day Briefing with something nasty. That's really why I'm here. We can't have egg on the Institute's face, Frank, not just at this particular moment.'

'Eggs are a lot cheaper than nuclear submarines,' Barbara snapped.

Harry held up his hand.

'Peace! I'm here. What have you two found?'

'We have a sonar trace of the Megalodon and an earlier sonar outline of what I think is the same animal. A thousand feet beneath this ship!'

'When … ?' Harry said, looking up from his plate.

Acreman smiled. 'Recent, Harry! They're both a few days old.' He stood up. 'I want you to see the tapes. I'm getting a bit tired of being the only neurotic around here. What about Vance?'

'Oh, I want Mr. Vance to see this,' said Harry wth relish.

Nothing more was said until they reached the communications room. Barbara set up the tapes and Harry watched them through in silence. Vance stood at the back of the room.

'What's the matter, Harry?' Acreman asked eventually. 'Do you need time to work out the alternatives? The Day Briefing starts in fifteen minutes. I'm going to be there.'

Harry, his voice suppressed, said, 'Yes, I suppose we must.'

'What we must do,' Acreman said gripping his arm, 'is get that sub up … *fast!*'

'And I want to hear your opinion,' Barbara cut in, 'before we go to that meeting.'

Harry looked around the room as though searching for an escape route. He took a deep breath and swung the chair around to face them.

'It seems I have about five minutes to teach you two the rudiments of political diplomacy. So listen! Firstly, I'm not expressing any final opinions because you two *are*. There may, just may, come a time when we *have* to be believed and if I erode my credibility by going along with theories … shut up, Frank … they remain theories until you have a positive sighting … that are desperately hard for any layman to believe, I won't be listened to when the time comes. It's like that dog I was telling you about. If I'd spent my time shouting at him, he wouldn't have jumped when I really wanted it.'

'So … ?' Barbara started.

'So this is what we do. We go to the Day Briefing. We show them the tapes. We emphasize our terms of reference here, which is to operate Cetacean Search in the interests of the *Jules Verne* and, now, her replacement. We make the point that *something* wrecked the *Jules Verne* and killed some of her crew. And, very politely, we point out that it is our duty to bring to the attention of the responsible authorities any potentially hazardous … anomalies.'

'Anomalies!'

Acreman's cry rang round the metal room.

'And that's it, is it, Harry? You see a Megalodon shark as nothing more than a potentially hazardous anomaly! Do you think that's going to cause them to bring the *Aquanaut* and sixty-nine people on board up again?'

'No,' said Harry stonily. 'The only thing that's going to cause that to happen is for you to produce the best picture you can get of a thirty-foot jaw—preferably wide open with the teeth dripping blood!'

'Or even better, with the *Aquanaut* gripped in them,' Acreman shouted.

'Frank,' Barbara said sharply, moving in front of him. 'Frank, Harry's right.'

'What!'

'Stop and think. Stop being angry. Think of the reaction last night.'

'Oh, shit,' Acreman said. 'I can't get beyond the faces of the crew. What's with you two?'

'Frank,' Harry stood up. 'Let's go to that meeting. You need to do that.'

'Why do I need it? According to you, no one's going to believe me anyway.'

'You need the time, Frank. Go on as you are and the whole Cetacean operation will be laughed off this ship. What will that achieve? Do it my way and at least we get the time to find the proof they will accept. They don't have any choice ... if we shout "Danger" ... they have to listen.'

Barbara nodded. 'He is right, Frank.'

Acreman stared at them for a long time. 'I see. I would just like to know, Harry, whether you believe me. Did we see what I think we saw on those tapes?'

Asquith grinned with relief and took Acreman's arm, pushing him in the direction of the door. 'You're the electronics whiz kid on this team, Frank. I would not know a computer projection from a "What the Butler Saw Machine". If you say that was a Megalodon, who am I to argue?'

Acreman reviewed this answer as they made their way up to the bridge to the Day Briefing. It was about as equivocal as parrot speech, but he conceded that, in terms of their eccentric boss, it almost amounted to confirmation. Except, Acreman reminded himself, Harry might not know much about computer images, but he knew a damned lot more than anyone else about the attack behaviour of deep-ocean sharks. He could have argued, Acreman decided, and he hadn't.

The Navy and government people who attended the Day Briefing watched the tapes in reverent silence. Harry was at his academic best and a good third of the words he used were incomprehensible to his audience. Some had no meaning even for Acreman and he was more than a little convinced Harry had invented them.

At the close of his address, the Project commander, Admiral Whitting, leaned forward politely. 'Professor ... you've made a good case for a special application of the Cetacean Search Team, and I personally cannot see that it would be anything other than our duty to implement that. I can't pretend to be qualified to assess those readings you've just shown us, but I can accept that they shouldn't be there. That's been confirmed by our own people. However ... I'm still a little hazy as to exactly what you're looking for. And I have a report here from my duty officer of a conversation with Dr. Acreman in which sharks were mentioned. Dr. Acreman seems to have become quite agitated. Now, Professor, I presume you know the armaments and capabilities of a modern nuclear submarine of the line. Sharks, to put it very mildly, Professor, are not our problem.'

Harry looked sternly at Acreman and smiled benignly at the assembled company.

'We *honestly* don't know,' he gushed. 'When one sees a mysterious trace of that kind, one's mind instinctively gravitates to the large species of marine predators. There are some very large sharks, Admiral. The whale shark runs to forty feet and I can see how Dr. Acreman, puzzling over this, might casually have mentioned the word "shark".'

Philbert, looking a little scruffy and very tired, sat up sharply, but fortunately the admiral had started to reply.

'I can see that, Professor, sure. Except I seem to remember our people expressing the opinion that if the trace is anything, it has to be a good deal bigger than forty feet.'

'Perhaps it was a whale,' said Harry, and before anyone could point out that the biggest whale was only half the size of the trace, he went on jauntily. 'Or perhaps it was interference from a source of which even a committee of this stature might not have been informed. I simply do not know. And I would, with respect, suggest that we might perhaps be wasting time until we have more reliable information. Or,' Harry paused for effect, 'until our animals have confirmed, as I suspect, that someone might have been using a vacuum cleaner rather closer to the sonar projector than was advisable.' Harry chuckled, as if to himself, and started to pack his briefcase.

No one spoke. Acreman was fighting an irresistible urge to hit him.

The admiral looked around the long table and suggested that the Cetacean Search Team be given the maximum facilities and that sonar communications run a double watch. There were general nods.

'Just to keep my paperwork straight,' Harry said casually, 'I'd like to propose that as an official minute, with a confidential copy to the Project Management Committee. I was with them a few days ago and I know that they are interested in this matter.' He waited long enough for the minute to be 'so recorded' then, with a small gesture to Barbara and Acreman, he scurried from the room.

'A whale shark,' Acreman said sarcastically, as they went down the corridor. 'An interfering vacuum cleaner. Honestly Harry, you made me sound like an idiot!'

Asquith was making his way back to the mess. He obtained a second breakfast and they gathered around a table. Vance had now got the message and he returned to his seat by the door.

'How can you eat that?' Barbara demanded.

'Brain food,' Harry grinned. 'Rescue operations exhaust me.'

'I suppose you think you rescued me,' Acreman interjected. 'Well, think again, Harry. All you've done is trap us here. There's not a damn thing we can do to find that beast.'

Barbara shot him a startled glance.

'What do you mean, Frank?'

'I know what he means,' said Harry, slurping coffee.

'So what do I mean?'

'You don't have any animals that can work deep enough.'

Acreman was aware that his mouth was gaping.

After a long pause, he demanded, 'If you have realized that, what the hell are we doing here! Why did you let me bring in my two best animals?'

'I still don't understand,' Barbara said plaintively.

'Yes, you do,' said Acreman. 'The maximum depth the dolphins will agree to work is about twelve hundred feet. Morgan, when he's in a good mood, will go to eighteen hundred feet—after that, he knows he's pushing his luck.'

'But those are their physical thresholds,' Barbara pointed out. 'Their sonar range is virtually infinite. They can get a sonar picture a long way down.'

'I suspect Harry's not going to be content with a sonar image,' Acreman said stolidly. 'Right?'

'Right,' Harry said with a smile. 'I would have thought we've all learned that lesson.'

Acreman had been thinking hard.

'Well, you can't do it with any kind of submersible,' he told Harry. 'Have you seen any of the photographs they have been taking from the *Jules Verne*? The darkness down there eats light. When they were surveying the location, they had flares as big as depth charges going off in chains a hundred yards apart. You see a murky halo around each light. The colour is completely milked out. In between it's as black as Hades.'

Harry nodded.

'And don't forget that our target … possibly several targets … won't be standing still. A submersible would be a sitting duck. Okay, maybe we could rig it up with sonar. But if it came under attack, it wouldn't be able to move fast enough —and it wouldn't know where to move. And with more than one target to think about … Oh, just forget it!'

'I presume,' said Barbara carefully, 'that our brief is not to kill this thing.'

'Oh, no,' said Harry. 'That would be a terrible waste.'

'You can forget it anyway,' said Acreman. 'We're dealing with a juggernaut.'

'You're wearing yourself out,' said Harry gently. 'I'm not thinking of a submersible. Or rather I have thought about it and your conclusions are correct.'

'So what the hell are we doing here then, Harry? This may be a big ship. It's still not proof against that thing. If it decides to come up underneath us, steel plate would go like tissue paper.'

Harry looked down at his feet and shuddered slightly.

'And I'm not that good a swimmer. All right, Frank. I'm letting you have your say. What's your solution?'

'Go away,' snapped Acreman. 'Just leave it alone. It has lived a quiet life for two hundred million years and hasn't bothered anyone. It was only when we started invading its environment—the old, old story—that it got nasty. Only this time it isn't chimpanzees or heron colonies or Australian wombats—it's a creature that is big enough to defend itself, thank God! There's a kind of justice in it, Harry. We had to meet something like it eventually. Maybe this time we will have the sense to go away.'

Harry looked sad. 'That will do beautifully for *National Ecological Review* but not for our lords and masters. Consider Vietnam.'

'What's Vietnam got to do with it?' Barbara demanded.

'It took us just a little time to accept defeat there,' said Harry mildly. 'Can you see the Pentagon backing down from a shark?'

'There may be no alternative,' Acreman said. 'And what's the Pentagon got to do with it?'

'Slip of the tongue.' Harry wiped the egg off his plate with a corner of bread. It was mixed with ketchup and Barbara felt her stomach churn. 'This is always the best bit. When I was a boy ... '

'Harry!'

He looked up, apparently startled. 'It is not our job to kill,' he said sternly. 'Not at all. I'd go further and say it was directly contrary to the ethical principles of the Institute. It's our job to study and defend marine animals.'

'When are we leaving?' said Acreman.

'Study,' said Harry with heavy emphasis.

'But how?' Barbara cried, totally exasperated.

Harry grinned.

'Get yourself a whale.'

Acreman exploded. 'What!'

'A big fat one. A sperm or a blue.'

Acreman giggled. 'Oh, sure. Go get me my shrimp net, Barbara.'

'Are you serious, Harry?' Barbara asked. 'No one has ever been able to properly study the big whales. They're just too big. You're talking of a sixty-foot animal. You can't keep them in captivity and they don't hang around long enough in the open ocean for any effective training to be contemplated. They just dive out of sight.'

'How far out of sight?' Harry asked casually.

'Don't answer that,' Acreman cut in. 'I can see where his evil mind's heading. It's not practical, Harry. No one's ever done it. It would cost a fortune.'

Harry's smile was now positively cherubic.

'I seem to recall a young scientist coming to my Institute a few years back and buying himself part of my costly facilities on the promise that dolphin speech was simply a stepping stone to communication with the large whales. I even remember the words … "They are simply large dolphins." '

'It would still cost a fortune,' Acreman said, close to panic. 'And I never said *"simple".'*

'Nothing that is worth achieving,' said Harry sonorously, 'is ever simple. And we have a fortune. Anything else?'

Barbara broke in suddenly.

'How deep can a sperm whale dive, Frank?'

'He knows,' said Acreman pointing an accusing finger at Harry. 'Five thousand feet … we think!'

'Deep enough,' said Harry contentedly.

'Do you want me to arm it with a giant bayonet, too—like they did with dolphins in Vietnam?'

Harry looked up with interest. Acreman held up his hand. 'Forget I said that!'

'Good,' Harry said, standing abruptly. He crooked a finger in Vance's direction. 'Come, sweet shadow.'

'You're not leaving *now*?'

Harry looked at the deck. 'Like tissue paper, you said?'

'There's a million things to arrange!'

'So arrange them. I am only a telephone call away.'

'Authorizations?'

'Consider yourself authorized.'

'To catch and train a sperm whale as part of the Cetacean Search Team. Barbara, you witness this insanity.'

'Just so,' said Harry.

'Nobody's going to buy this, Harry!'

Harry was already heading off. 'As an alternative to a bloody great sub-eating Megalodon, I think they'll buy it with considerable relief.'

By the entrance to the mess, with Vance at his elbow, he paused. The expression on his face had changed and so had the tone of his voice. Acreman hoped that it was simply the fact that Vance was now in earshot, but he wasn't sure.

'You have to be right about the Megalodon, Frank.'

Acreman led Barbara back to the table where he finished his cup of lukewarm coffee.

'What have we let ourselves in for now?'

She had her chin cupped in her hands. Acreman studied her face and was surprised to find that it expressed concentration and interest rather than the anxiety that was giving him stomach cramp.

'Harry's up to something,' she said eventually. 'I don't know what, but it's something. In amongst all that verbal garbage he pumps, there was one thing definite. He ducked your question about us just moving out. Vietnam … I ask you! We should be moving out. I think, Frank, that for whatever reason, Harry's behind this scheme. And that's probably all we should be thinking about. If you take it on from there, it's marvellous. We've got the funding not just to look for a Megalodon species, but to attempt to contact a large whale. A double first, Frank!'

'Half of that is more than big enough for me,' Acreman said. 'And there was something else he was definite about. I do have to be right about the Megalodon. If I'm not, it's the end of all this.'

'Probably. Frank, can you contact a sperm whale?'

He stood up. 'Theoretically, yes. But why don't we go and talk about all this with our friends?'

On their way to the dolphin pool, Barbara asked, 'Is there *anything* we should be doing about the Megalodon? This ship's so big I keep forgetting it's floating.'

Acreman grunted doubtfully. 'My fear is that we already did something. You attract sharks by dumping things in the sea that they like to eat.'

'The new sub?'

'If you like, but it's probably worse than that.'

'How can anything be worse than that, Frank?'

'Because sharks aren't cloned from seaweed, sweetheart. We keep talking about *it*. We should be thinking about *them*.'

4

They moved through the planes of deep cold peacefully.

Had the water not been salty, they would have been entombed in ice. Their vast eyes, fixed open, stared ahead: the blood-fused retinas, the size of basketballs, took what little light there was and printed images that took a long time to reach a huge, but at the same time, minute brain.

Few other things would have been able to see at all. The Megalodons were cruising, six thousand feet down. Red vanishes from the marine light spectrum at a mere one hundred feet, the yellow-greens a few hundred feet deeper and the last trace of blue at fifteen hundred feet. At half the depth the Megalodons were cruising, most things would experience a darkness blacker than anything imaginable in the earthly world.

But unlike many other species which simply abandoned an optical sense in this twilight zone, the Megalodons had enhanced their vision by evolving large numbers of plates silvered with microscopic crystals of guanine behind the massive irises—photo-reflecting mirrors that used every scrap of the ghostly light.

But eyes were not all they had to see with, in fact they were the least important in these stygian deeps. Along their flanks and across their flattened snouts were thousands of lateral line pits and crypts: porelike apertures in the shark's skin that were detection mechanisms of extraordinary sophistication and power.

These ampullae were sensitive to changes of both pressure and temperature and also to taste sensations. The Megalodons, even when moving at extreme depths where there was simply no light, could detect the movement of a fish fin at one thousand feet, minute changes of frequency vibration, variations in the sea's acoustic waves and any minor alteration to the water currents in which they swam.

They also had a highly developed sense of smell. Two deep grooves on the underside of the snout fed olfactory receptors which occupied two-thirds of the Megalodon brain. They could easily detect particles of axoma dispersed several parts to the million in water.

And all these acute senses were primarily tuned to the taste and smell of blood. They could find a particle of blood in ten million to one hundred million parts of water.

They could hear through pits that would not normally be recognized as ears, and which were receptive to a range of cycles well outside the human limit; from a hundred to seven thousand cycles a second.

Only in one sense could the Megalodon be regarded as primitive—its tiny brain. In every other sense, it was perhaps the most finely tuned hunter-killer ever evolved by nature.

Millions of years had committed the Megalodons to the deep Fracture. Once the seas had teemed with predators and only the explosive development of massive cartilage and muscle had kept the Megalodons ahead, and even then it had been a closely run race. The fast-swimming sea lizard, *Icthyosaur*, with its saw-blade snout, had savaged the Megalodon ancestors of the remote past. With their better swim bladders and delicate fin structure, the Megalodons had evaded this assault by living ever deeper.

This special niche of dominance had been obtained at a price. Very little food existed naturally and like that much smaller species of the deep, *Argyropelecus*, the hatchet fish, the Megalodons had been forced to enlarge their mouths and their teeth.

A third of their bodies were now taken up by this enlarged head and their mouths could open to a maw of forty feet, and were lined with a full set of sharp teeth, varying from eight to fifteen inches in length.

In fact, the Megalodon, like the hatchet fish, was on its way to becoming one huge, toothed mouth.

In spite of all this evolutionary striving, the Megalodons were still lucky to be alive. For at least the past fifty million years the sea's natural harvest of animal protein had been insufficient to sustain so large an animal.

A unique characteristic of the great Fracture had been responsible for their survival.

The Fracture was a deep, submerged trench the size of the Grand Canyon. At its northeast end it was wide and open, its walls rising as peaks to within a few hundred feet of the surface. These seamounts and guyots were well known to sailors because of the peculiar effects they had on the currents and weather patterns in the busy shipping lanes eastwards to Asia and the Antipodes. Thirty ships a week passed through the Zone and most of them disgorged something, among them oil tankers who would use these troubled waters to disguise the illegal dumping of oily ballast.

All this strange food, human waste in great quantities and accretions of tarry oils that could be reduced to rich protein by the powerful enzymes in the Megalodons' stomachs, was swept down the trench until a narrowing of its southern end caused it to accumulate on the bottom. Here the Megalodons, who in common with other sharks were scavengers, had learned to graze like cows on the detritus of a race that had grown to dominance without either being aware of the other.

When the harvest was poor, the Megalodons could, and would, rise from the still planes of the deep bottom and hunt in what, for them, were the shallows. But these forays involved paying a price of sustained pain. To eyes sensitive enough to work in the deeps, anything resembling normal light was searing, agonising brilliance.

Thus, they invariably chose the night for their rare expeditions out of the dark tranquillity of the familiar deeps.

When the Megalodons did ascend, they were animals driven by the desperation of starvation, furious with the torment of the pain behind their great eyes. They would strike up on sweeps from their vast fifty-foot triangular tails to hit, sightless, mindless, schools of barracuda, other sharks and sometimes the occasional sleepy whale. They performed these attacks without aggression, without violence. Theirs was simply the natural process of survival and when they had fed they would flee gratefully back to the bottom and there, like the essentially gentle animals they were, digest their food for several days.

Recently, the Megalodons had been forced to venture into

the hurtful light less frequently. The food had increased—a seemingly endless supply of protein-rich waste had come floating down to them.

In the peace and serenity that sufficient food engendered, a strangely atrophied impulse had stirred in the giant male—the desire to mate. Now, eighteen months past that time, the adult pair enjoyed the unusual experience of company; a young male.

He was different. Almost ninety feet long, he was agile and hot with energy. He swam almost continuously, running close to the surface, playing games that were joyful enough to override the pain of light. He investigated. He had no patience with the incomprehensible nagging vibrations that had started to invade the Fracture in very recent times. These vibrations filled the water all around the Megalodons but when, impelled by the strange feeling in their sensing pits, they went in search of the source, they found nothing.

The adult pair learned to live with this irritation. There was a special cave they knew, shielded by rock, which relieved it somewhat, and they began to spend much of their time sheltering there. But the young one was not so content. He shook his huge head with fury and ran at the rocks and the thick sea forests in which he thought the source of the vibrations might be found. When he simply caused explosions of rock and sand, the vegetation slid around his speeding body without resistance, the young one grew even more frustrated.

He knew nothing of frequency-amplified vibrations from tightly focused laser beams. He only knew that something he could not find was stimulating his attack mechanisms and causing a continuous ache in his brain.

Now some relief had come. The vibrations had ceased. The family was at peace, and food continued to flow down in abundance. The young male enjoyed this time of calm and fed well. Soon he forgot the vibrations. His youthful drives began to stir.

He returned to his games in the depths, making token attacks at tall spurs of rocks, diving on waving growths of weed with his huge mouth glistening open.

But these were familiar games. He began to look for something more interesting.

Aboard the *Eros*, because there were no windows in the steel tank walls, communication with the dolphins and the orca was via Janus hydrophones and hastily rigged closed-circuit television cameras and monitors. This method lacked the intimacy of contact that had been established back at the Institute and both humans and Cetaceans felt uneasy with the arrangements.

Acreman, Barbara Monday and the two handlers, Dave Spurling and Louise Putnam, sat watching inadequate silver and glistening black and white images dance on their monitor, while Spurling fiddled with the controls.

'That's about as sharp as I can get it,' he announced eventually. 'Basically, I need more light.'

Acreman nodded impatiently and spoke into his Janus microphone.

'I am sorry this place is not as good as the other.' The two dolphins stopped swimming and came across to a watertight monitor that gave them a picture of the human team. The Janus hydrophones were alongside the set. The young orca continued to swim nervously around the huge tank.

'It is interesting, Acreman,' the young male, Macho, replied. 'I am getting strange images of an *outside*. What is this place?'

'We call it a ship. You remember we have pointed them out when you were swimming in the sea pool.'

'So the outside is the sea.'

'Can you tell that with your sonar, Macho?'

'Yes. I would rather be outside there, Acreman.'

'You will be soon. That is why we are here. As soon as I have told you what we are to do, you can go outside. But there you will only have radios so it is better that we first talk here, using this equipment.'

Barbara leaned towards the microphone. 'How are you, Doris?'

'I am living well again, Barbara.'

Acreman looked at the two young handlers and wondered how they would react to what he was about to say.

'Macho. Remember your numbers lessons—matters of size?'

'Yes, Acreman.'

'Please judge the size of this tank.'

Over the hydrophones the human team heard a ripple of sonar clicks.

'One hundred and fourteen feet, six-point-three inches.'

Acreman drew a deep breath: 'Think of a sea animal as big. Have any of your kind ever seen an animal in the sea of the same length as the tank?'

Dave Spurling spun around in his chair to stare at Acreman. The dolphin had still to make a response.

'Macho?'

'Define "any of your kind".'

'I don't understand,' said Acreman.

'I do,' said Barbara. 'Not of *your* kind, Macho. Of another kind of that size.'

'No,' the dolphin replied instantly. 'There are some of our kind nearly that size. But we have not seen another. Perhaps we have thought of one.'

Acreman sat up quickly.

'*Thought*, Macho?'

'*Remembered,*' said the dolphin. 'Not of now.'

'You remember an animal of that size?'

'Many.'

Barbara joined in excitedly. 'When, Macho?'

Bubbles. A waggle of the head. 'How long is memory, Barbara?'

'How long have you been with us, Macho?' Acreman asked sternly. He was never sure whether expression carried through the Janus circuit.

'One of your years almost.'

'How many years is this other memory? How long in years?'

'I cannot count it.'

'Many years?'

'More than years. It is a memory, like a dream.'

'Inherited memory,' said Barbara excitedly. 'Like they think pilot whales strand themselves on certain coasts because they have inherited a memory from millions of years back when those coasts were open seaways. Before continental shift.'

'Totally unproved,' Acreman snapped. 'Let's not guess.' He flipped the Janus microphone again.

Macho said: 'Acreman wait. The orca is communicating.'

Acreman cut in the underwater hydrophones in the far end of the tank and they heard a barrage of pure cetacean clicks and whistles. Then the huge black and white shape of the orca zoomed to the camera, its formidable teeth bared.

'This big thing says it has a memory,' Macho said through

the Janus. Acreman was certain he picked out a note of condescension in Macho's voice. Morgan, in spite of his size, was only three years old. The ridiculous appellation 'killer' was denied on a daily basis by the whale's friendly baby games and what Barbara called a crying need for company.

'Morgan,' said Barbara. 'Hi, baby.'

'Good morning, Barbara.'

'It's not morning, Morgan. Night. No light.'

'Good night, Barbara!'

'Night, baby.'

Acreman looked at her and wondered how she managed to be so objective a scientist yet so anthropomorphic about the orca.

'Morgan,' he said. 'Listen and answer.'

'Yes, Acreman.'

'Have you a memory of a big animal in the sea?'

Macho cut in. 'He doesn't know "memory", Acreman. Talk through me.'

'He'll never learn if we don't talk to him, Macho!'

'I'll give him a sonar picture of my memory, then he can say yes or no. He can do that much.' Again the hydrophones resounded to a barrage of sonar clicks as Macho transmitted the sound-picture of his memory. They all waited in silence.

'Morgan,' said Acreman. 'Yes ... no?'

'No,' said Morgan after a long pause.

'His brain is too small,' said Macho.

'His brain is twice the size of yours,' Acreman snapped. 'Try again, Morgan.'

Another long pause while the orca wiggled his big head in front of the camera.

'No ... yes, yes. No, no, yes, yes, yes yes.'

'What the hell's that?' Acreman asked. Barbara had spent the most time with the orca.

She was evidently delighted.

'Good, baby! Good. Wait.' She turned to Acreman.

'That animal's going to get very confused about its identity if you keep changing its name,' Acreman said. 'What's with the indecision?'

'It's digital,' she answered excitedly. 'In the beginning, when we can't get through with variations, we do it digitally. So "very good" in the early stages is "good, good". I think we're getting a kind of temporized answer here, digitally. Like "I'm not sure" only it's "I think not but I saw something like it." Morgan's very honest.'

'That's right,' said Macho. 'His brain's too small.' Acreman hadn't realized he'd left the Janus mike open. He reluctantly addressed himself to the dolphin again.

'Okay, wise guy, can you get Morgan to give you a sonar impression of what he did see?'

'Yes,' said Macho. More sonar clicks, several times repeated.

'Now we'll see who's got the big brain,' Barbara said. Macho was weaving in front of the window, blowing bubbles; obviously in some mental trouble.

'Macho, do you have it?'

'Maybe, Acreman.'

'So let's have the maybe.'

'It's big. Like a sponge, like a bottle, like a fish.'

'Jesus Christ!' said Dave. 'Like a fish! What is this, Frank?'

'Quiet, Dave. Yes, Macho. As big as the size I gave you?'

'Bigger Acreman, bigger than the tank.'

'Define "bottle", Macho.'

'Thin front, thick middle. Hard, like a bottle.'

'And the sponge?'

'The image is poor—full of holes—very deep.'

Acreman cut the Janus switch.

'Go and dump about a ton of prime halibut up there, Dave.' Then, as an afterthought, he triggered the switch again.

'Macho, is this like *your* old memory?'

'Yes, Acreman.'

'But has Morgan seen this recently?'

'No, Acreman. But you know he lives deeper than we do.'

'There's nothing wrong with his brain, Macho! Dave's bringing you guys a treat, and I'll get them to winch you out.'

'No, Acreman.'

'But you just said … '

'No, Acreman! Morgan says *that* memory lives in a deep place—like this!'

Aboard the U.S. Ohio-class nuclear submarine, *Aquanaut*, the sixty-nine-man crew sat in the cold limbo of the condition called *Silent running*.

From captain to the most lowly mess hand, no one moved.

No radio played in the mess. None of the fifty tape recorders kept by the crew against the endemic loneliness of submarine life gave off a single tinny note. No cigarettes were lit, no matches scratched, no cups rattled, no loads were moved. Every man in the crew sat at his battle station in the kind of silence that alone brought home to the crew exactly where they were. For only the sounds of human activity, the alien sounds of an alien group, separate the crew of a submarine from the dreadful fact that they are deeply submerged; dead men but for the artificial aids that noisily surround them under normal conditions.

Silent running is the condition reserved for the most extreme danger a submarine can face—when the enemy is overhead, listening for its target, depth charges primed and ready to go. Some aboard the *Aquanaut* were old enough to know this condition from their days in active service. A third of them had run the gauntlet of the Vietnam war. The captain, O'Halloran, had been a young ensign in submarines in the final stages of the assault on Japan.

He stood now, his cap reversed against the column of the conning tower; the traditional position for him, even though his con was already over two thousand feet below the surface and as blind as everything else on the sub. The *Aquanaut* was his last command and this, his last voyage, was not a voyage at all, simply a descent.

But that descent was also deeper than O'Halloran had ever made, or than he would ever have contemplated making were his craft not specially strengthened for this one dive. Except that O'Halloran, who knew how priorities could become weighted by expediency, doubted that the *Aquanaut* was as strong as they claimed her to be.

Which was why he was making the descent under the condition called *silent running,* even though that condition placed almost unbearable stress on his crew, and there was no enemy that he knew of within a thousand miles of the *Aquanaut.*

As she sank ever deeper into the maw of the Molokai Fracture, his doubts about the strengthening of the *Aquanaut* expressed themselves as a cacophony of small sounds.

Her plates creaked. Edges of metal that had never been intended to move, flexed minutely under the enormous pressure and screamed at cycles that seemed to penetrate directly to the nerve centres of the brain.

The dead silence of the crew augmented the sub's natural sounds and distorted them to frightening abnormality. The vessel seemed to pant as air was rapidly cycled through her air filters. Instruments fitted with audible warning indicators buzzed, rang, and howled at frequencies no louder than was intended but which, in the flat silence, seemed to speak of imminent disaster.

The voices of the few men authorized to speak from the various command and steering positions grew steadily more muted as the *Aquanaut* dropped ever deeper away from the world of air-breathing man.

'Stop all engines,' O'Halloran said quietly but with firm authority. 'Confirm our trim.'

He was small and slim; custom-made, it seemed, for the cramped conditions of the Submarine Service. At first glance, he seemed almost too slight for the weight of responsibility that rested on his narrow shoulders. What he had was all used. His thin face was finely muscled, with few folds, his waist was slim and when he moved it was with a quickness that belied the fact that he was middle-aged. His eyes, a clear blue, moved rapidly; flickering, it seemed, to every aspect of the ship's control systems. In summary, he was vitally alert.

As now he needed to be, as never before.

Even in her strengthened condition, the *Aquanaut* was absolutely incapable of descending to the sea floor. She would have burst like an overripe banana even halfway down that pressurized pit.

Her destination—her final resting place—was that shelf of rock jutting one hundred feet out from the Fracture's northern wall that had formerly accommodated the *Jules Verne*. According to O'Halloran's briefing, it was the only place capable of taking a vessel the size of the *Aquanaut* at a depth of eight thousand, eight hundred feet. It was also a good thousand feet below the *Aquanaut's* depth capability.

There was, they had said, no choice. The *Aquanaut* had been specially strengthened for the additional depth. So they said.

But she had not been strengthened for an extra fifteen hundred feet, O'Halloran had pointed out at the briefing, and were he to miss that narrow sliver of support there would be at least a thousand feet of extra pressure, more likely fifteen hundred before the descent could be reversed and corrected.

They had made no effective answer to this point. They had smiled nervously and talked of his experience. That he was the best; that the men who would be monitoring them from the surface were the best.

O'Halloran, standing silently at the conning tower shaft as he had always done when the enemy was within range, had not replied to these platitudes. He had accepted that this time his best would either be good enough or he and his crew would die.

The trim corrected, he resumed the descent.

So far the *Aquanaut* had taken a day and a night to descend four thousand, five hundred feet. Surface command had ceaselessly demanded to know what was wrong. What was holding them up? O'Halloran was holding them up. He was doing his best.

The young Megalodon was restless. The pain in his head had gone but the weeks he had endured it had disturbed his metabolism. The normal life of the Megalodon family was tranquil. They swam quietly up the twenty miles of the Fracture, mouths open to scoop up the liberal detritus. Then sometimes for weeks on end, depending on the plentitude of the current's harvest, they rested on the bottom, their gills barely moving. At other times, they went into the cave.

When the vibrations ceased, the adult pair returned to their pattern of behaviour as though they had never been. But the young one readapted less easily. He had enjoyed the flush of energy that came from increased oxygen conversion during high-speed runs when he had moved in order to escape the pain. Like all children, he had discovered and enjoyed games, and he remembered these games.

So while his parents rested on the bottom, the young one cruised the Fracture, just for the thrill of moving. He was not hungry so did not bother to investigate the congealed accretions of high-protein grease, vegetable matter, wood and fragments of decayed flesh that the current rolled into loose sandy balls along the cliff walls and the deep bottom.

Until one day a new image changed the nature of the sea far above him in the watery, milky sky.

The young Megalodon's senses were not capable of any definition. He could not sense texture, or shape. He reacted only to the marginal variation of electrical conductivity through its lateral pits, variations to which its primitive brain was tuned—a circuit no more complicated than a doorbell.

The silent bell that now rang in the brain of the young Megalodon was loud. He was able to judge that the object was a great distance away. So large a current variation at such a great distance spoke of an object of great size.

Alongside the young male, the two comatose adults stirred briefly and moved their huge heads in the direction of the mass. Even their slightest movement was enough to stir several tons of sand. And then they settled again. Better experience of judging the messages of their lateral pits told them instantly that the object was too large even for their huge maws. It could not be taken comfortably as food. And it hung in the painful light of their sky. They settled back to the bottom and another cloud of particles misted up around them.

But the young one remained restless.

The ship-to-surface intercom crackled. The voice that came through to O'Halloran was thready. *They forget that our communication systems are also getting well out of their depth,* O'Halloran thought.

'Say again, Control,' he said urgently.

'Control to *Aquanaut*.' This time the voice was clearer as the sub's operator tuned his equipment.

'We have a flicker of activity at the bottom. Nothing to worry about. Our computer prognosis gives seventy-five per cent to that heavy current running on the bottom, twenty-five on minor subterranean activity or submerged landslip. Do you copy?'

An icy hand grabbed O'Halloran and he spun around to the first mate, who had the con.

'Stop all engines. Stop 'em! Hold your trim. Attention all hands. This is the captain speaking. I want absolute silence. Suppress mechanical warnings until further notice.'

He moved across the bridge to his sonar operator, who had slipped off the heavy earphones.

'Do you copy, mister?'

'No, sir. I'm pinpointing the shelf on all systems. Your orders, sir.'

O'Halloran nodded. The sonar technician had been given a very specific brief; to find the shelf and hold it. Nothing else in the sea had any priority as far as the *Aquanaut* was concerned. And O'Halloran knew that more complex sonar scanners on the surface *Eros* were monitoring the general situation.

'Shall I reset for the bottom, sir?'

'No. You hold that shelf. If you lose it, we go back and start again. Is that clear?'

'Yes, sir.'

O'Halloran returned to the radio. 'All hands ... you may return to partial Silent running. *Aquanaut* to control.'

'Control.'

'We are set to our target. We have no copy of your activity. Do you have any more?'

'Negative, *Aquanaut*. Prognosis remains the same. We now have some blurring but computer prognosis equates this one hundred per cent with residual disturbance from the previous activity.'

O'Halloran forced his breathing to a more normal rate. He touched his forehead. It was slightly beaded with sweat. He looked around the bridge. It was hot in the room. Everyone was sweating a little.

'*Aquanaut* to Control. Is Commander Suskin available to come on set?'

There was hardly a pause. Suskin, O'Halloran's friend for three decades, came through.

'Hallo, Charlie. I've been right here since dawn.' And for all of the time that the *Aquanaut* had been beneath the surface, bar three hours of uneasy sleep snatched the previous night. Suskin saw no need to mention this. Charlie O'Halloran was about the best sub captain in his squadron, but he had one failing. He was cautious to the point of nervousness. That's why he, rather than another skipper, had command of the *Aquanaut*. It was also the reason Eugene Suskin was living in his control room.

'No, Eugene. *We've* been right here since dawn. What's this stuff about bottom activity? I want your judgment, not some computer readout.'

'Nothing abnormal, Charlie. We've had it before off and on.

76

Remember, you're sliding down the side of a mountain. Bits fall off it just like they do in the Alps. Maybe you nudged a rock.'

'We didn't nudge anything, Eugene!'

'Sorry, Charlie. I know you didn't. But it doesn't have to be that at all. You know the funnel effect of the Fracture. Under you, there's a bottom current running nearly ten knots. That's enough to move rocks about and disturb the sand.'

'I know about the current too, Eugene. We're already fighting the shadow of it here. Trim's getting tricky. Eugene, are you absolutely damned sure there's nothing we could set down on that's closer to the surface?'

''Fraid not, Charlie. Before we positioned the *Jules Verne,* we surveyed the whole Fracture. And there's other reasons why we have to have you exactly there. You know all there is to know, Charlie.'

O'Halloran looked at his microphone for a long time. The one thing he didn't know, the one important thing, was just what the hell had happened to the *Jules Verne.* Officially, she had been clipped by a rock slide and had fallen off the end of the shelf, ramming her bow between two spurs of rock a hundred feet below the shelf. O'Halloran had seen the lengthy postmortem report. And postmortem was right. With holes in her bow, the pressure had got in. Water went through the *Jules Verne* like solid steel rams. Three members of her crew had been blown to bloody bits. Five others had drowned.

But, O'Halloran mused, *what does it take to push a heavy submarine off a wide piece of rock once she'd settled down?* Underwater avalanches, it seemed to him, were becoming something of a placebo—an instant answer to things that couldn't be answered.

'Number One ... resume your dive,' O'Halloran said. He leaned his hot forehead against the cold steel of the con shaft, feeling the agony of the ship through the particles of the metal.

The young adult was swimming. Stirred by the images from his lateral pits but subject to the conditioning of his species, he had overcome his first impulse to investigate the mass and had stayed in range of his parents.

He swam a mile-wide circle, keeping the older Megalodons within sense range. The image of the mass had also faded;

77

there was no longer movement to stir the sea's natural electricity.

Halfway through a turn that would bring the young adult back to the family resting ground, the currents stirred again.

Already in motion, already launched towards the ceiling, the young adult turned, half by instinct, half out of youthful curiosity. As his vast head turned in the direction of the mass, the lateral pits focused, strengthening the impression of the mass. Images invaded the limited mechanism of that primitive brain. All other considerations were swept aside. The great flag of a tail lashed once, twice. As the shark rose, its special metabolism ran stored oxygen into its vast mass of bone and muscle tissue. Its gill flaps closed, making it more streamlined and increasing its speed. At almost thirty knots, it shot towards the mass, lifting through the black sea like a spear. The light began to cause pain. Irises a foot across closed behind the lidless eyes to cut out the light. The shark swam a course dictated by the impulses of its ampullae, blind, incapable of deviation now that its limited brain had locked shut; directly up and under the sub.

For the last two thousand feet of its ascent, the shark was no more controllable than a torpedo. It was fixed, mind and body, on the attack. The current stirred by the huge tail sped back down to the bottom and caused a hurricane of sand.

Inside this pall, the young adult made a high-speed pass three hundred yards away from the *Aquanaut*'s port side.

This is the basic pattern of a shark attack. At first, a blind reaction to a possible food source. Then the pass, during which the food selection mechanisms in the shark's brain assess the target for size and availability. All these processes were followed by the young Megalodon which, in spite of its size, was only a shark.

Its ampullae read and reacted to the solid black bulk of the big sub. Nerves in the brain clicked out. This could not be eaten!

Reality returned! Pain returned. The young adult pointed its head down and, with one further flick of its tail, it dropped directly below the *Aquanaut* and returned to the depths, entering its own sand screen within seconds of its pass.

Ensign Larry Mannheim was seated at a fixed microscope in

the marine bacteria lab when the backlash from the Megalodon's first pass hit the *Aquanaut*.

It was later calculated that the impact equated to the sub being picked up by a giant crane to a height of ten feet—then dropped!

The microscope tube entered Ensign Mannheim's right eye and penetrated his brain to a depth of three inches. He was the first to die aboard the *Aquanaut* but at least his death was instantaneous.

Every man aboard the ship was thrown. O'Halloran, conditioned by half a lifetime's experience, felt the first rush of water against the hull through the metal of the con and he hugged it instinctively. But he was wrenched loose and thrown into the radio bench.

A steel plate sixteen feet long and nine wide buckled and exploded into the forward mess hall, where ten ratings of Yellow Watch were taking their breakfast. Eight of them drowned within the next few minutes, one died of shock and drowning when he was sucked through the hole, losing a leg and half of his right side in the process. A seventeen-year-old Marine cadet, George Penrose, was blasted through the mess deck's watertight doorway two seconds before the water-triggered automatic mechanisms slammed the door shut. He arrived, totally unconscious, to join the piled up, variously broken forms of the other six members of the Yellow Watch who had finished their meal and were digesting it in the room behind the watertight door.

The *Aquanaut*'s pumps went to work instantly on the invading water but her bow went down ten degrees under the weight and her slowly turning engines pushed her into a dive, so that within a further ten seconds she was two hundred feet deeper than at the time of the Megalodon's pass, and diving faster with each moment. Pressure increased in ratio and, when the mess hall filled and the water was compressed, it burst the watertight door to the forward engine compartment.

The *Aquanaut* was now pointing straight down into the stygian blackness of one of the world's deepest sea holes.

In the galley, Chief Cook Masters, who was two years away from retirement and had been offered, and refused, another posting when the *Aquanaut* was chosen for special duty, was thrown hard against his cooking range and his spine snapped. The aluminium fresh-water tank that ran the length of the galley ruptured and covered the galley floor with just a few inches of water. Chief Cook Masters, totally paralyzed, drowned in that.

When the final count was taken the dead numbered twelve and a further seven had broken limbs. Cuts and bruises were not even counted.

Suskin, seated bleary-eyed before the *Eros'* sonar screens, was watching the white sausage that was the *Aquanaut* when the screen went slightly milky along its left-hand edge, and the sub itself moved half an inch sideways.

Suskin stared and turned sharply to the operator.

'Is this thing on the blink?'

A red light flashed on the computer console above the sonar screen and a klaxon siren went off.

The operator, his mouth agape, was pointing dumbly at the screen. The white sausage, still set in a halo of mist, had moved across the screen and was now vertical.

'They're diving,' Suskin yelled. 'What the hell!'

And as he watched, the *Aquanaut* slipped off the edge of the screen.

'They're fucking sinking!' He leaped across to the radio console, grabbed the microphone from the stunned operator and started yelling.

'Condition Red. Condition Red. All hands to action stations.'

He hit another bank of switches.

'Hallo, *Aquanaut*. Come in, *Aquanaut*. Charlie! Are you receiving me?'

There was no response.

'Keep calling him,' he snapped, handing the operator his microphone. Suskin ran across to the sonar screens.

'What's ...? Ah, you have them again.'

'Different view, sir,' the operator stuttered. 'They're down four hundred feet and still diving. If they don't stop her within the next few minutes, they'll pile straight into that shelf!'

'What the hell is going on?' Suskin bellowed. 'What's causing this? We didn't see a goddamn thing! They must have had an explosion.'

Men in flak jackets had begun to pour into the control room.

Beneath these bizarre outfits, Suskin spotted the suited legs of government officials and the uniforms of Navy brass.

A tall, capped figure strode through the mêlée—Whitting. A Marine sergeant with a huge pistol marched alongside, clearing the way. By the door, two more Marines with carbines took up their emergency stations.

His face blanched white and his mouth set to a thin, bloodless line, Whitting came to a halt in front of Suskin and said icily,

'You best show good cause for this, mister!'

Suskin reached forward and turned him to face the sonar screen.

'There's your cause! The *Aquanaut* is sinking. She's into a lethal dive.' He turned to the sonar operator.

'Report!'

'No change, sir. The rate of descent has slowed slightly. No, wait … Look, I think her bow is coming up, but they've got less than thirty seconds to stop her.'

O'Halloran heard Suskin's call as a vague echo reaching towards him through a mist. He fought unconsciousness but found he could not move. As his vision cleared, he realized that Grierson, the radio operator, was lying on top of him. His head felt as if it was about to burst.

Two of the bridge technicians were crawling towards him. Their problem, O'Halloran realized with horror, stemmed from the fact that they were clawing their way *uphill*. The *Aquanaut* was going down vertically.

One of these men was Chief Mate Riley. 'Help me, sir. Lend me a hand.'

Pushing Grierson's unconscious form to one side, O'Halloran tried to stand up.

'Don't try that, sir. Just reach out and pull me over!'

O'Halloran fell to his knees and did as he was instructed.

Behind Riley, Leading Seaman Brent, the engine control rating, found a foothold on the corner of a desk and pulled himself upright.

'I can reach the engine controls, sir,' he yelled. 'Do I do something?'

'No,' the chief mate bellowed back. 'Sorry, sir. You get yourself together. If we lose engine power, we lose the pumps.'

O'Halloran felt the adrenalin of fear push aside the veils that had wrapped themselves around his brain.

'Trim,' he yelled. 'Chief, get to the trim controls. Blow all stern tanks.'

Riley let go of O'Halloran's hand and allowed himself to roll back down the deck, scrabbling like a crab to reach the port side and the trim controls. He climbed over the still form of another crewman and stood up, reaching forward quickly to pull down two large silver levers. The sub shook; there was the sound of a small explosion in the stern. But her bow still kept pointing down.

'Front planes to hand arise, chief. Now you, Brent. Gently, gently ... both engines half astern. Hold her ... hold her. Now ... Brent. Now both engines full astern. Pull, you bitches. Pull!'

Beneath their feet, the deck began to level.

As soon as he could walk across it, O'Halloran leaped to his radio console.

'Damage control. Report in ten seconds. I say again, in ten.' He flipped another switch. '*AQUANAUT* TO CONTROL. WE HAVE AN EMERGENCY. I SAY AGAIN, WE HAVE AN EMERGENCY. WAIT ... OUT.'

5

Suskin heard O'Halloran's voice and he stood rooted to the spot, suddenly oblivious of the frantic activity going on all around him. *I must call June,* he thought. *Tell her Charlie's okay.* Then he realized that Mrs O'Halloran knew nothing of Charlie's position. He looked at his watch. *Don't keep me waiting too long, Charlie,* he prayed. *Just get her goddamn bow UP.*

Almost as an echo of the prayer, he heard the sonar technician call jubilantly. 'She's coming up, sir. The bow's coming up.'

And then the radio crackled and Suskin heard O'Halloran again. The sub captain's voice was level, controlled. It struck old memories in Suskin's brain. It was the voice of a submarine commander at war, the level tones a man will use when he has come to terms with an option of death and is handling it.

'*Aquanaut* to Control. This is a Class-A Emergency.'

'We read you, *Aquanaut.*'

'We have a large pressure rupture forward. Irreparable. There is water in the ship in sections one through four. Three and four will respond to pumping. We have four minor leaks to pressure, all reparable. We have high casualties, presently reported as twelve fatal, minimum twenty seriously injured. We are commencing to surface. Priority request all support and medical facilities. Ensure surface clearance, as my manoeuvrability is considerably impaired.'

'You can say that again, old buddy,' Suskin said under his breath.

Behind him, Admiral Whitting was fidgeting.

'Absolutely no report on the cause, Commander! Suggest you call him back for that at a suitable time. I have to make my report.'

Suskin looked at him angrily. 'There's not going to be a suitable time before they surface, sir. Charlie'll have to bring her up even slower than he took her down.'

'I'm not asking for a written statement, Commander. Just give me something I can use to keep the Project Management Committee off our backs while we tidy this up.'

Suskin looked at the admiral and handed him the microphone without comment. 'We have different priorities, sir,' he said tersely, leaving the sonar control position to check on the medical facilities. *We're going to need a field hospital,* he thought gloomily.

Behind him, he heard Whitting's Marine say, 'Hallo, *Aquanaut.* Will Captain O'Halloran stand by for Admiral Whitting?'

The radio crackled.

O'Halloran's voice, still level, still very much in control, came through. 'Not now, Control. Out!'

Whitting's pale face flushed and he turned to face Suskin. 'Then you give me something if you please, Commander.' His temper was not helped by the slight grin on Suskin's face.

Suskin walked across the wide steel deck to the computer banks, Whitting following closely.

'What have we got, Maxwell?' he asked the computer operator. 'Have you had time?'

The man turned a puzzled, weary face.

'Plenty of time, sir. Just no information! I've been programming constantly from the beginning of the alert. We have nothing more positive than we had to start with. A lot of bottom activity—a real sandstorm. But nothing more than that. Nothing solid at all.'

'Then I'll tell you what you're looking for, because I saw it happen. Something very solid swiped that sub sufficiently hard for it to be thrown several feet sideways. We have the best instruments in the world, and that thing you're playing with is supposed to be able to read those instruments. So what's it reading?'

Dumbly, the operator punched several buttons and a picture grew on the screen. It showed the white sausage of the sub in its original level position and then, as they watched, the screen altered and what looked like a spiral sprang up directly beneath the ship and brushed against it.

'Can I explain, sir, that that's not actually what happened.

What I've done is to programme the actual movement in an object of the sub's given mass ... ' He stopped. 'Am I making myself clear?'

'I play chess,' said Suskin. 'What are those spirals?'

'Forces. Moving water. Projected, of course.'

'Is it accurate?' Whitting demanded. 'Come on, man. We're looking for something definite.'

The operator sighed. 'All I can tell you definitely is that currents ... forces ... exactly as per this projection, moved the *Aquanaut.*'

'Just forces?' Suskin queried. 'What caused them? You'd need a hell of an egg beater to stir up that kind of storm.'

'I agree,' the operator nodded. 'But we have no evidence of anything solid, although the computer is persistently promoting an answer based, again, on these movements.'

'So give,' said Suskin.

'If a solid causal object had come up directly below the *Aquanaut,* it would have caused this pattern. And we would not have seen it, or, more accurately, registered it on our sonar because the mass of the *Aquanaut* would have been in the way. Sonar cannot penetrate solid metal masses.'

'And that funny misty effect we saw?'

'Sand disturbance bellying up from the deep bottom,' Maxwell said more definitely. 'I have a hundred per cent confirmation there.'

'But no egg beater,' said Suskin. 'Does your electronic friend like the hidden object idea?'

'Partially, sir.'

'It has other ideas?'

'Seismic activity,' said the operator. 'It ... er ... likes that best.'

Behind him, Suskin heard Whitting say, 'So do I.'

'Underwater earthquake?' Suskin suggested.

'Or a minor volcanic explosion,' said Maxwell.

'It would account for the sandstorm,' said Whitting, his voice rich with satisfaction. 'It even casts a new light of reason on the *Jules Verne* incident. It's much better.'

Suskin leaned forward. 'Does this thing have information about earthquake activity in the area?'

'Yes, sir.'

'You want to ask it for me?'

Maxwell played with his button banks.

A line of figures glowed on the screen.

0004762

'Does that say what I think it says?' Suskin asked very gently.

Maxwell looked embarrassed. 'The incidence of seismic activity this far from the islands is, or has been, exceptionally low in recent geophysical time. The rock face that the *Aquanaut* has been descending is what's called a guyot—an extinct volcano that's been quiet for so long it's been levelled off by subaqueous weathering.'

'That's what I thought.' Suskin turned to the admiral. 'It's one of the reasons it was decided the *Jules Verne* and now the *Aquanaut* could hold that station.'

'There's always a first time,' the admiral said gruffly.

'Sure,' Suskin admitted. 'And now we have a second time—and a dozen Navy boys dead!'

'Commander, you're letting your emotions get the better of you. I'll stick to the computer evidence until we get something better. Unless you have another suggestion, of course.'

Suskin shook his head. 'I'll wait until we can talk to O'Halloran. There's just one crowd I think we should consult ahead of that. Did we have any of those dolphins in the water when this was going on?'

The computer operator looked up.

'I'm afraid not, sir. I called the Cetacean Search in the hope they might give me information to improve my programme. The team is not active at the moment.'

'How "not active"? Aren't they part of this show?'

The operator looked very unhappy.

'I was told they've all gone off to catch a sperm whale.'

Suskin fought for control. 'That's just about all I need,' he said with a ragged laugh.

Acreman had taken his team up on deck after the conversation with the dolphins.

'I owe you two some explanations,' he said to Dave Spurling and Louise Putnam. 'But there's something more immediate we have to do first, so bear with me. Our animals aren't equipped to do what we've been asked to do here, so we've decided to try and bring in a sperm whale.'

There was a long moment of stunned silence.

Davé looked at Louise. She giggled nervously. 'Can it be done, Frank?'

'I expected you to ask "what's the point?" '

'What is the point?' Dave frowned.

Acreman explained about the Megalodon prognosis, apologizing that he had not had the opportunity to tell them sooner.

'We've tried to hold things up temporarily, but we've hit a brick wall. The naked ape still thinks it's invincible,' he said sourly.

'Against a thing of that size?'

'Probably more than one,' Acreman said soberly. 'I don't want to scare you but you all have enough biology to know sharks don't engage in virgin births.'

'Are we after a live specimen?' Louise asked.

Acreman shook his head. 'I'm not even allowing myself to think about that at this stage. Certainly, I can't see how. No, all we can hope for is a positive identification. Theoretically, that's not difficult—the existing Cetacean Team could do it in an hour if the water wasn't so damned deep. That's why my ... ' he stopped, slightly embarrassed. 'That's why Professor Asquith's suggestion of a sperm whale has a grain of possibility. It can go down as deep as we need.'

He stared at them searchingly. 'I'm sorry I've got you all into this. Barbara and I have been talking it through and at best it's a problem of logistics. Size. We just have to scale up everything we know about capturing and transporting whales.'

Acreman walked across to a large wall map of the Pacific. 'I suggest we don't think about that for the moment. Let's just approach it as a logistics exercise. Now it's spring, so we have a pretty good idea where to look. As I think you know, whale food is a paradoxical commodity. We tend to think that plants grow best in tropical heat, but that's not the case with vegetable plankton. It's synthesized from carbonic acid and water with the aid of sunlight and oxygen. And carbonic acid is more soluble in cold water than in warm water. In the tropics, you get about five thousand micro-organisms per gallon of seawater. In Arctic waters, it can go as high as five hundred thousand. Animal plankton eats the vegetable plankton and krill eats that, so do fish and, of course, whales.

'So the two populations of big whales, Arctic and Antarctic, will be heading for their summer feeding grounds. I've checked the charts and it seems our best bet is to go north and try for one of the Arctic animals. It's nearer than the Antarctic and we can go to work off one of the Aleutian Islands with support from the facilities in Alaska. I've established that we can fly from Oahu to Barrow, then to a strip called Dutch Harbor in the Fox Islands. There's a U.S. Coastal Patrol vessel based there and a small helicopter squadron that watches out for Russian trawlers in the Bering Sea.'

Barbara interrupted. 'Aren't the Arctic whales smaller than the Antarctic population, Frank?'

He nodded: 'The Antarctic convergence is the richest food belt on earth. There are warm currents from the Atlantic, Indian and Pacific oceans hitting very cold water and dumping salts along the convergence. But the Arctic sperms will be big enough for our purpose and they're a thousand miles nearer ... which brings us to the real crunch. Let's assume that the techniques we've used for catching killer whales, scaled up, will work with a sperm. How the hell do we get it back?'

They discussed the problem for the next half hour and got nowhere. No aircraft was big enough to safely ship a sixty-foot sperm. It could just about be squeezed into the biggest Hercules, but as Dave pointed out, what would happen if it flapped its tail?

Acreman was well set to call Asquith and tell him it wasn't on when Louise Putnam made her suggestion.

'Wouldn't it be a good idea to see whether the ship's computer could produce an answer?'

Barbara laughed: 'You should know, dear!'

Louise flushed pink with embarrassment.

'Go on, call him,' Barbara said, more seriously. 'What have we got to lose?'

Louise went to a phone and made an obviously intimate call to Gary Maxwell. Barbara looked at Acreman and winked. Maxwell appeared a few moments later, carrying a clipboard, and listened to Acreman's outline of the problem, rather obviously avoiding looking at Louise.

'Any hope?'

'It's not a difficult programme. Our memory circuits have all the military equipment configurations. I really only need to establish what we have that could lift and fly that load. You want me to do that?'

'Sure,' Acreman grinned. 'Do you have some other reason for being here?'

Maxwell looked at Louise. 'Do you want to come upstairs while I do this?'

'Can't we all come?' Barbara asked sweetly.

Maxwell was now as pink as the girl. 'That's what I meant.'

Fifteen minutes later, Acreman stared at the printout: 'What the hell is that?' There was just one line of print on the screen.

Maxwell produced a thick manual. Acreman stared at the photograph. 'What on earth is it ... a giant liverwurst?'

'It's a dirigible,' Maxwell said. He read from the manual. 'MK-10 Low-Altitude Helium Dirigible. Developed 1976 as a tank transporter for use in regions where landing facilities are unavailable. Maximum lift capability: one hundred and twenty tons. Engines two. Maximum speed: two hundred and twenty knots.'

He looked up at Acreman. 'Anyway, according to the computer, it's your only option.'

'I thought those things went out with the Red Baron. Don't they blow up?'

'Not any more,' said Dave. 'They use helium instead of hydrogen.'

Acreman smiled evilly. 'Get Harry for me!'

By the time the call came through, he was feeling positively buoyant. Barbara watched him carefully. 'Don't push your luck, Frank.'

'Harry. Harry, you remember how you told me that nothing was impossible. Yes, you did, Harry. Okay, we've licked the problem of transporting the whale. But it requires a little organization. I want a MK-10 dirigible tank transporter. You have to get it to Dutch Harbor in the Aleutian Islands—that's right, the Aleutians—in two days at the outside. And I want a Coastal Patrol ship of trawler size and three choppers on stand-by. Also a sling like we used for the orca of one hundred feet—right, one hundred. You'd better tell them to use carbon steel. And a heavy-gauge purse seine net.' He paused, grinning hugely.

Watching, the others saw the grin began to slip. 'What? Oh, Christ, Harry, if you want anything like that, you'll have to arrange it yourself.'

Acreman put down the phone.

'What did he say, dragon-killer?' Barbara demanded.

'He said to make sure "Marine Studies Institute, Hawaii" is painted on the side of the dirigible.'

'Serves you right,' Barbara said. 'So we go?'

'Yes, damn it—we go!'

Some kind of order had been restored aboard the shattered *Aquanaut* by the end of the first day. The casualty list rose to twenty during that time, however, when two torpedo technicians died while carrying out routine maintenance on the *Aquanaut*'s forward torpedo tubes. Between them and the rest of the ship was a solid wall of water, contained in the ruptured mess hall.

Once the sub's nose had lifted, O'Halloran elected not to try and pump out this section. He needed all his pumps to handle the minor pressure leaks that had erupted in various stations when the *Aquanaut* went bow down. Two-thirds of the ship was now dry, or at least not sufficiently wet to be dangerous and, with the bow buoyancy tanks blown full of air and the stern tanks full of water, the *Aquanaut* was maintaining a roughly level equilibrium, provided O'Halloran was very gentle with the engines.

But that meant that no one could get to the Golding brothers working on the torpedo tubes and they could not get out. Fortunately, when the return to the surface began, the brothers reported themselves in good shape. Jamie had suffered a cut to his head and Scott had a sprained wrist, but they were fully conscious. And for two men trapped fifteen hundred feet underwater in a submarine that might suddenly fill from bow to stern, they were remarkably cheerful. O'Halloran told ship's intercom to keep up a steady broadcast of music and he brought Mess Steward Walker up to radio control.

'You disc jockey on games nights, don't you, Walker?'

'Yes, sir.'

'Well, I want you to keep those two boys alert and interested. This mike links you to the bow section and they're the only ones down there. It's not your biggest audience, but it's the most important you'll ever have. And I want a two-way chat. If anything changes in their condition, I want to know about it.'

O'Halloran then went on a lengthy inspection of his broken ship, feeling increasingly bitter as he reviewed the white faces of his subdued crew. He listened to the sharp whistle of pressurized water coming through the outer skin, and the laboured beat of the engines as they fought against the heavy load of water in the hull.

The *Aquanaut* was a dead ship and she was probably his last command. What a hell of a way to end thirty years' service. And was any of it his fault? He had warned against taking this combat vessel down to depths that exceeded her specifications.

All of it *was* his fault, O'Halloran grimly admitted to himself. He was in charge and he had agreed to make the dive. Reluctance didn't count.

But at least he would get her up again, God willing. The closer they crept to the surface, the lower the pressure on the hull. Mallory, the ship's doctor, was a demon at his work and had reported that unless there were unforeseen reactions to shock, the casualty list could be closed.

'First Officer to Captain. Come in, please.'

'O'Halloran, Mr. Forbes. What is it?'

'I think you should return to the bridge, sir. We have … er … abnormal behaviour in the bow.'

O'Halloran scrabbled as fast as he could up the companion ladders to the bridge. On the way, he called to Mallory to come with him. When they reached the bridge, they heard the Golding brothers singing!

O'Halloran listened, frowning.

'They sound drunk! Is there any liquor on this ship, Mr. Forbes?'

'No, sir!' the first officer said emphatically. He knew every member of this crew. Most had been hand-picked volunteers for this mission. None of them would have broken the golden rule of the Submarine Service. 'And there certainly wouldn't be anything of that kind in the torpedo room,' he added unnecessarily.

'They sound drunk to me,' O'Halloran repeated. 'How long has this been going on, Walker?'

'It started about an hour ago. Not like this, sir. At first, they just got more chatty. Then I noticed they were slurring their words but I thought it might just be their end of the radio. When they started the singing, I advised the first officer.'

O'Halloran took the microphone. 'Hallo, the bow,' he said sternly. 'This is the captain speaking. How are you boys doing down there?'

The singing stopped and was replaced by giggling, a loud hiccup and then, after a pause of several seconds a long, thin, agonized scream. O'Halloran reached forward abruptly to cut the speakers.

Mallory, white-faced, had stepped to his side.

'Captain ... it's ...'

O'Halloran's eyes had swung up to the bank of pressure gauges. He nodded, turning reluctantly to Mallory.

'I know ... pressure's bleeding out of the torpedo compartment. Is that it?'

Mallory nodded 'Yes. The drunkenness is nitrogen narcosis, the so called "raptures of the deep". That scream is one of them getting the bends.'

'Is there *anything* we can do for them?' O'Halloran demanded harshly.

The doctor shook his head. 'If I could get them into a decompression chamber within the next five minutes, they might survive with no more than minor narcosis of certain bone joints. Provided, of course, that the nitrogen from their blood that's forming as bubbles in their bone joints isn't doing the same in their brains.'

'With the state of this hull, we need at least twenty-four hours for the ascent,' O'Halloran snapped. 'If I try it any faster, she'll rupture, bow to stern!'

'I know that, skipper.'

O'Halloran shook his head in a frenzied moment of frustration.

'What the hell did this to us?' he cried. 'I'm stuck in the middle of a conspiracy of silence that's killing my men!'

Mallory put a restraining hand on his shoulder and took the intercom microphone. 'Run the ship, Charlie. Get us up. Leave the medical business to me. Hallo, the bow. You Golding boys, this is Dr. Mallory. Can you hear me down there?'

After a moment, a thin voice responded.

'Doc ... Doc, Jamie's gone to sleep and I keep getting this pain between my shoulders that I reckon'll knock me out if it happens again ...'

'Okay, Golding. Don't talk any more. Up front of you—it's

painted bright red so you can't miss it—is a big first-aid box. Open it. Take out the white box. Inside there's a big hypodermic syringe. Take it out and give yourself an injection into the muscle just above the knee. Shoot straight through your pants and take it all. Okay, Golding, do that now, it's going to kill the pain.'

Mallory waited a moment, then switched on the intercom speaker. All on the bridge listened to the silence for a long time.

'What was in the syringe?' O'Halloran asked eventually. 'I need to know for the log.'

'Something to make him sleep,' said Mallory, his eyes steady. 'I'll make my own endorsement to your entry.'

'Thanks,' said O'Halloran. 'But it is still my responsibility.'

He went down into the bowels of the ship to continue his inspection. He didn't much like the sounds that were coming from the port drive shaft and he'd been slipped a note by radioactivity control. The pile was overheating, due to a lack of cooling water pressure. O'Halloran was not surprised. The pumps that drove the cooling water through the pile were presently doing other things.

Back on the bridge, O'Halloran stood quietly before his Systems State board. The quivering needles of the depth gauges were hypnotic and he had to force himself to look away to the other important gauges, dials and telltales.

The flooding and pumping gauges showed ninety-five per cent capacity, a dangerously heavy work load but one that had to be maintained if the ship's ascent were to continue. He glanced at the fore and aft planesmen, seated before their joysticks. Both had their sticks pulled hard back as the big hydroplanes fought against the weight of the water in the bow. O'Halloran would have liked to increase his speed to give the planes more lift but dared not run the risk of forcing more water into the ship.

Behind him, he heard a muttered conversation about the Golding brothers and when he turned he caught a glance from a systems technician that seemed openly accusing.

'Stop the chatter,' he snapped and picked up the command microphone. 'Marine Captain Stacey, this is the captain. I want an armed Marine guard posted at number four watertight door. No one is to open any WT doors or air-conditioning vents, even if tapping is heard.' He waited for the 'Aye, Aye, Sir,' and was about to start another tour of the ship when a red light went on in a line of bulbs directly above the Systems State board. O'Halloran experienced a moment of real physical nausea.

'Atmosphere control—report!' The red light denoted radiation, the one aspect of this huge finely tuned machine that O'Halloran secretly detested.

'Lieutenant Stanstead, sir. We appear to have a rupture of a cooling pipe gland.'

'What's it spilling, mister ... and where?'

'Grade four contamination, sir. But it can't be more than a trickle. It will be working its way into the bilges under section nine, the standby generators.'

O'Halloran spun around. 'Evacuate Emergency Generation, Number One ... Now!'

'But, skipper ...'

'It'll either run on its own or not. I'm not having men burned for nothing. Get them out! Stanstead, can we flush out those contaminants without making things worse?'

There was a pause. 'It can't hurt anything that's not immediately alongside the hull.'

O'Halloran grimaced. 'Number One, commence flushing nine and keep it circulating. Let me know if it affects our trim.'

In ten minutes, the red telltale blinked out. O'Halloran experienced a surge of relief. With so many other problems, he had no right to feel better, but somehow the fact that his ship was clean of radioactive contamination made him feel a whole lot better.

'Steady as she goes,' he said unnecessarily. He walked across to the sonar operator. 'How's your postmortem?' The technician lifted his hands in despair.

'It's just plain uncanny. I don't even have a trace until the last second or so, and then suddenly this huge image. But no sounds! No engine noise, no sonar signature. Nothing. A ghost—like the ghost of a submarine.'

O'Halloran patted him on the shoulder.

'Don't let it get you. We'll leave them to worry about what it was, topside. Let's be thankful it's gone away.'

The Soviet Delta-class ballistic missile submarine *Red Ensign* was some six hundred miles south of Alaska when she received her emergency command to surface in a force nine gale.

Captain Uri Markov, Commissar Beltyin, the torpedo and sonar technician, and Chief Engineer Yivshenko made their way rapidly up the many stairs linking the *Red Ensign*'s three decks, pausing briefly while the flying bridge hatch was broken open and their ears popped with the change of pressure. They were ready when the deck aerial lifted to its full extension and the long-range transmitter began to receive a direct high-speed coded signal from the Soviet Naval HQ in Murmansk.

Decoded, they considered a message which, though it struck Markov as somewhat garbled and cryptic, still made him shiver with real apprehension.

It seemed that what were termed 'significant' levels of radiation were emanating from their target RV.

'What does it mean?' Engineer Yivshenko, a youngish, university-trained entrant who had never seen active service, inquired. 'Has there been a nuclear detonation?'

'It does not say that,' Markov pointed out. 'We are warned that a radioactive trace has been noted in the area designated as our RV. We are ordered to delay our RV until further information is available.'

The elderly political officer smiled grimly at the young engineer.

'Maybe it is the Third World War we have been expecting for so long. You may yet be a Hero of the Soviet Union, Comrade Yivshenko.'

Yivshenko's face blanched white. 'No!'

'No to being a hero, or no to the war? When it does come, this is how we will hear of it.'

'Leave him alone, Beltyin,' Markov growled. He had never quite learned to live with the idea that there was a man aboard his ship he could not always command. 'We don't want to start rumours.'

He ordered the surface aerial retracted and they made their way below.

On the bridge, he approached the technician monitoring the Delta's sophisticated three-dimensional sonar display, its range over forty miles.

'Is there anything happening in our RV sector?'

'We are too far away, Captain. It is three hundred miles, at least. Here ... ' the technician pointed to a neon blip on his circular screen, 'are two U.S. destroyers and this is a NATO

Swordfish proceeding to Pearl at a depth of two hundred feet. All behaving normally.'

'Do they know we are here?'

'I doubt it, Captain. Certainly their sonar and hydrophones do not have our range. The British ship is ancient. It is possible their satellites picked us up when we surfaced.'

Markov shook his head. 'With only the flying bridge clear? No, not in that storm.'

He used his command microphone. 'Engines one-half and hold your course. Prepare for *silent running* in five hours. No excessive noise as of this order.'

He thought of Beltyin's coarse joke. What if it was not a joke and the next time he surfaced, the world had come to an end? Markov shivered and felt momentarily ashamed. *You will be very busy long before that time,* he reminded himself, looking up at the pressure gauges monitoring his sixteen SSM–SSN9 (MK11) nuclear ballistic missile tubes.

After his abortive foray in pursuit of the large prey object, an expedition that had caused him much pain, the young Megalodon male sought the gentle darkness of the deep bottom.

Above him, he was aware that the movement that had first so impelled his instincts had not stopped. But his limited memory retained the impression of a thing too large for even his enormous jaws and, as he settled into the soft shale lining of the Fracture, his sensing pits told him that the object had now drifted even further away. Soon it was beyond a level where even his feeding instincts and adolescent energy would have been capable of overriding the pain of the light. Slowly, he lost interest.

He became aware that his parents were not in their traditional feeding ground and he began to swim slowly up the long length of the Fracture in search of their company and some food, for he had not eaten now for three days.

Over the several million years of their evolution, the Megalodons had paid one heavy price for their deep-water home. They were, in the normal sense, blind. Their sensing pits were effective eyes when it came to detecting objects that moved in the water, but static objects, like the crags and spikes of rock protruding from the Fracture, had to be avoided by instinct and with great care.

This, and the fact that the bulk of their food came to them and required no hunting, had resulted in the Megalodons developing a swimming technique like the giant rays. They moved along slowly in almost permanent contact with the bottom, and such was their size, their movement cloaked them in a thick pall of shale and sand.

Deeply buried within the instinct/mind of the Megalodons there was a memory of another time, a time long passed. Then, others close to the size of the primal Megalodons had existed. Enemies. They had come in a kaleidoscope of shapes, armed with a confusing variety of body weapons. Mostly middle, or surface dwellers, these enemies had had scales, or bony plates protecting their snakelike bodies. Some had had spikes protruding from their snouts, all had had highly developed teeth, some generated lethal electric voltages, others attacked with long claws as sharp as razors.

Against these enemies, the primal Megalodons had had only teeth, of limited use against their well-armoured opponents, and their size. But the price of their size was enforced occupation of an arid environmental niche, the deep Fracture. But sometimes in that other age, the middle and surface predators, driven by extreme hunger or feeding instincts even more ferocious than the primal drive of the Megalodons, would be forced to hunt in the depths

So the Megalodons had learned to hide and to camouflage. The latter had been an evolutionary development; the former, a lucky break.

Any animal the size of the Megalodon must accept that it will be used by smaller marine creatures in a symbiotic relationship. Over the years, the Megalodons had accepted these riders, shell encrustations and service partners. Thus, the family of three now presented a very strange appearance. They did not look like sharks at all.

They were completely covered, snout to tail, with a layer of living and dead molluscs. Varieties of seaweed clung tenaciously to this calcium skin and flourished, some of the strands growing as long as thirty feet. Small species of blind fish, many with luminous dots glowing in various parts of their boneless bodies, swam among this forest. Blindworms, some three feet long, moved through channels in the layers of dead shells, while crabs, most of them nearly transparent, occupied those that were abandoned.

When they settled for the purposes of digestion (and considerably more than half of their lives was so spent), they were simply rock gardens. The weed growth settled and waved upright. The little fish, most of which had evolved either suckers, or the ability to hide in the molluscs' caves during periods of movement, came out and fed in these silent gardens. Only the gills of the great sharks moved and this movement was deeply buried in the weed jungle.

All along the Fracture were rocks which, to all intents and purposes, were identical to the still Megalodons. Only when the Megalodons opened their vast maws and the huge teeth and tender pink interiors of their mouths were exposed, did they become in any way different to the general seascape.

Lying thus, their maws were like the opening to a cave, thirty feet across, leading into a rock garden two hundred and fifty feet long and sixty feet wide, with a height of thirty feet. This opening was lined with teeth and through the veil of weed, lidless eyes, deathly white, stared fixedly ahead.

Carved aeons ago by volcanic activity in the southern base of the trench, the floor of the cave where the young one's parents sheltered still possessed some residual heat and it was this that first attracted the Megalodons. To an animal which had come to terms with temperatures only a degree or two above zero, this warm floor was a welcome relief. That it was lined with a glistening sand of almost pure alluvial gold and that it was slightly radioactive were of no interest to the Megalodons whatsoever.

Unfortunately, the cave was bypassed by the main current and the Megalodons were obliged to leave it to feed. But if they had fed well, or if the normal water temperature dropped, or if any disturbing activity occurred, they would seek the warmth of the cave and there lie dormant, sometimes for weeks on end.

The heat of the cave was not quite sufficient to keep their cold-blooded systems active, and the Megalodons had never properly learned to hibernate. But it did afford them long periods of total peace.

After scouring the Fracture to no avail, the young Megalodon turned his head in the direction of the cave. He entered and found his parents resting there. He moved behind them and settled on the floor. His primitive mind accepted that, after the excitement of the day with the nagging pain still behind his eyes, he should relax here for a time. His parents, however, had spent their day more sensibly, feeding on detritus.

Very soon, the young male would need to leave the cave to feed. And his simple mind had acquired a new image. A large food target. He had attacked once, but the texture of the object had not been to his liking. A second time he had made an attack pass but instinctive caution, and pain, had dissuaded him from following through the attack. But now the young male's nervous system was familiar with pain and with the large food object.

Familiarity breeds contempt.

Suskin looked at his notes and wondered whether it wouldn't be simpler to allow Whitting to proceed with his threat to court martial the entire communications section. At least a few new heads could be applied to the problem and Suskin would get a judgment of his results or, more accurately, of his lack of results.

The situation with the *Aquanaut* had stabilized. She was now a thousand feet below the surface and O'Halloran had allowed the rate of ascent to increase to a few feet a second rather than the marginal lift of the preceding twenty-four hours.

Since the death of the two torpedo technicians, ghastly and still only to be presumed, there had been no further casualties aboard the craft and all the injured were reported 'comfortable'. The problems with the nuclear pile had been handled. As the sub rose and the pressure on her hull decreased, the small leaks had made less water and the pumps were able to increase their output of cooling water into the pile. Admittedly, O'Halloran was still running the boat as though the entire Japanese Navy were about to launch depth charges, but after all he, Suskin conceded, was still down there.

Looking again at his notes, Suskin would still willingly have swapped roles with O'Halloran.

Once the primary emergency had passed for the *Aquanaut*, Whitting had descended on Suskin like the proverbial ton of bricks.

'We have now lost two Ohio-class nuclear submarines,'

Whitting told him unnecessarily. 'Even *I* don't know the real cost. More to the point, Commander, we are obliged, I stress *obliged*, to locate a boat on this station. I want some answers, Commander, and I want them fast or I'll court martial your entire communications section for gross dereliction of duty.'

But Suskin knew this was not an option open either to himself or Whitting. Whitting was a Navy administrator, not the type that went down with sinking ships.

For the past twenty-four hours, once things had improved for the *Aquanaut*, Suskin had subjected the Fracture to every form of electronic surveillance open to him. He had gathered the tape recordings of sonar sweeps up to, during and after, the moment when the white sausage moved sideways and a fifth of O'Halloran's men had died. His computer analyst, now rapidly approaching a nervous breakdown, had reprogrammed his box every whichway without improving the original prognosis. They had relayed the programme to the U.S. Coast Guard Ground and Geodetic Survey Complex, but these monster silicon brains had also drawn silvery spirals and committed themselves no further.

There was absolutely nothing solid.

Maxwell, the computer analyst, was sitting listlessly opposite him.

'It still doesn't feel right,' Suskin said. Maxwell flinched as though a shell had exploded overhead. 'There has to be something solid.'

'That is not an automatic assumption,' Maxwell said mechanically, as if he had become an extension of his own machinery. 'Earthquakes, volcanoes, can create terrible pressures and pressure effects. Krakatoa killed six thousand people—the tidal wave was almost seventy feet high. If you wish, think of that as solid—it flattened the buildings. They say the entire Minoan civilization was destroyed, marble temples and all, by the volcanic collapse of Thera. What's this obsession with solid objects?'

Suskin did not fail to note that Maxwell had stopped calling him 'Sir'. Under the circumstances, it was understandable.

'And anyway,' Maxwell added wearily. 'The scans did show some solid objects and the computer's taken them into account.'

'Rocks,' said Suskin contemptuously. 'I'm not talking about

a few rocks on the bottom. They were twenty thousand feet below the *Aquanaut* and, with the blanking you were getting from sand disturbance, we can't even be sure of them.'

'We can be sure of those two very big slides,' Maxwell said doggedly. 'At about the time of the pressure wave, we have clear images of two rock sections moving away from the point which the computer promotes as the source of the activity. The computer has finite recollection of the sonar reflections off all known materials, organic and inorganic. It labelled those objects as *rocks*. It doesn't make mistakes at that level.'

'Even with the sand disturbance?'

Maxwell shook his head. 'They were sufficiently large to reflect a quite definite echo pattern.' He thumbed through several pages of figures. 'In fact, I can do a little better ... the variations on the echoes indicate quite positively, typical mollusc infestation of the rocks.'

Suskin sighed. 'Whitting's not going to like it.'

'He's going to have to lump it.'

Suskin looked up sharply. 'Careful, mister!'

'I'm sorry, sir,' said Maxwell dejectedly. 'But I just don't understand this refusal to accept the evidence. It's very depressing.'

'We're in the same boat,' his commander reminded him. 'The reason they won't buy it is because they have a real good reason for wanting a sub down there. I can't tell you more, but you've seen what's being spent and you've seen the security we're carrying. You'd just better accept that this is big business for our country.'

'I still don't honestly see how they can contemplate siting a submarine over a subterranean volcano,' Maxwell persisted.

Suskin looked at him. 'Maybe you'd better get some rest because that's exactly what you are going to have to get used to. And they're going to be asking us the safest way of doing it.'

'There is no safe way, sir!'

Suskin nodded. 'We're in the Navy. I said "safest". Not safe.' He went on quickly. 'Our big problem with your volcano theory, Maxwell, is the lack of a previous history.'

'I can't offer anything further on that, sir.'

'Maybe we need a volcanologist. Do these things suddenly spring up like mushrooms?'

Maxwell's pale face flushed.

'I already did that on my own initiative. I needed expert information for my programme. The Seismic Sea Wave Warning Station in Honolulu is the centre of a network of seismographic detectors ringing the entire Pacific, and I trained with one of the analysts working there.'

'And you've spoken to him?'

'Yes.'

'Was that call cleared?'

'It went through,' Maxwell said defiantly.

'Be careful, mister. You wouldn't be the first young officer to be locked up for using his own initiative. So what did your friend have to say?'

'He wasn't very helpful.'

'Come on, Maxwell. Give!'

Maxwell's face was now bright pink. 'Seismic activity can be pretty accurately forecast nowadays, thanks to computers. Most of the major fault lines in the earth's crust, like the San Andreas, are well-plotted and monitored constantly. And, in a sense, volcanic activity is something of a chain reaction. It's possible to make computer projections, of likely seismic outbursts.'

'Good,' said Suskin heavily. 'You just got your master's. Now what did your friend say about our little volcano?'

'No way.'

'What!'

Maxwell bit his lip. 'The volcanoes here are guyots, blown out and capped off. The Fracture is, in fact, a great chasm—a split associated with the formation of Mauna Loa. Mauna Loa is still active and a fuse for the whole area. Any pressure goes up its spout like a chimney. We're just old scar tissue held down by an immense weight of sea. My friend says that, before we even got a tremor here, the whole of Southern California would have fallen into the sea.'

'And it hasn't,' said Suskin.

'I beg your pardon.'

'Pity,' Suskin said to himself. 'Now *that* would have diverted their attention. Why haven't you come out with this before, Maxwell?'

The analyst's voice grew shrill. 'Because it is still totally negative. I can only work with the information I'm getting. I have a positive prognosis of seismic disturbance, supported by rock movement on the bottom and evidence from the submarine of major water disturbance. My evidence is actual, not theoretical.'

'But we've still got it wrong, haven't we, Maxwell?'

'I think so, sir.'

Suskin grinned. 'Well, there's something. I thought maybe you were an android and that light-show over there was your daddy.'

'There's no need to be insulting. I'm only doing my best.'

Suskin leaned forward and patted his shoulder.

'Now, now, Maxwell. In fact, I just paid you a compliment. How would you fancy humouring me for a little while? Before Whitting descends on us. I reckon we've got about half an hour.'

'I'm not sure what you mean.'

'I'll give you a few ideas for Big Daddy. See what he has to say. Nothing official. Just between you, me and him.'

Maxwell looked puzzled but stood up and made his way across to his console. Suskin followed.

'I said to you a while ago, that we needed something solid. What I'd like you to do, if you can, is to turn your sums on their backs. Instead of asking the computer to project an opinion of what could have caused the water movement, I'm going to give you a possible cause and see whether the computer agrees that it fits the water movement. Okay?'

'You'll need to be fairly specific.'

'Well, I can't be,' said Suskin carefully. 'Remember, this is just a game to fill the time, Maxwell. But here goes. You have the known water pressures. Ask the computer what size of solid object moving near the sub could cause such movements.'

'Yes, I can do that,' said Maxwell. He played with his keyboard, and five lines of figures appeared on the screen.

'I just wanted one answer, Maxwell.'

'These are variables. Three thousand tons at ten knots at range half a mile and so on.'

'What's the smallest?'

'Two hundred tons at twenty-eight knots range two hundred feet.'

'Okay, good,' said Suskin. 'Now, ask if there is any way an object of that size could have approached the sub without them, or us, seeing it.'

This time the programme took much longer. Suskin looked at his watch. He did not want the officers, due for the Day Briefing, breaking in on this, particularly Whitting.

Maxwell sat back. A soft bell pinged and the screen printed 'AFFIRMATIVE'.

'Good Lord,' said Maxwell. 'I don't see how that's possible.'

'Is that all we get?' Suskin cried. 'I want to know how!'

Maxwell hit three more buttons. The computer drew three straight lines and one wavy.

'Oh, I see,' said Maxwell. 'Interesting.'

'Explain it!' Suskin growled, suppressing an urge to put his hands round the analyst's throat.

'By coming up directly under the sub no more than a foot to two feet away from the wall of the Fracture. We could not have seen it because the mass of the sub—all metal—would have blocked the echo. The sub could not have seen it because they were using close-proximity sonar very tightly focused on the shelf.'

Suskin picked up the phone to the bridge, and asked for the information centre.

'Commander Suskin in communications. Can you tell me exactly when Dr. Acreman of the Cetacean Search Unit will be back aboard?'

Suskin thought he heard a short laugh.

'I don't think you're going to believe me, sir.'

'Try me,' Suskin grunted.

'Dr. Acreman is presently six hundred miles north of us, proceeding at two hundred and twenty knots … in an airship.'

'What the hell's he doing in an airship?'

'It's dangling his whale … sir!' said the operator jubilantly.

Suskin cut in, shortly. 'Now I'm telling you something, mister, and this you'd better hear and believe. The moment Acreman hits the deck, you call me. Right?'

'Aye, Aye, sir!'

6

The most difficult decision Acreman had had to make about the catch was whether he should be doing it at all. Acreman's respect for the great whales was as near as he had ever come to a religious feeling.

He suspected that he loved the dolphins in a genuine, if anthropomorphic, way. But since they had learned to talk, he had stopped worrying about anthropomorphic thinking—the crediting of animals with human characteristics—which all good zoologists are taught to avoid. As far as Acreman was now concerned, a talking dolphin was very close to man. Different, but close, and definitely superior in many ways, particularly in the general beauty of their natures. But, he acknowledged, inferior if you rated man for his ability to build artificial things. Acreman had never fallen into the trap of downgrading this unique human talent simply because so many of the things man had built had spawned ghastly byproducts like plutonium waste and the bomb. Man had also built antibiotics, which now kept the dolphins healthier than they had been in the open sea, and some men used their hands to make more things than his own brain could handle.

Dolphins, on the other hand, were definitely sane. Acreman considered this to be the result of their making the right choice at the start of their evolutionary history. They had decided to live in the sea. Man, who opted for the land, had soon over-populated its limited surface which, after all, occupied only three-tenths of the earth and the fierce competition, the killing and the conquering, had largely shaped man's emotional brain. On the other hand, the dolphins had not been forced to change the sea world to suit them as man had been driven to change the land. The dolphins had simply changed themselves so that they could fully use the size and freedom of the sea. It was not surprising they were so consistently 'nicer' and so easy to love.

But the great whales, like the sperms, even though they were, zoologically, just large dolphins, were something else.

It was as if they had somehow expanded themselves, mentally as well as physically, to fit the enormity of the ocean. Man had never been able to do this. Even the men who went to the moon had been ordinary men encased in massive technology. The whales were the largest species ever to have lived on the earth and Acreman thought they were, in fact, inhabitants of another planet.

He had often wondered whether the Janus machine would work with the great whales. They possessed the big, sophisticated cetacean brain and they were very vocal. But part of Acreman was secretly relieved that the great whales were not readily available for a language experiment. They were simply too large to keep and feed for the period of close contact necessary for the early stages of Janus learning.

Or so it had been up to now.

Their helicopter had been circling the school of sperm whales for twenty minutes while the Cetacean Team studied it through binoculars.

Acreman watched a large male slide to the surface, blow, pause and then disappear again to feed.

The sea looked ugly. The waves had a swollen, bloated appearance and even from the helicopter it was possible to judge their considerable size. But Acreman was an experienced diver and he knew that, twenty feet down, there would be little movement.

However, he still could not relish the prospect of the sickening plunge through the spume-flecked grey shoulders of that heaving mass of water. He also knew that he was going to do it, and he started a meticulous check of his equipment.

He muttered a silent apology to the whales. *It may be a pity for you that we exist,* Acreman thought, *but we do and you'll have to learn to live and die with us because it's not in our nature to stop. The best we ever do is pause.*

Locked into racks behind their seats were twin-seventy aqualungs with enough air for an hour underwater, depending on how much work they had to do. Acreman strapped on a thirty-five-pound weight belt to compensate for the buoyancy of his wetsuit. Barbara needed only twenty-five pounds and she would stay warmer longer than he. Even slim women had thicker subcutaneous fat layers than men. The best divers in the world were women.

Around his neck he pulled on a life jacket with its own miniature air bottle and an emergency mouthpiece. The bottle would inflate the jacket and pull him up to the surface like a rocket if anything went wrong. If the problem involved his air supply, he could breathe the air in the jacket through the mouthpiece.

To his right thigh he strapped a large knife with a chisel tip, and a snorkel. His left wrist carried a depth gauge, a waterproof watch and a length-of-dive warning device.

Finally, he leaned forward awkwardly to slip on flippers. Suiting up for a dive was a damned tedious business.

The helicopter pilot had been watching him.

'I want to hit the water a hundred feet ahead of the school,' Acreman instructed. 'Dave, we'll go first and see what it's like down there. If there's a bad current, we'll not manage much more than a pass.'

The pilot asked, 'From what height do you jump?'

Acreman thought about it. He didn't want to frighten the school of whales.

'Forty feet.' The pilot looked startled but accepted the instruction, and dipped the helicopter towards the sea.

'Where do you want the backup boat, Frank?' Barbara asked. 'I think we should be down there, waiting, when you come up.'

'Watch our first pass and see what the current does. That skimmer can do twenty knots and it's probably our best bet. Dave and I won't dive on the first pass so, depending on how quick we get pushed behind, you make your drop. Then we'll wait for you and come back on the school in the skimmer. Then maybe we'll do a dive, probably on lines under the inflatable. The animal I'm most interested in is swimming between the two animals in front. I'm assuming that means it's the school leader. But we have to check.'

'How do you judge a whale's age, Frank?' Louise asked.

He stood up and braced himself by the port door. Dave Spurling took up a similar position on the other side.

'You measure the rings on their teeth,' he said. 'Dave … GO!'

Acreman was too busy holding himself together to be aware of the few seconds he was in space. Jumping from so high he had to enter the water correctly or do real damage to his spine and maybe break both ankles. He needed to enter the water heels first with his flippers tilted upwards. And he did not have much chance of correcting his alignment because he needed to keep both hands clamped on his face mask to prevent the impact from ripping it loose. So he threw himself flat into the chopper's slipstream and, when he felt the considerable weight of the big aqualung pulling him backwards, he pointed his toes, closed his eyes and gave himself up to a moment of pure terror. It was something he had learned not to fight.

The immediate, biting clutch of the cold sea drove this veil from his mind. Even in the heavy suit, the change of temperature was dramatic and, as he sank below the surface, he had a terrible feeling of breathlessness.

Discipline took care of him in those first seconds in the sea. Keeping one hand clamped to the top of his mask, he blew hard through his nose, and the water that had been forced under his mask blasted out through the soft nose seal. His free hand lifted his mouthpiece above his head and triggered the air valve, blowing the tube clear. By this time, he was feeling pressure in his ears and he gripped his nostrils through the mask and blew hard until the pain disappeared.

He took two long, deep breaths and gently cracked the valve on his life jacket. The jacket took up a little air and his rate of descent slowed. Acreman let in more air until he was hanging stationary in the water, thirty feet down.

He looked around. Dave was also hanging in space, thirty feet away. Visibility was about a hundred feet, much better than Acreman had dared hope.

Thirty feet in front of him, approaching fast, was the huge bulk of a sixty-foot whale, its mouth slightly open to show a formidable array of teeth. There was another animal sixty feet below with large silver air bubbles dribbling out of its blow hole, and another of enormous size only about ten feet away swimming parallel with Dave. Dave was watching it, unmoved.

Acreman felt a surge of elation. This position was exactly right. The current, as far as he could tell, was not particularly strong, although the whales appeared to be swimming much faster than they had judged from the air.

The whales also looked much, much bigger than from the air. That, Acreman had to remind himself forcefully, was because the masks magnified by almost a third.

The whale that had been heading directly for him was holding its course! *Dear God,* Acreman thought, *can it even* see *something as small as me?* He reached for the life jacket air valve.

But in that moment, Acreman realized that the approaching animal was the bull he most wanted to see.

Fighting a flood of alarm with an even more powerful blast of total wonder, Acreman stayed where he was.

The bull swam on until it was less than ten feet away. Acreman could see the slow horizontal rise and fall of its tail, and then the whites of its eyes.

Then a familiar sound calmed Acreman's spinning brain ... the high squeak of the whale's sonar pulses.

The whale stopped—the pause was momentary—and scanned him with another sonar burst of lower frequency. The wide head moved to one side and then the other to give each of the large eyes a full glimpse of him, and then, with a surge of air bubbles lifting from the blow holes, it slid beneath his feet.

Had Acreman emptied his life jacket, he could have descended onto the whale's back.

The big dorsal fin missed him by no more than a few inches, but by then the whale had increased the angle of its dive. Acreman spun around to watch. Ahead, the two large females were circling. Suddenly, Acreman felt a sudden surge of water and he was pushed up ten feet by the upthrust from the whale's tail, now some thirty feet beneath him.

He hung in the water until all the whales were out of sight. Six others passed him in that time, but none of them came close. Acreman had the impression that word of their presence had been passed on. He felt immensely satisfied. He knew his dolphins could do that. It was a primary requirement for the whale if it was to fulfil their intended purpose. But mostly his satisfaction came from the conviction that the whale had seen him, acknowledged his presence, bypassed him politely and gone on its way without fear.

He signalled to Dave and filled his life jacket.

As he broke surface and transferred to his snorkel, he saw the bright orange outline of the skimmer sliding down the side of a wave only thirty feet away.

'I thought I told you to wait until we'd made our first pass,' Acreman protested as the rubber hull came alongside.

'I thought you said you weren't going to dive,' Barbara said curtly. 'What's with this chauvinist bullshit? Did you see them?'

'Fantastic,' Acreman grinned, pulling his mask off.

'Come on, then. Open her up. It's our turn!'

Acreman wondered whether this wasn't becoming a dangerous way to run a dive, with everybody in charge and nobody taking his orders. Then he looked at Barbara, and at Louise, sitting tensely beside her. He smiled and wound up the engine. What was this chauvinist bullshit? They were both fitter than he was.

To Barbara's considerable chagrin, Acreman's liberal decision resulted in Louise riding a whale for the first time.

They pursued the whales for nearly three miles, carefully timing their dives. The school was keeping roughly to the original lineup with a very big bull doing patrol duty a mile out on the right flank, and their target animal was a few hundred yards behind the lead females. Acreman was coming to the conclusion that the school consisted of two families—the three animals in the lead and the second group of six swimming about three-quarters of a mile behind. By bringing the skimmer around in a wide arc, they managed to position themselves between the two groups and held this position to see whether the school would break up. It went on, undisturbed.

Very carefully, Acreman began to narrow the distance between the inflatable and the target bull. He was diving and surfacing about every eight minutes.

Part of the kit that had come down with the inflatable was a radio direction finder. This was no larger than a cigarette pack with a two-inch stub of aerial, its base consisting of a large blob of impact epoxy 'super glue' which stuck tenaciously to any kind of skin tissue.

On a whale, which sheds skin as part of its hydrodynamic process, the packs were good for about two weeks. Louise's job was to tag the target bull.

Acreman waited until they were less than two hundred yards behind and held this position for two further dives. The next time the bull went down, he gunned the engine and surged forward. At the appropriate time, he signalled Barbara and Louise to dive.

Acreman's timing was right again. By the time the two girls were established below the surface, the bull was coming up directly beneath them. He saw Barbara and paused to scan her exactly as he had done Acreman. Louise had entered the water a few seconds behind Barbara and the current had carried her thirty feet backwards, so that the bull did not see, or apparently detect, her.

The young dolphin handler did not panic. She saw what was about to happen and held still. The bull rose beneath her. Louise reached down and positioned the radio direction finder two feet behind the great dorsal fin. Then, very calmly, she spread her legs and rode the whale as it took her weight.

The reaction was immediate and violent. The bull flapped its tail twice and, thirty feet above and sixty feet behind, Acreman and Dave were almost thrown from the bobbing boat.

Louise was upright for no more than three seconds before the whale's forward lunge spread her flat. But she still had a grip on the radio direction finder, now stuck like a limpet, and the great fin allowed her to slipstream.

The ride lasted only about sixty seconds before Louise let go and swam back to the surface.

Her face was wreathed in smiles when she struggled back into the boat. Barbara clambered in a few moments later, and Acreman saw with some relief that she was also smiling and excited.

'I could have stayed on much longer but I was worried about the finder pulling loose. You get a lot of protection behind the fin. But the power ... it's quite incredible. It's like being in a very fast lift. I'm sorry, Dr. Acreman. I *had* to do it.'

'We'd all have taken the chance,' he assured her. He looked at his watch. 'Okay, everyone. That's it for now. According to my calculations, we have about six minutes before we freeze solid.'

When they hit the jetty, Acreman was told all the catching equipment was ready and the crews waiting to be briefed.

They were introduced to two helicopter pilots, a Naval officer, Gus Gustaffsen, who captained the icebreaker used for patrol work, and the airship pilot, a young, fresh-faced Texan, called Jim McSweeney.

Through the snow-curtained window, Acreman could see the ship, now grown to the two-hundred-foot silver sausage he had seen in Maxwell's manual, pulling gently between two large radio masts to which she had been moored. Beneath, a fragile cabin of interlocked geodesic frames supported two small prop-jet engines. The whole thing, in spite of its bulk, looked very insubstantial.

'Is she ready to go?' Frank asked McSweeney.

'Yes, sir. Everything you asked for's been done. We've taken off the tank ramp but left the two winches. They can handle your sling okay. It's a pneumatic system and we can move things about pretty neatly.'

'How about the wind?'

'I've worked her in much stronger winds than this.'

'Did you manage to do anything about the special pump and hose I asked for?'

McSweeney nodded. 'There's an Eskimo sergeant here who's a better fixer than Bilko. He found a portable fire pump that we can run off our electrics and three hundred feet of fire hose on a reel. I just hope they don't have any emergency landings here for a while. Can I ask what the hose is for?'

'We have to keep the whale wet and cool.' Acreman nodded in the direction of the sea. 'They actually enjoy those conditions. I've calculated that our slipstream will keep him cool enough, but it will also be very drying. The hose gives us access to sea water if that doesn't mean you have to fly too low.'

'It's best to stay low. We aren't pressurized and ...' He paused. 'If anything should go wrong, I reckon you'd want to give that whale a break. Right, Doctor?'

'Of course. And will it be okay for me to climb down onto the sling?'

Again McSweeney nodded. 'That's one of the joys of airships. In the old days, they used to walk along the tops of them in midair. We go a good bit faster but you won't have any problem getting down on the sling. Actually, the winches can bring him up to you if you want. I intend to keep him pretty close under the fuselage to avoid drag.'

'And they really can't blow up?'

'No, sir. You could put a match under that baby.'

'You seem to like these ships.'

'I love 'em, Doctor. They have a lot of style.'

Acreman took a place at the head of a makeshift conference table. He explained to the helicopter pilots that they would be dropping the huge purse seine net around the target whale. He and his team would be in the third helicopter and would instruct them when to drop it.

'The net's been specially adapted for us. It's now a one-hundred-yard ring, completely open at the bottom. The top's weighted and strung with oversized orange floats. When it's dropped, the weighted top falls fastest, with the bottom flaring out like a skirt. Understand, we're not trying to trap the whale—just throw a fence around him to slow him up long enough for us to get the sling/raft under him.'

The two helicopter pilots nodded. 'With your permission, sir, we'd like to practise a dummy drop in the bay this afternoon.'

'Provided you can recover the net in time,' Acreman said. 'We'll be doing it for real tomorrow morning. Otherwise, the whale will be out of range.'

The sonar control screens were active again, but not with the *Aquanaut*. She was limping to the repair yard at Pearl with two heavy Navy tugs chugging along beside her like mother ducks.

It was only twenty-four hours since they had 'buried' her dead. On board the *Eros*, Whitting had taken over. Suskin stared at the admiral, who was standing rooted like a tree in the middle of communications control, wearing what Suskin thought was probably his version of battle-dress—an elegantly tailored boiler suit, bedecked with badges of ranks and his medal ribbons. He still wore his cap with its heavy crusting of braid. Suskin had never known him to leave it off. He suspected the admiral was hiding a steel skull cap which, in turn, was protecting a brain of plastic cogs.

But the sonar screens were running again and Suskin was reluctantly forced to transfer his attention to them. This time, he only had a pinhead to watch, not the substantial sausage that had been the *Aquanaut*.

The pinhead was a Navy deep-diving bell with no name, just the number, *XT-4*. Inside it were two highly experienced salvage divers, Leading Diver Willy Maine and Diving Chief Petty Officer Max Wiseman. Maine was twenty-seven, Wiseman thirty-eight. Suskin looked at the pinhead and wished he didn't know them as well as he did, or that, like *XT-4*, they were just numbers.

Whitting was standing over him because finally his excuses had grown so wishy-washy that Whitting had decided he was incompetent and had told him so, and taken over.

In a way, Suskin didn't mind that much. Twenty deaths on his conscience was enough! This time, Suskin had a nagging conviction that something would happen. Whitting would be responsible.

The *XT-4* was part of the *Eros'* secret equipment. The ten-foot bell lived in a huge silo in the bottom of the ship, guide rails holding her clear of the black disc of water at the bottom. It was open to the sea. Her crew climbed aboard and then the rails slid down into the water and she was on her own, apart from a heavy support wire and a thick umbilical of radio, TV and life-support systems.

As eggs go, she was extremely tough. Her diving capability was almost fifteen thousand feet, two-thirds the depth of the Fracture, and her spherical shape was much better suited to pressure than the hull of the *Aquanaut*. For observation she had two windows of six-inch armour-plated acrylic but these were useless below six hundred feet so she had a battery of low-light TV cameras strung like a belt around her middle. She could turn full circle using high-pressure water jets but was otherwise completely dependent on her cable. Designed for very deep observational diving, the *XT-4* had no hatch other than the heavy circular steel entry port. There was no other way her crew could get out. But then there was no way they would want to get out once she was down where she was designed to go.

The men were diving by the system known as 'deep saturation' and breathing a strange mixture of oxygen and helium that gave them Mickey Mouse voices. If everything went completely normally they would take three days to return to the surface to ensure they suffered no blood pressure problems. And even then the crew would have to spend another three days getting their metabolism desaturated in a decompression chamber.

It was, Suskin thought as he watched the pinhead on the sonar screen, *one hell of a way of earning a living.*

If only he could think like Whitting and believe that all they were doing was following orders.

These orders had been quite specific. The Project Management had flown in three supermen when they'd finally got the *Aquanaut* back to the surface. These three—short-cropped hair, aquiline noses, high-buttoned shirts, thin ties and thin mouths—had listened without comment to O'Halloran's description of what had happened to the *Aquanaut*. Equally silently they'd heard Suskin describe the available sonar information and the computer's interpretation of the accident. When he went to the briefing, Suskin had carried with him two readouts of the state of the trench at the time of the accident and, later, evidence of the missing rocks. But he had not presented that information. The supermen had been brusque and Suskin realized that the hearing of the evidence was merely a formality.

'Gentlemen,' their spokesman said without emotion. 'This position is unsatisfactory, very unsatisfactory. The Project is of national importance and it will and must be pursued. The presence here of these extensive support facilities is seriously jeopardizing security ... we're soon going to have trouble explaining you away.

'As it happens, we thought we were blown just a few days back. One of our subsonar devices seemed to be indicating a course and speed for a Soviet Delta that would have brought her right here. But she should have been here by now, as we're assuming it was coincidence and she's gone elsewhere. That situation can't last much longer. We all now have to give this thing our best shot. It may well be our last.

'A third Ohio-class, the *Poseidon,* is proceeding to Pearl as of this moment. After taking on the special equipment from the *Aquanaut*, she will be coming here ... directly.

'You have, at best, four days to complete any investigations you may wish to make of the survey location—the shelf. The existing reports, which we have had assessed by our own experts, are no way sufficient to support any interruption of the Project. They are totally insufficient.'

'So far as the Project Management is concerned, you have just been unlucky. Or careless.'

Suskin caught his breath. The spokesman heard the sharp intake and turned.

'Yes, sir. That is our assessment. The record of seismic activity in this area is minimal. It has been suggested to us that your findings are, quite simply, wrong.'

Suskin could contain himself no longer.

'With respect,' he broke in harshly. 'That's just too damned easy. We have positive evidence of large rock movement—just what do your experts think is causing it?'

There was no change of expression on the spokesman's face. He looked down at his notes.

'Reviewing the *facts*, Commander Suskin,' he said with heavy emphasis. 'We believe the most likely cause is that loose rock formations were disturbed by the two submarines. We think one of these slipped and actually caught the *Jules Verne*, while another, quite possibly from the same loose formation, came away when the *Aquanaut* slipped past it on her descent.'

'But that boat was hardly moving,' Suskin insisted vehemently. 'O'Halloran had her on *silent running*—the engines were just ticking over. What the hell could have caused a land slip of that size?'

Again the spokesman considered his notes. 'Security does not permit me to go into details, Commander, but I would ask you to accept that the *Jules Verne* was using equipment that might have loosened unstable local rock formations. The *Aquanaut*, we think, inherited part of that earlier problem. The pressure disturbance of a craft of her size, even going very slowly, would have been substantial. As you may know, Commander, Alpine landslides can be caused by no more than the weight of a man on an unstable layer.'

Suskin knew he wasn't going to get anywhere. In fact, he was no longer that sure of himself. The explanation sounded a damned sight more plausible than the seismic activity theory. And he had not known the *Jules Verne* had been using dangerous equipment.

'Do you now accept that, Commander?' the spokesman asked with studied patience. 'We are aware that there have been discussions of other possibilities that frankly we believe should be treated with extreme scepticism. The Committee has agreed to support a secondary search facility using the Cetacean Unit. But again, I must emphasize that we regard this as extremely speculative.'

So much for Acreman, Suskin thought. *He's already been relegated to the idiot fringe. But I'm one step away from being relegated to that box myself.*

'I'm not arguing the assessment,' he compromised. 'I'm mainly concerned with preventing it from happening again. I suggest the Project, no matter what the priorities, could not afford to lose a third sub, and it's my job to try and ensure we don't.'

'Very understandable, Commander, and of course we don't want any more losses. But we've gained experience, and there's nothing in these reports, now we know the problem, to halt our plans. We've already worked out a new approach path for the *Poseidon.* Instead of hugging the face, she'll dive some distance away and tack on to the shelf. That way, if there is any further movement, it'll be well clear of her.'

Other than when she's sitting on the shelf, Suskin thought. But he said nothing.

Whitting spoke up.

'Mr. Chairman, we don't have a lot of time. I've given this some thought and I think we should make a new inspection of the face and the shelf using our diving bell. She's tougher than the Ohios and her cameras would show us any loose rock in that vicinity. She might even shake it up a bit and clear away any hazards before the *Poseidon* goes down.'

'That seems an excellent plan, Admiral.'

Except for the two men in the bell, Suskin thought.

But the spokesman was already gathering up his notes. 'So, gentlemen, you may expect your new charge by the weekend. Good luck.'

Now Suskin, with Whitting in personal command, was watching the *XT-4* have her go, and so far everything was desperately normal. Suskin felt considerable disquiet and it had nothing to do with the hazards facing the diving bell. He was aware that half his mind wanted something to happen and he didn't like that thought one bit.

'*XT-4* to Control. Are you reading our TV?'

'Control to *XT-4*. Everything's fine. How's your life-support?'

'Couldn't be better. Did you see anything you didn't like the look of? It all seems pretty solid to us.'

Suskin looked at Whitting. The admiral shook his head tersely.

'We concur, *XT-4*. What's your depth?'

'Coming down on eight thousand feet. We are about where the *Aquanaut* bought it, right?'

Suskin was relieved that the *XT-4* crew knew the relevance of their present position.

'That's right,' he said. 'Keep your eyes peeled, boys.'

He leaned forward and studied the bank of television screens monitoring the face. The rock was a brilliant white and looked more like a snow slope than anything else. Suskin knew that this was millions of tiny white shellfish. In the folds of the white rock, there were various growths of weed and other plant life, like anemones, and the colours of these plants were bleached out now that the depth was increasing. But there were still a great many fish, some of them showing colour. The total anonymity of the deeps had yet to be reached. The rock face looked as solid as, well, rock. He walked over to Whitting.

'They're there, sir. I can't see any evidence of slippage.'

Whitting looked angry. 'I don't know what you expect to see, Commander. It just slipped. It wasn't dynamited loose.'

'Surely there would be some change of colouration. The white encrustations wouldn't have got to the underside of the loose material.'

'You seem determined to prove us all wrong, Commander. I don't know what I'm looking for, and neither do you. But I know what I'm seeing. That face looks perfectly solid to me.'

'I thought we were looking for the cause of the two accidents.'

'Correction. We're looking for any reason that would prevent the *Poseidon* from making a safe descent. I don't see any, do you?'

'Well, no, sir,' said Suskin reluctantly. 'But that's only one way of looking at it.'

'It's my way, Commander, and this is my operation.' Whitting shifted his head to take in the sonar screens. 'And I don't see any evidence of volcanoes either. The bottom's as solid as the face.'

Suskin knew that to be true, too. He had nothing to fight.

'So may I order them up? They're now a hundred feet below the shelf and we won't be going down there.'

Whitting shook his head.

'While they're down there, we'll check it out properly. We're still well within the bell's specification. Let them go down another thousand feet. That'll give me a safety margin that nobody can argue with.'

'It will also add another day to the decompression time,' Suskin said hotly. 'As well as making them almost invisible on our screens. *XT-4*'s not that big, sir. This equipment is designed to watch a sub thirty times her size.'

Whitting looked at him contemptuously.

'Don't argue, Commander. Just do it!'

Suskin addressed his microphone.

'Control to *XT-4*. We'd like you to continue on to the nine thousand five hundred foot mark. Watch your camera controls, you'll soon be into very low light.'

There was a long pause.

'*XT-4* to Control. Assume you appreciate we're on saturation routine.'

'We know, boys. We need the pictures. I'll have a bottle of champagne waiting for you in the chamber.'

'Aye, aye, sir. Keep the sun shining for us.'

'We will, boys. Just take it slow and careful.'

All three Megalodons lay almost unconscious on the warm floor of the cave.

They had not eaten so well for almost a century and the adults at least were virtually incapable of movement. Their brains were incapable of appreciation and they rarely knew satiation, but the bonanza of food that had descended like manna from the sky twenty-four hours previously now suffused them with simple organic contentment.

Their lethargy was increased by the fact that they had not needed to stir to take advantage of the food that had come down to them. They had used no energy.

The big canvas-wrapped packages of almost pure animal protein had been carried by the current to where they lay and there were weights in these packages that caused them to bounce along the bottom until they reached the open mouths of the waiting sharks. And the packages kept on coming until the Megalodons were almost too lazy to open their mouths. The huge male had consumed five, his mate four and the young male the remaining three.

The Megalodons, like their modern relatives that lived near the surface, had retained the facility of being able to regurgitate their stomach linings to reject indigestible objects. At the end of the feast, they performed this necessary function and the floor of the cave was now strewn with the chains that had been used to weight the parcels, the brass buttons, and the scraps of cloth caught in this waste metal.

A rag of Old Glory floated against the cave roof and was circulating slowly around the walls on a rising current of warm water.

The *Aquanaut*'s chaplain would never know that his burial service had been a lie. Her dead crew would never revert to ashes.

The young male was restless.

Unlike his parents, he had not eaten sufficiently to be comatose, but then being a young animal, he rarely had the patience to feed so doggedly.

He lifted gently off the floor of the cave and slid slowly towards its mouth.

He had not been mistaken. Now, the faint changes of current he had felt, perhaps only sensed, in the enclosed cave were definite. His lateral line pits tingled to the impulses. But he hesitated because his senses told him that the new food source was again in that difficult and hurtful plane, the bright sky. He was also able to judge that the food target was much smaller than the one he had investigated before. He stayed where he was. It was not worth the pain. He could still remember the pain.

But the impulses were growing stronger.

'*XT-4* to Control. Nine thousand feet. It's as black as pitch down here. Unless we get right up against the face, you won't see a damned thing.'

'Control to *XT-4*, this is Admiral Whitting. So get her close. That's what you're there for.'

'*XT-4*. We're picking up considerable current movement. I don't see how we can get close and not bump. Our jets aren't strong enough to control that kind of movement.'

'Control to *XT-4*. We must have those pictures, Mr. Wiseman. Continue the mission.'

'*XT-4* ... Out!'

The young male could resist no longer. In fact, he had no powers of resistance, only senses of warning, and now the call of the food target was overriding the warnings. In any event, the food target was much closer, hardly in the sky at all.

Had he not fed so recently, his feeding impulses would have been driving him to the target now. Instead, he slid from the cave and moved his huge head around in the direction of the target and, slowed by the last thread of painful memory, settled to the sandy bottom. After all, the target was still closing and soon it would be in a dark place that would contain no pain at all.

'Sir!'

Suskin spun around. Every nerve in his body stretched as thin as the long cable going down those unimaginable depths to the tiny bell. Huntingdon, the chief sonar operator, was staring at his screen with his mouth open.

'Sir! It's happening again. Bottom activity. Look!'

Suskin, with Whitting directly behind him, leaped across to the sonar screens. The bell, now a single white pinprick of light, was three-quarters of the way down the screen. Below it, misting the previously solid lines of the trench bottom, was a milky haze. As they watched, the haze thinned, lifted again, then thinned. Through the electronic mist, there hardened a more solid outline.

'Was that there before?'

'No, sir. It just started up a minute ago.'

'I mean that rock, was that there before?'

'No, sir. That's new.'

'Damn!' Suskin cried and he hurtled back to the radio. 'Control to *XT-4*. Stop your descent. I say again, stop your descent. Go to emergency life-support. Tank up!'

'Sir ... the cloud ... it's rising!' Huntingdon cried.

'*XT-4*,' Suskin bellowed. '*XT-4* … get her UP. Max—emergency lift two hundred feet. GO!'

With a trace of reluctance—almost lazily—the young male slashed the vane of his tail sideways and inclined his giant snout upwards. The long weed strands flattened and he became a streamlined torpedo. His pits were screaming. The target was so close!

He could not resist. His tail began to beat faster. In thirty seconds he had rocketed into the sky. As he lifted, his eyes began to be of use. But this time there was no pain. He saw the food target and his primitive mind measured and decided. He had already made one investigation of a food source like this, it did not need a second. He turned and flashed along the face of the Fracture. His huge maw, lined with teeth half-mooned like giánt scythes, opened.

'*XT-4* to Control. We see nothing. What's up?'

'Just lift her, Max. Don't talk. Lift her!'

'Control. Lifting. Wait. We're getting current, hell, buffeting from the side! I'm swinging my lights … What! What in God's name? Control … Control … There's another sub coming at us. No … too fast. It's got weed all over … like a rock. Stop … stop it! For Christ's sake, stop it! It's got huge white …'

The line went dead. All that came through the speakers was a soft hum.

Into that silence, Huntingdon said, 'They've gone. Something fell down on them. Another rock. I saw it move across the face of the trench.'

Suskin sat back in his chair. He wanted to be sick. Whitting took the microphone and started raving for damage reports from the crew manning the *XT-4* lift system. Suskin sat back and waited. He knew he would be busy soon enough.

Whitting lunged round on him.

'Commander, take over here. That cable must have parted. I'm going down to see what's happened.'

'You mean, *XT-4*'s not on the end of it any more, I think, sir.'

'That's what I said, man.' He stormed out.

Suskin moved lethargically over to the sonar controls.

'Another rock, Huntingdon?'

'Well, yes, sir. Well, that's what it looked like to me.'

'Run the picture for me.'

Suskin watched silently while the tapes were rewound.

'Okay, you can switch it off now. Where's the rock?'

'It's gone, sir. It went down the face. There was more bottom activity when it hit, but now it's gone. Do you think there could be an overhang down there?'

'Maybe,' said Suskin. 'Or a cave.'

'You don't seem very surprised, sir.'

'Oh, I'm petrified, Huntingdon, I'm not surprised. Did you notice anything funny about that rock just before it hit *XT-4*?'

'No, sir. I don't think so!'

Suskin sighed. 'Run the tapes again. Maybe you can tell me how a bloody great rock can travel along the wall of the Fracture ... sideways!'

He returned to his seat and waited for Whitting to return. He felt defeated. He now knew Acreman was right.

Willie Maine and Max Wiseman learned what Acreman suspected about twenty seconds before they died. They knew they were being attacked by the biggest shark of any nightmare six seconds before it hit them. The rocks and weed became shark when the impossible mouth opened ten feet in front of them, in the full glare of their lights.

They glimpsed a flash of delicate pink, the icy triangles of teeth as the Megalodon turned to slash and only then, in the last millisecond, were their minds capable of accepting the image *SHARK*.

By then, the teeth of Megalodon were shearing through the steel of the *XT-4*'s hull like a knife through butter and her crew were desiccated by water jets compressed to steel needles.

All the young male knew was confusion. The object he had taken into its mouth was at first repugnant and his initial instinct was to throw it aside. But as he dived for the trench floor, satisfaction came. Moments later a rich flow of blood ran down the sides of his teeth onto his palate.

He flashed along the bottom and turned into the cave. A thin red stream leaked out of the Megalodon's mouth and was quickly dispersed by the current. The Megalodon opened his mouth and dropped the now tasteless food object. It crunched to the floor of the cave and the comatose adults turned slowly to look at it, then settled back without interest.

It rolled a little and came to rest alongside the male adult. In this context, it was about the size of a basketball.

When there had been no further movement on the screens for nearly ten minutes, Suskin heaved himself reluctantly to his feet.

'Mind the shop here. I'd best check the admiral isn't keelhauling them.'

He walked through nearly a quarter of a mile of steel passages before dropping down a set of steps to the bowels of the tanker. He noted dismally how quickly the huge lift mechanism was turning.

Whitting, rigid and white-faced, stood watching the cable as it wound onto the great drum. The *XT-4* lift crew were similarly stunned. Only the man on the cable control was animated. He gripped the handles of the winch with unnecessary pressure, praying, Suskin knew, that the loose wire would suddenly snatch and tell them that the rapid take-up was only slack.

But the big wheel continued to turn easily and fathom after fathom of cable wound onto the drum until, eventually, the winch operator stopped it and announced dispiritedly, 'That's it, sir. We've lost them!'

Suskin moved forward.

'We know that, mister. We need to know why. Let's have the end up.'

The winch operator nudged his controls until ten feet of wire hung down from the wheels, the end looking like frayed string. The wire was carbon fibre around a stainless steel core. It could only be cut with the most advanced kind of acetylene torch.

Reaching up, Suskin fingered the frayed cable. It looked as if the *XT-4* had been plucked off the end like a grape. A glitter of reflection caught his eye and he instructed the winch operator to lower more cable. Suskin heaved the frayed end over to the bright light. Down one side there was a sharp indentation, as though a chisel had been run down the wire. At one point, the cut went right through, exposing the steel core. He let the cable slide back onto the deck plates.

'Cut me off the last fifteen feet. Be careful not to damage this part here where it's marked; or the end. We'll have some forensic work done on this.'

Whitting stopped him as he made to leave the winch room.

'I'm taking it there's nothing we can do for those men, Commander?'

Suskin nodded.

'That's right, Admiral. We don't have another *XT-4* unit and the *Poseidon* won't be here for another three days, always assuming in the light of all this, you'd risk putting her down.'

Whitting looked agitated. 'That decision is not ours to make.' He stared at Suskin. 'It would be in both our interests to ensure continuity of record on this.'

Suskin looked at him with disgust.

'I'm not really sure what that means, sir. I'll want it on record that I was opposed to our using the *XT-4* in the light of the unexplained potential hazard.'

Whitting's eyes bulged. 'All right, Commander, so recorded. My log will, of course, then show that you agreed to participate, once having stated your reservations.'

Suskin nodded.

'I did, didn't I?' He turned and left Whitting standing. As an afterthought, he stopped by the door. 'But I promise you, it's the last time!'

It was almost the last time for Acreman. Everything had gone well with their preliminary approach. Winds were light and the helicopters had no difficulty with the huge ring of the purse seine net. The whales had continued their southerly migration.

Gustaffsen's icebreaker, which had remained on station with the tagged whale for the past twenty-four hours, had lost the school once in the night but, on Acreman's advice, had held its course and, midway through the morning, the whales had reappeared.

When the flight came up on the school, Acreman studied the waves. He was relieved to note that they were much smaller than the last time he'd dived. But he also had to accept that the water would be much colder this close to the ice fields. Even in their special wetsuits, he doubted they could afford to be down there much more than eight or nine minutes.

The whales rose and dived rhythmically, and Acreman

125

recorded the length of these dives was the same as before. When all three helicopters had formed a triangle behind the school, he reluctantly turned to study the vast bulk of the airship, hanging a hundred yards behind them.

Acreman still couldn't properly accept it. That morning, when he had first seen it fully inflated, its size had intimidated him and filled him with doubt. He could not believe that a thing of that size could do the delicate job he was asking of it.

But at first light, McSweeney had lifted off for a test run. The airship did not seem to fly. It was as if she were suspended on invisible strings and that her movements, backwards and forwards, were on equally invisible runners. When McSweeney brought her directly over Acreman and the others and ran the big sling down with a hiss of pressure to within a couple of feet of their heads, Acreman recalled the sci-fi movies of his youth when the ramp came down from the flying saucer. With their great net, the helicopters had managed about one hundred and fifty knots on the way out, and the airship had had no trouble keeping up with them.

Aware that his stomach was beginning to tighten and that he could delay no longer, Acreman turned to Dave and the girls.

'We'll go down on the next dive.'

Acreman and Dave would go down first, signal for the net drop and wait for the girls to come down with the skimmer once the ring was floating and the whale was coming up into it. They had between three and four minutes to get into the boat, locate the whale as it completed its return to the surface and tell McSweeney where to drop the sling.

'We don't have any time for mistakes,' he told the others. 'Not a moment. So let's get it right.'

They stared back at him.

The young bull surfaced, blew a thirty-foot vapour spume and vanished.

'Let's go,' said Acreman and allowed himself to fall backwards through the port hatch. Again, he let the fear take over as he dropped. Again, the water bit like it was trying to consume him. But this time, Acreman knew what to look for and, having completed the routines that gave him air, he blew out his mask and looked down.

The whale was already coming up. It had shortened its dive. One corner of Acreman's reeling brain immediately registered why. He could see the bottom! It had shelved rapidly in the last few minutes and they were now hanging over a plateau no more than one hundred feet deep. The whale would be blowing in less than a minute.

And it was coming up fast, directly beneath him!

There was no time for the agreed routine. Acreman, who was no more than twenty feet down, held hard to his nose, blew and opened the air bottle on his life jacket. He shot to the surface so fast that the jacket lifted him three feet out of the water. Waving frantically, even as he surfaced, he gave the signal to drop the net.

Everything seemed to happen at once. The net fell slowly like a huge theatre curtain and a ring of spume, like a salvo of gunfire, lifted all around him.

Two black shapes and a large orange parcel fell out of the lead helicopter and hit the sea a hundred yards away

And the whale surfaced *under* Acreman, blowing so that the spume misted his mask.

Then he stopped.

Abruptly, there was silence, total silence. Even the ordinary sounds of the sea were cut off by the heavy rubber of Acreman's diving mask.

He felt a slight stirring as the whale moved his huge flippers to hold position. But the mighty tail did not move. Reaching down gingerly, Acreman found he was standing on its back. He looked around quickly. The big fin, hanging slightly sideways without water to support it, was some ten feet in front of him. Moving more slowly, Acreman went forward, kicking gently with his flippers. He came up to the fin, reached down and, with his mask just clear of the water, was able to get a grip of the radio direction finder aerial.

Acreman, who had never responded to the more esoteric suggestions that the cetaceans might be capable of ESP, now prayed to God and hoped that these others might be right.

'Stay still, sonny,' he muttered into his mouthpiece.

Dave surfaced twenty feet away and signalled, 'Are you okay?'

Acreman held up his thumb and forefinger in a circle—the diver's affirmative. 'Stay where you are,' he called. The whale stirred again, and Acreman saw the huge head move slowly from side to side. A rattle of sonar clicks ran through the water. But still the whale did not swim. *He knows the net's there*, Acreman thought.

A dark shadow suddenly blocked the light. Looking up, Acreman saw the huge bulk of the airship no more than twenty feet above them. In the background, he heard an outboard engine start and, without looking around, he waved the skimmer away. 'Get them out of the boat, Dave,' he called. 'Tell them to swim in. I think if we're quick, we can do it.'

Dave nodded, and hanging in his life jacket, held up both hands to halt the approach of the skimmer.

Acreman was thinking furiously. Logically, he should now abandon his bizarre position and swim to the head of the animal to direct the lowering of the sling. But something told him that this would be a mistake. Acreman was obsessed with the notion that the whale was quiescent because he was on its back. It was a gross manifestation of the well-documented love of contact shown by other cetaceans. *But not surely*, Acreman asked himself, *by a thing so big only its instincts could tell it he was there?* And yet he stayed where he was and called softly to Dave.

'You mark the drop. Go forward twenty feet in front of his head. Tell Barbara that it must be lowered very slowly and gently. No disturbance. Don't drop it like we thought. This is a different situation, okay?'

Dave signalled an affirmative and swam out to the skimmer, which was now holding about a hundred yards away on the left.

Hurry, Acreman thought, *he can't stay still for long*. But the whale seemed to have no desire to move. His head scanned almost continuously and the sonar click patterns were now regular. But the huge tail lay still in the water and Acreman had no difficulty holding his position.

Dave swam around in a circle, keeping well clear of the animal, until he was holding the position Acreman had directed. The black shadow shifted above them and slowly edged forward so that Acreman could observe without having to crane his neck. He watched the sling slide down, stop a foot or so above the water and then vanish.

What the hell do we do now? Acreman thought. *The whale must move forward over the sling*. He had a giddy thought that what he needed was a pair of spurs!

Suddenly the young bull flapped his tail. Once, to break down the massive inertia; a second time to gain way.

Acreman stared ahead with total disbelief. He was moving directly towards the sling. Now he was over it. Acreman looked left, right—the support cables were moving down the body and would soon be level with him.

He was so stunned he nearly missed the moment. The support cables drew level, lifting like huge steel triangles on either side.

'Blow the flotation bags, Dave. Blow them!'

Acreman heard a sub-marine rumble. Above him, the support cables twanged as tension was lost. His feet were taken from under him and he fell sideways, clawing for a hold on the radio direction finder box. Then he was out of the water and Acreman realized that the lifting mechanism had worked and the whale was out of the water too. And he had actually ridden the whale through the whole process.

And still the whale didn't struggle!

Acreman lay flat, holding his breath, looking down the length of the animal as he bobbed gently in the now fully inflated raft/sling. The huge head lifted, the only gesture of protest that Acreman could detect. He spread his arms wide. But even spreadeagled, he was unable to touch those huge flanks.

'Boss … are you okay?' Dave was shouting to him.

Acreman got to his knees reluctantly. The extraordinary reality that he was lying astride a sperm whale was only now beginning to invade his mind, and he was loath to give it up. But he realized that he was doing no good where he was and he slid gingerly sideways, anxious not to damage that smooth skin with the metal cylinders on his back. As he reached the edge, he threw himself sideways and was immediately aware of the deadly cold of the water. What was he doing? Dave had been in all the time. But a glance at his watch showed that the whole incredible business had taken no more than five minutes. The girls had edged the skimmer alongside and were now staring down at him anxiously.

'Frank,' Barbara called. 'Frank. We saw him come up under you. You should have got out the way. Get in the boat now. He's quite secure.'

Acreman looked at the great head and saw that this was true. He swam to the boat and climbed in.

'There was no time,' he said shakily. 'And no need. That's the incredible part. Barbara, they do the same as the dolphins. He knew … he had to know!'

Barbara threw him a coat. 'Come on, Frank. Don't worry about that now. We saw what happened. Didn't you hear him sonaring? He spotted the net as soon as it hit.'

'So why didn't he dive … or try to escape?'

'Don't know, Frank,' Barbara said, edging down the boat to kneel in front of him and help with the straps. 'Just because it's a big one, you don't have to get so carried away. Anyway, now's not the time. Nothing's going to happen till you give the signal. Do we lift him?'

He looked round carefully.

'Is everything in the right place? How's the tail lying?'

'Everything's fine, Frank. Dave checked. It couldn't be better.'

But still Acreman hesitated. He was filled with a feeling of intrusion. *Why?* he wondered. How many dolphins and killers had he lifted out of the sea without a second thought? Was it just that this beast was so big, or that it had treated him with respect and now he was about to betray it?

'It's getting pretty cold in here, boss,' Dave said.

'Take him up,' Acreman said. 'Barbara, I'd just as soon you did it.'

She gave him a strange look and stood up in the boat, the walkie-talkie in her hand. She nodded to Louise, who was sitting by the engine, and the skimmer nosed over to collect Dave. His face was blue when he pulled off his mask and he was kneading his fingers frantically. Then Louise gunned the skimmer well away from the raft and they watched as it began slowly to lift out of the water. The whale lifted his head and tail so that for a moment he was arched; groping, it seemed to Acreman, for the support of the cushion of the sea that they had now robbed him of. Then he settled with a series of high-pitched moans and the sling lifted over their heads.

A shower of water splashed across Acreman's face and, for a ghastly moment, he thought the whale had been injured. But when his vision cleared, he saw that Barbara was using the walkie-talkie again and a powerful stream of sea water was showering down on the huge load from below the airship.

Minutes later, with the sling nestling under the airship, a

line with a canvas sling snaked down from the rear hatch of the cabin and hung a few feet above the water. Louise ran the skimmer across to it.

'You go first, Frank,' Barbara instructed.

Without comment, he looped the sling over his shoulders and was winched up to the cabin.

'Welcome aboard, Doctor, and congratulations. I've never seen anything done that well in all my time in the service.'

'How is he?' Acreman demanded, pulling off his air cylinders.

'He's certainly alive,' McSweeney confirmed. 'I can't see much more than the head, but that's moving plenty and how about those eyes ... ? Man, I could turn on to a girl with eyes that lively.'

'And the ship? Can it handle him?'

'This ship?' said McSweeney innocently.

'We've got a long way to go.'

'You just worry about your whale, Doctor. This ship will get us where we want to go. In fact, as soon as we can get one of your people to strap the stern of that sling to our aft frame, I'm ready to be off.'

Barbara had just come up on the winch and was standing in the rear hatchway. She turned and walked along the narrow ramp of aluminium frames to the stern of the airship and began to wind in a loose rope attached to the rear of the sling. She worked on the rope with deft expertise and soon had it tightly secured.

'All fast,' she called.

Dave and Louise appeared together at the port hatch, clasping each other inside the sling.

'You okay, Dave?'

'Best way I know of handling frostbite, boss!'

Acreman helped them in, then, leaning out of the hatch, waved thanks and good-bye to the circling helicopters and the icebreaker, which had now moved in to recover the purse seine net and the skimmer.

He nodded to McSweeney. 'Let's take him home. I want someone on watch the whole time. I'll take first stint.' He buttoned his coat tight at the collar, donned a wool cap and clambered down onto the steel frame.

The whale was blinking slowly. As the engines increased

their noise, he abruptly shut his eyes tight. Acreman heard movement behind him and turned to find Barbara clambering down the frame.

'We should do this singly,' he said. 'We've got a long way to go and it's going to get pretty cold out here.'

Barbara looked at the whale.

'I was thinking about him. I'll go back in a minute. He should have a name,' she said.

'What do you christen a baby this size?'

'Didn't the god Apollo take on the shape of a dolphin when he established his shrine at Delphi, Frank?'

'Right! And he was a big daddy of the gods. Apollo it shall be.'

'He seems okay,' Barbara said after a long pause.

'We might have to do something about his eyes,' Acreman said. 'He's blinking a lot. It's the air stream. I hadn't thought about that.'

'How do you build goggles for a sperm whale?'

Acreman grinned.

'We'll rig a bit of window plastic on an arm in front of the head. There's a window in the rear hatch door that will do. Otherwise, he seems fine.'

'Isn't this weird, Frank?'

'Nobody would believe it,' he admitted. 'I'm not sure I do.'

'How big is he do you think?'

'About sixty feet!'

'Is that big enough? I mean … well, it's not just weird, is it? I feel sorry for him.'

'The old problem.'

'Yes.'

'You know Doris doesn't agree.'

'I know she doesn't. But Doris doesn't have any of our ethical problems. She's a lousy judge.'

'Anyway,' Acreman said, holding her hand. 'He's big enough. He'll be capable of diving several thousand feet without trouble and with his sonar … he'll spot it if it's there.'

'And you think he can handle the journey? McSweeney says it will take about fourteen hours.'

'Oh sure. I have no doubts about that. In the old days when dolphins were shipped around the world some of them were out of the water for as much as forty-eight hours with no ill-effect.'

'Yes. I know.'

'You don't sound very convinced.'

'I suppose I accept that part of it. But what honest right do we have to subject him to those things?'

Acreman thought for a long time.

'I don't know. But part of me is resisting thinking of them like that. I know it's difficult because they belong to a species that seems to trigger an automatic fear syndrome in humans. We have to find out more about them. If you can see the need for that, Apollo might just be the only friend they've got.'

7

Harry Asquith had been free of Vance for less than a week when the government agent returned to the Institute from the *Eros*. Harry had spent most of that time in bed and some of it alone. He felt he had earned a holiday.

Harry was beginning to regret his involvement in the search programme, even though the Institute's bank account was positively bulging. If the flow continued, Harry was even toying with the idea of buying a stretch of the Amazon for his study of the electric mudfish, *Gymnachus*. He had heard that such things were possible in South America.

But even the thought of such exotic fishing rights was not enough to compensate for Vance. Harry's right hand twitched whenever the man's pallid face came into view and this was no nervous spasm. Harry was a fine anatomist and his cutting hand was suffering a reflex desire to open Vance up. He suspected the Institute could then claim the discovery of both the world's largest and smallest brains.

Vance arrived in the middle of Harry's Sunday lunch; a Polynesian pork curry dressed with pineapple and tiny flowering orchids. Harry pointed at the meal when Vance slid in and stood silently over him.

'Have you no soul?' Harry demanded.

'You're wanted,' Vance reported. 'We can grab a snack on the plane.'

On entering the Pentagon, Vance took a big plastic security tag out of his pocket and held it aloft like a flag. With Harry scuttling to keep up, they hurried through the checkpoints and were in the Project's main offices in minutes.

Hope Ward was waiting at his desk, just sitting and staring. Harry began to suspect that Vance's trouble really was big.

Hope Ward confirmed it. He told Harry about the *XT-4*

accident, adding, 'And we have the *Poseidon* due there in sixteen hours.'

Harry was not sure what response was expected of him so he waited. Hope Ward waited too.

'I see,' said Harry with great emphasis.

'I thought you'd appreciate our dilemma,' said Hope Ward.

'Ye … es,' said Harry.

'When is Dr. Acreman due there?'

'Did you see it on television?' Harry asked eagerly. 'Wasn't that magnificent? Imagine, a great whale against the background of an Arctic sunset. I must say I was moved!'

'It was also unauthorized,' Hope Ward said. 'But we'll discuss that later.'

'Quite,' said Harry. 'I knew nothing about it. A local leak, I suppose. You can't keep something that big out of the headlines.'

'Perhaps not,' said Hope Ward. 'However … '

'Yes.' Harry leaned forward attentively.

'In the next sixteen hours, I have to decide whether the *Poseidon* takes up her station. What would be your recommendation?'

Harry thought quickly.

'It is … um … a military decision. I really think you should do whatever you think best. I'm hardly qualified.'

Hope Ward winced. 'We're paying a great deal for your advice, Professor. I think you're going to have to do a little better than that.'

'Please tell me how you think I might help,' Harry said. *Think of the money*, he reminded himself.

'We have to decide what status we now give Dr. Acreman's hypothesis,' Hope Ward said levelly.

'As opposed to ignoring it?'

'We don't ignore anything. To this point, it had a purely hypothetical status. The *XT-4* incident might change that.'

Harry wished he were somewhere else. He realized he had allowed himself to be lulled into complacency. He still secretly believed that Acreman's theory was exotic fantasy, a heaven-sent money-maker for the Institute. And even if it wasn't, Harry had seen no need for any action on his part. If there were Megalodons, surely the Project would realize they could never locate survey vessels, in particular submarine vessels, in that position. And if the worst came to the worst, Harry had his ace—the powerful National Ecology Trust—waiting in the wings and ready, in fact downright eager, to rush to the rescue of the Megalodons and Asquith's reputation. Harry had calculated that, if the Trust intervened, the Institute would be 'investigating' the Fracture for the next fifty years. The way the money was coming in, Harry reckoned to be on the Amazon within twelve months, leaving all this silly business to Frank Acreman.

Without waiting for an answer Hope Ward proceeded to confirm Asquith's worst fears. 'One of the options being proposed is the use of a nuclear torpedo, Professor!'

'Good God!'

'Can you think of a better way of sterilizing that station, or any other that's as quick?'

'It's downright lunacy! There'll be Soviet submarines homing in on an explosion of that kind from all over the world. Also I would have thought the market for radioactive gold was a little limited!'

Hope Ward smiled. 'Well now, Professor, what have we smoked out! There's a note in your file saying that you're no fool politically. Personally, I'd begun to have my doubts.' He glanced at Vance. 'I presume that reference to a Soviet submarine was purely to make your point?'

'Yes,' said Harry, momentarily bemoaning blowing his cover. 'Why?'

'We suspect there might be a real one nosing about,' said Hope Ward. 'But that is no concern of yours.'

'The dolphins and the other cetaceans are.'

'Agreed. That's why you're here.'

'You have not properly considered the value of Dr. Acreman's whale to the safety of the new submarine and, as such, the successful completion of this entire project.'

Hope Ward looked genuinely puzzled. 'Go on, sir.'

'If you were a shark, sir, and could choose between a solid metal object and a very large piece of animal protein, which would you choose?'

Hope Ward sat in stunned silence. 'You're openly proposing the use of that whale as a decoy duck, Professor?'

Harry nodded. 'You will, of course, understand if I insist that that is for your ears alone. You can imagine what the ecology lobby would make of it.'

Hope Ward winced but recovered quickly. 'You don't have to worry about my keeping quiet, Professor. A whale's a damned sight more expendable in my book than a costly nuclear missile.'

'I hope your security is good,' said Harry, looking meaningfully at Vance. 'I think I can claim to have cooperated to the point of almost putting my reputation in jeopardy. A lot of people might be getting to hear about those sharks soon. I don't want any leaks laid at my heels.'

'No need for concern, Professor. In fact, I wonder if you'd give me a few minutes alone with Mr. Vance here.'

Harry nodded and went through to the outer office. Before Mandy could say anything, Harry spoke.

'The most extraordinary thing has happened to me, my dear. I've developed this terrible allergy to tea. I suppose I've been in America too long.'

She stared at him stonily for a moment, but finally hurried out of the office. Eventually she returned with the coffee he had been hoping for.

It helped to calm the pangs of seasickness Harry was already imagining. But there was no escaping the reality. His next stop would have to be the *Eros*.

Hope Ward sat silently for a moment, facing the flag behind his desk. Turning around, he told Vance to take a seat.

'That's a clever man, Vance. You'd do well to remember it.'

'We have plenty on him if we want it.'

'I don't care what we have on him. He has too much on us, and this situation has become extremely delicate. Moscow station is saying that there is *interest*.'

'I'm not surprised,' Vance sniffed, feeling more at home. 'They have a good idea what we do with our big subs. We've also had the *Eros* sitting out in the Fracture Zone for too damned long.'

'I know that, Vance! But since the Afghanistan thing, our Moscow people have had to keep their heads right down. They just aren't that quick anymore and that means this interest they've reported has probably been around for some time.'

'Time enough to get a ferret in,' Vance said.

'Exactly. You can stop watching and go hunting.'

Vance didn't move.

'That's all, Vance. Go to it!'

'I think you've forgotten the limits of my initial briefing.'

'Okay, I'll extend you into the politics. But remember, Asquith knows nothing of this side of it … '

'Asquith doesn't talk to me anyway.'

'Right. Now, if we find what we're looking for out there in the Zone, it's going to trouble the Soviets a lot. Instead of the dollar going up and down like a yo-yo, we're going to be calling the tune again. The Arabs can charge what they like for their goddamned oil and it won't matter to us.

'So the economics look good … but on the political side, there are problems. The Fracture Zone is just under three hundred miles off the Hawaiian coast, which puts it an awkward one hundred miles outside American territorial waters. Those waters are open to all comers at the moment and there are a lot of international fishing agreements and such stuff to which the Soviets, among others, are interested parties.

'But if we confirm our finding in the Fracture Zone, Congress is prepared to arbitrarily extend our territorial waters to a three-hundred-mile limit. If we do it without anyone knowing what we've actually come up with in the Zone, we'll get away with it. There'll be a lot of flak and we'll have to tie up the International Court of Justice for a couple of years, but nobody's going to make real trouble over a mess of fish.

'On the other hand.' Hope Ward paused and took a deep breath. 'If the Russians were to find out that those fish are gold-plated and will give us control of the international money market, then … well, then I reckon the flak might just go radioactive.'

Vance looked like he was made of concrete.

'Can you see that, Vance?'

'Yes', he said. 'I'm debating whether I can handle something that big, solo.'

'At this stage you have to,' Hope Ward said firmly. 'The trick is not to attract attention. If there's just you, the other side will assume it's small stuff—no offence meant, Vance. The bill for extending our waters is drafted and will go through on an emergency basis. The moment it's clear, we'll put a ring of ships around Oahu that a tunafish couldn't get through. They're there already at Pearl Harbor. We're within an ace of it, Vance. The primary geodesic readings are fantastic!

But we can't pull a stunt like this until we're absolutely sure.'

Vance nodded.

'So.' Hope Ward held up his left hand and counted on his fingers. 'Your order of priorities is now the *Eros* and any ferrets that may have been planted there. Acreman—I'm still secretly worried about that guy. If this Mega-thing turns out to be for real, he's going to be famous and he's not going to like giving it up. And Asquith. I've noted what you've said about his habits and, while I think they're just part of his act, they could make him a soft touch.'

'I think I should proceed to the *Eros* directly,' Vance said.

'I agree.'

Vance stayed where he was.

'We have less than sixteen hours.'

'I'm on my way. I just need to know whether you bought that line from Asquith about the whale protecting us.'

'He didn't say *us*, Vance. He said the sub. Are you scared of that thing? Anyway, forget it. I've been in this business long enough not to buy anything outright. You can rest assured we won't be relying exclusively on Asquith's opinion.'

The intercom buzzed on Hope Ward's desk. He listened, appeared nonplussed for a moment and then answered. 'Tell him yes, Mandy.'

Hope Ward stared at Vance. 'That was Asquith, asking if you'd give him a lift out to the *Eros*.'

'How did he know … ?'

'He worked it out. Or he can read minds. Watch him, Vance!'

The young male played with the ball that had been the *XT-4* for almost three days.

At first, he had left it to lie among the other detritus that had accumulated in the cave over the long years.

But as time went by, the young male's interest in the diving bell returned and he began to nudge and explore it with his sensing mechanisms. The most sensitive part of the Megalodon's anatomy was the soft inner lining of its mouth. He sucked at the ball and discovered that there was flavour.

Eventually he exhausted the juices and finally, in frustration, he spat out the ball. The last tastes had been the best

For a Megalodon, it was animal protein in its most delicious form. It was human putrefaction.

The young male now had nothing to assuage the mounting pangs of hunger. He lay uneasily beside his parents, facing the cave mouth.

Since the loss of the *XT-4*, two days previously, Suskin had kept the floor of the Fracture under continuous sonar observation.

He came to know those remote depths like the proverbial palm of his hand.

It was not an easy observation. Suskin learned that submarine valleys, like their dry counterparts, suffer storms. Sometimes the sonar screens were a white fog of heavy sand particles, avalanches and solid blankets of moving substances which Suskin assumed were weed or huge shoals of fish.

He consulted the deep-water experts aboard the tanker and was told that the Fracture floor had a fierce current that varied in intensity according to the time of the year, ice melts, and even the time of day.

Ostensibly to test the *XT-4* lifting mechanism, Suskin, on his own initiative and without informing his superiors, had a low-light TV camera lowered fifteen thousand feet into the Fracture. But after three thousand feet, the camera saw nothing and Suskin had it winched up.

He had VTR equipment wired into the sonar screens to make continuous recordings of their images and, soon after dawn every morning, Suskin rose and did a pre-breakfast review of what the cameras had picked up during the night.

But apart from what Suskin had now come to regard as normal bottom activity, nothing untoward moved down there. He could not believe that the solid image that had appeared at the time of the *XT-4* incident had been a coincidence, or a malfunction of the equipment. Nor would he accept that the three solid shapes that had appeared briefly after the *Aquanaut* accident were also freak conditions.

It was as if the sea bottom was opening up and swallowing everything, Suskin thought.

He ran through the last few minutes of the previous night's tapes once more. There was a fair amount of activity, but all of it insubstantial. He had learned to differentiate between sand

and items more solid. He had even learned to listen to the sonar pings and believed he could now tell when they were hitting thick seaweed, which sometimes gave a solid impression on the screen.

The thing that bugged Suskin most of all was the total disappearance of the *XT-4*. Not so much its crew now, but the metal bell itself. It added a new and disturbing element to the problem. If it was hidden, what else was hidden?

He checked another set of reports on the progress of the two approaching craft, the new sub, *Poseidon*, and Acreman and his crazy airship.

From the night log he read that the *Poseidon* had completed fitting out her geodesic lasers and would be with them the following morning, in twelve hours' time.

The airship had stopped to water the whale off Alaska somewhere. *What the hell had that involved?* Suskin wondered. She would be joining them sometime the following morning, depending on the head winds. That was a sight Suskin definitely did not intend to miss.

As he left to go for his breakfast, he glanced again at the sonar screens. The base of the cliff had swelled out!

Suskin blinked and looked quickly away, refocusing his eyes on anything that would confirm he wasn't seeing things.

He looked back. It was a definite, solid bulge.

Suskin leaped across to hit the necessary buttons and looked up again.

The bulge had vanished. The flat face of the cliff was back to normal. Suskin waited another five minutes.

He shook his head violently and decided he was spending too much time alone in this room. *Go and get some food and a strong cup of coffee*, he told himself forcibly. But he left the VTR running.

At the door, he glanced back. The face was normal.

Watering Apollo had been done in something of a panic. The flight until then had been remarkably uneventful, almost too good to be true, Acreman thought. They had stumbled across the perfect method of transporting large cetaceans. Necessity had mothered an invention. Their speed had not been sufficient to disturb the animal. After the initial series of high-pitched calls, he had become almost completely quiet and, so far as they could tell, was actually enjoying the view. They had fixed up the windscreen and he had stopped blinking. Barbara cleaned it thoroughly every time she came on watch, which Acreman thought was probably unnecessary but Barbara insisted on doing it.

'We're being lucky, Frank. Don't blow it for want of caring. You don't know what's happening in his head.'

'Do you?'

'I've been trying to imagine it. You know when we ship dolphins in planes, even when they're watched over like babies, they still thrash about and they never stop calling and sonaring. Maybe it's claustrophobia. We forget that they're never contained in small spaces. And that goes double for big whales. Maybe Apollo's staying quiet and happy because we haven't got him in a tin can. He can see the whole horizon. That's what whales are used to.'

Acreman's private belief was that it was the hose that was keeping Apollo happy. In a sense, he wasn't out of the sea at all. The free end of the big fire hose was trailing in the sea and its other end was swamping Apollo at the rate of three hundred gallons every few minutes. He might not be swimming, but he was more in the water than out of it.

Louise Putnam had produced an ingenious idea for monitoring Apollo's breathing and heartbeat. One of the pieces of equipment they'd had on the skimmer was an underwater microphone working to a portable amplifier. It had been included in case they had needed to hunt for the school by sound.

When Acreman and Barbara had consulted about doing respiration tests, they had not come up with anything practical for an animal the size of Apollo. Then Louise had casually asked whether they had a microphone. No one had seen the point until she climbed down on the frame and simply held it against Apollo's side. The heavy, regular thumping that came out of the receiver had almost deafened them. They had taped it to the frame so that now they could monitor the beats continuously. Apollo had continued to breathe normally.

As they approached the Alaskan coast, there was a moment of alarm and anger when a light plane buzzed out of the sunset. McSweeney let loose a stream of curses about amateur flyers

142

when the plane made its first pass, but when it came back and began to circle the ship, he got on the radio and started bellowing for information. After two wide circles, the plane vanished. Apollo seemed totally unperturbed by the incident.

'Wouldn't you know!' exploded McSweeney.

'Wouldn't you know what?' Acreman demanded.

'We're on TV. That was a bunch of film boys.'

'Do our people realize that?'

'They do now.'

'Can they do anything about it?'

'Not sure they want to. The plane's winging it back to Anchorage and it took its time telling Control who it was.'

'I suppose it doesn't matter,' said Acreman. 'Apollo seems all right.'

'Enjoy it,' McSweeney grinned. 'This trip could do great things for airships.'

'And whales,' said Barbara pointedly.

An hour later, she said abruptly, 'Oh, my God, Frank. Dehydration!'

A tremor of concern struck Acreman.

McSweeney thought it was a joke. He looked down at the cascade of sea-water and said so.

'You don't understand,' Barbara said urgently. 'They don't get their moisture from drinking water—they can't, it's salty. It comes from the tissue of the food they eat!'

'An animal of this size must be able to manage for a long time,' protested Acreman.

'We don't know that, Frank. And we can't afford to guess. We have to feed him.'

'Oh, shit,' said McSweeney. 'Now, that is going to be difficult.'

'Why on earth didn't we think of it before?' Barbara said.

'Well, we didn't,' Acreman replied sharply. 'And I agree we can't risk it. Not having come this far. But where do we get a sufficient supply of fresh fish, and how do we get it into him in the sling?'

'Damn it, Frank. We have to let him go!'

'No,' he said, not even considering the idea.

Earlier that day, Suskin had come through on the radio and Acreman had taken the headphones.

143

'Dr. Acreman, this is Commander Suskin. I wouldn't normally attempt to have a conversation with you under these circumstances, but I would like to know your exact time of arrival. Over.'

'We can't be very definite, Commander. Is it that important? Over.'

'Yes, it is, Dr. Acreman. We've lost another item in what I think you would regard as very suspicious circumstances. Over.'

Suskin had refused to say any more over the open radio link so Acreman asked McSweeney for their ETA. He asked Suskin whether the holding net had arrived.

'Affirmative. It was dropped in here yesterday by helicopter. We have it all set up on the lee side of our ship. Professor Asquith supervised it. Over.'

'Harry's there?' asked Acreman in confusion. 'Over.'

'You sound agitated, Doctor. I think we should close down now. Affirmative to your last question. Over and out.'

Acreman knew that, if Harry were back on the tanker, Apollo was needed. For reasons he could not properly define, he did not pass any of this information on to the others.

'So what do we do then, Frank—let him die?'

'We don't know that he will die. I don't want him to die. Dolphins can stand hours and hours out of the water without any problem.'

'Only if they've been well-fed before transport,' Barbara snapped. 'And this animal is a hundred times bigger than a dolphin. It needs a hundred times more water—gallons!'

'He was feeding before we picked him up.'

'Even so, Frank. I don't think there can be any such thing as a justifiable risk. Not this time!'

'How much are we going to need, Doc?' McSweeney asked.

'About a ton of small fish or squid. And a goddamn big spoon.'

'I don't know about the spoon, but there is a ship with a trawler stern immediately below us.'

Acreman stood up shakily. Could it be done? Could they just open Apollo's mouth and pour food—and thus water—into his huge belly? He did not know. Apollo was the first. Everything they did with him had to have its first time. He turned to McSweeney.

'Tell me if this is impossible. Could you lower the cradle just into the water then tow it behind that trawler?'

Don't know,' McSweeney said. 'The drag will be massive. I wouldn't have motion for long, not with these little engines. The inertia would eventually stop us dead and I'd have to throttle back, otherwise the nose would come down and we'd simply dive into the sea.'

'A hundred yards would be enough,' Acreman said. 'The problem will be to get him to open his mouth. I don't think he'll do it while he's still and there's no way we can open it for him. But if he's in the water moving and there are fish coming at him, he should open his mouth instinctively. And maybe it'll stay open when we stop. Anyway, he'll at least have got something in him.'

'You want me to give it a try?'

'We first have to persuade that trawler to chuck its catch overboard. That's going to be a real fun trip. I wonder what nationality she is.'

'Portuguese,' said McSweeney. 'The *Juarez* out of Lisbon. I've got them on the radio.'

'Well, that's promising. The Portuguese catch herring in these waters. Does anyone speak Portuguese?'

'No need,' said McSweeney. 'They have an English-speaking radio operator. You can bet they know we're here.' He lifted his microphone and explained their situation.

McSweeney listened, then turned with a smile to Acreman.

'Nice people. The captain says, "From one fisherman to another, why don't we swap catches?"'

'Seriously. What does he want for his catch?'

'Twenty thousand American dollars.'

'Tell him he's got it. Did you explain what he has to do?'

There was another rapid exchange, and McSweeney brought the huge ship down with consummate delicacy. Fortunately, the sea was relatively calm, the waves dipping no more than three or four feet. There was no real feeling of descent but suddenly Acreman saw the trawler ahead of them. Her crew had gathered in the net and it now hung like a huge silver blob halfway up her stern, ready to be spilled as soon as they were given the command.

Acreman stood by the port hatch and watched the last ten feet of sea approach. There was a huge splash which completely engulfed the cabin and rendered the windows momentarily opaque.

Acreman, with no glass between him and the sea, was drenched, but as Apollo hit the water, he saw the silver blob on the trawler's stern burst open like a split grape. Almost immediately, the sea all around was a mass of silver fish. They were at least getting their money's worth.

Leaning out, he stared down at the whale. The nose of the airship was well down and the engines were roaring, their sound reflecting loudly off the sea. Apollo's head was ploughing through the water and McSweeney had positioned his craft perfectly. But the whale's mouth stayed shut.

The gap between the silver harvest and the huge grey-black head of the whale narrowed and closed. Apollo's head was surrounded by fish. Suddenly, he blew and Acreman was momentarily blinded by fine spray.

'Open your goddamn mouth,' he roared in frustration.

And the whale obeyed.

It tilted down like the ramp to a transport plane. His tail beat once and the airship lurched forward.

'Christ, he's swimming,' Barbara yelled in Acreman's ear. 'Frank, we'll have to cast him off if he does that.'

Acreman spun round to the pilot. 'Do we have to be this low? He'll pull us in any moment.'

'Loose the winch,' McSweeney called. 'It's got a hundred feet on it.'

Acreman pulled the winch lever by his hatch door and the airship lifted rapidly. Soon they were thirty feet above the sling. Apollo moved his tail again. The motion moved him forward several feet and the airship was pulled with him.

'Frank,' Barbara begged. 'Please let him loose.'

'We can't,' he said urgently, aware of her concern and suffering it himself. 'Anyway, look! He's feeding. He can't be that distressed!'

'I hope they get that trawler underway soon,' McSweeney called. 'We're catching her. They seem to be hypnotized.'

'Wouldn't you be?'

Looking down on Apollo, Acreman realized he was not moving any more than he needed to keep his head in the mass of herring. His mouth stayed open. Only when the harvest had thinned and there was just an occasional flash of

146

silver, did the black ramp close.

'I think he's done.'

'Is he going to want to come out?' Barbara asked.

'Let's try it. Up, captain?'

'Pull the handle,' McSweeney grinned. 'He comes or he doesn't.'

He came. There was no further tail movement. Apollo lifted until his sling clicked against the airship. Dave went to the stern and secured the holding rope. Apollo just blinked. The engines roared and the huge ship lifted. The men on the trawler waved.

Acreman looked down on the huge black shape of Apollo and thought of Doris hanging eager-eyed behind the viewing window and he heard the clipped voice of the Janus machine. He thought of Macho and his arrogance. He remembered the muscled bulk of Morgan and his gentle nervousness.

'Hold on, fellow,' he said to himself and Apollo. 'Soon we'll be among friends.'

Barbara took his arm.

'You remember what Doris said about not understanding fear. I think the big whales must be the same.'

Harry Asquith, invisible, or so he hoped, in a mountain anorak borrowed from the giant who commanded the *Eros*' forward winches, sat looking at the horizon. He was perched like a gull on the most forward point of the ship's bow, and was hoping that Vance would not find him.

Normally a view of the sea, uncluttered by decks or people, had a calming effect, but this morning it was not working. Firstly, there had been the new Vance. Harry had decided, during the flight out, that Vance's recall to Hope Ward's office had been for a battery change. The man was transformed. There was an eagerness about his normally still presence that Harry disliked intensely.

Once upon a time, Harry told himself wistfully, a scientist could have sat here and watched the dolphins leap. Now the sea was full of submarines and Acreman's bobbing net.

It was all coming to a head and Harry, who was occasionally honest with himself, accepted that it was his own stupid fault.

He looked down the long cliff of the tanker's bow. The U.S. Ohio-class submarine of the line, *Poseidon*, lay like a matt-black turd in the flat calm of the sea, two hundred yards to port. A grey plastic sausage snaked out to her through which people could walk, if they had superb stomachs and gimbals instead of hipbones.

Harry was waiting for Acreman, but Acreman was late. The kindly tail wind that had been assisting the airship had died on them. The dirigible was now some two hundred miles away on the northern edge of the doldrum in which the *Eros* lay.

'Professor Asquith?'

Harry spun around so fast he nearly fell off his perch into the sea. He thought it was Vance. It was Suskin. Harry had met him two or three times and had been impressed with his sincerity.

'How did you find me?'

'I'm sorry, sir. I didn't realize you were seeking privacy. Your assistant, Mr. Vance, told me where I could find you.'

Harry glowered. Vance definitely had a new battery!

'It's all right, Commander. I was indulging in a moment's contemplation before my people get here. You've heard of their wonderful achievement with the airship, I trust.'

Suskin grinned. He had heard many strange stories of this Englishman. He was, it was said, eccentric, a word Suskin didn't properly understand. The only eccentrics he knew got their lift out of badly brewed grapes. Asquith obviously wasn't a wino but he was definitely peculiar. He was meant to be brilliant. Suskin had once heard that Albert Einstein read *Superman* comics on his way to work. Asquith was probably like that. Suskin watched him and thought Asquith was reacting like he'd just stolen someone's wallet.

'Most people call me "Gene",' Suskin said.

Asquith winced. 'I don't think I could manage that, Commander. We'll use Suskin, if that's all right. It's quite common where I come from.'

Suskin smiled. 'Whatever you like, Professor. You don't mind me calling you "Professor"?'

'No, I quite like it. I've had a bad experience with my dignity this morning.'

'Well, I've certainly heard about your boys and their whale. Incredible. Is that what you're waiting for up here, Professor?'

'Yes. But do you know where Mr. Vance is?'

'Oh sure. He's in communications.'

'What's he doing there?'

'Well, maybe I shouldn't be saying this, but I think he's watching you through the TV. You know, we cover the whole ship. That's a pretty dangerous place you're sitting, Professor.'

Harry had forgotten all about the endless TV monitors. Worse than that, he did not like the idea that Vance was getting so good he had even worked out a cunning way of watching Asquith.

'Are you sure he's got the necessary clearances to be down there?' Harry said nastily.

Suskin raised an eyebrow. This entire exchange was very puzzling. He wondered whether persecution mania was an aspect of eccentricity. 'I understand that he *is* Security, Professor. He's certainly down on our books as that.'

'He should be down as a bloody nuisance,' said Harry without thinking. But he collected himself and said, 'Sorry, Suskin, bit fraught this morning. Worried about my whale. Understand?'

'Oh, sure, Professor. Maybe I've chosen a bad moment.'

'Not at all, not at all. If I can be of any help.'

'Well, sir,' said Suskin carefully. 'I really want to talk to you about sharks.'

For a terrible moment, Suskin thought Harry was going to fall into the sea again. He twitched as though he had been touched with a live wire, and his face went grey. Suskin reached out and took his elbow.

'I really think you should come down, Professor. You don't look at all well. A touch of seasickness, maybe.'

Harry climbed down, with Suskin's assistance, and flopped onto a metal bollard. What the hell did this man know about the shark hypothesis? Harry thought it was information confined to the very top brass. Was it all over the ship? If it was, none of his contingency plans would work. But perhaps Suskin, who had considerable responsibilities, knew a lot more.

Harry looked at the gleaming outline of the *Poseidon*.

'Is she ready to go, Suskin?'

'She is.'

'And the special equipment's functioning?' Harry asked casually.

Suskin nodded. 'Everything's ready. I know she stopped in at Pearl to take on some gear from the *Aquanaut.*'

Harry felt a little better. Suskin was patently honest.

'I don't know what you've heard about sharks, Suskin. There's been some theorizing, I know. But scientists do that rather glibly.'

'I think there is something down there, Professor.'

Harry looked up sharply. 'You've made independent observations?'

'Sort of. It's more putting two and two together. You know we've had two unexplained incidents since you were last here. One took the *Aquanaut* out. Now we've lost our *XT-4* unit.'

'I've read the reports,' Harry nodded. 'The emphasis would appear to be on *unexplained.*'

'I don't think so. I've been virtually living in communications since the *Aquanaut* ran into trouble. And there was something said by the boys in the *XT-4*. I think there's a hazard down there.'

'But you mentioned sharks. I thought perhaps you were quoting.'

Suskin looked Asquith squarely in the eye.

'Come clean with me, Professor. I get the feeling you know more than you're telling. And things keep happening which support what I've said. And they're going on. Isn't it true that this whale you're bringing in is going to escort the *Poseidon* when she dives?'

'Yes, he is. But only to enhance observation. With respect, Commander, you must accept that your equipment has limitations. Cetacean sonar is much more sophisticated than anything man has ever devised. And, as you know, we've found a method of communicating with the cetaceans that allows us to be aware of what they find with their sonar. The whale's being brought in because he can dive very deep. Our other animals can't.'

Suskin nodded impatiently. 'I know all that. But you're still ducking the point. All my readings, and what was said by Max Wiseman aboard the *XT-4* just before we lost contact, caused me to believe that there's a living thing down there that's attacking our units. I can't think of any other way of explaining it.'

'Have you considered how big a shark it would have to be to fit the description you've just given?'

Suskin grimaced. 'I know it seems ridiculous. That's why I

wanted to speak to you before I let it go further. I don't want to be laughed off the ship. But I can't sit back and let that sub go down if I know something the others don't.'

'None of us can afford to be laughed off the ship, Suskin. I think your caution is very wise.'

'I just want to know one thing, Professor. Is it possible?'

It was fortunate that Suskin did not know Harry very well. A look of supreme innocence fell like a thin curtain across his face. Everyone at the Institute knew the look. It made Harry the world's worst poker player.

'We have to accept that anything's possible in the sea. We know so little about it. We're like schoolboys trawling for shrimps on the beach. But I can tell you with absolute honesty that there is no *living* creature fits the description you've given me. Far and away the largest thing we know of is on its way here now—a sperm whale. When he arrives, I'm sure you'll understand what I mean, Suskin.'

'Then what the hell is causing all those moving images?' Suskin demanded. 'What was it that came flying across the face of the Fracture and hit the *XT-4?* What did they mean when they called out about something opening … something with white in it?'

Harry let him finish. He was seriously disturbed. None of the reports had contained these details. He assumed Suskin had suppressed them for fear of ridicule.

Suskin stood like an angry schoolboy, sure and unsure at the same time. Harry addressed him affectionately.

'But we have the consolation of knowing that if, and I must stress *if*, there is something down there which fits your description, our whale should find it. Now surely the mature thing to do until we know more is to wait for that information. In fact, I'm at a loss to think what else we can do.'

'There are sixty-eight officers and enlisted men going down in the *Poseidon*,' Suskin said doggedly. 'The two men who crewed the *XT-4* were personal friends of mine. Old friends!'

Fortunately fate then presented Harry with a distraction, a distraction of such magnitude that even Suskin was diverted. The huge silver airship with its extraordinary cargo suddenly loomed over the horizon.

'Will you just look at that!' Suskin cried.

'Magnificent,' said Harry with absolute satisfaction.

Acreman and his crew were not altogether unaware of the impact of their arrival on the crew of the *Eros*. As the airship drifted closer to the ship, her decks filled with madly waving ants. The conning tower of the sub opened and soon there were figures standing all along her hull.

But Acreman and the others were now dead-tired, and they had long grown used to the idea that an airship could lift a giant whale. Frank ignored the reception committee and peered anxiously down to check that the holding net was suitably positioned.

After their encounter with the trawler, the remainder of the journey had been uneventful. As night fell, there had been a slight increase in the rate of Apollo's breathing but he had soon adjusted to the change of light and Acreman had decided that Barbara's claustrophobia theory might well be right. In the darkness, Apollo could not see as much and, whereas in the night-darkened sea he would have continued to 'see' with his sonar, here in the air he could not.

He soon settled down and once, during his watch, Acreman saw one of his eyes close. Cetaceans, who must constantly rise for breath, cannot sleep for extended periods like humans. Instead they take continual catnaps, resting one side of their bodies at a time. Acreman was pleased to think that Apollo might be catnapping. It was the best evidence yet that he was surviving the transport well.

In fact, he had survived extraordinarily well and, alone on the windy frame, Acreman found himself contemplating where the whales fitted into the family of the cetaceans. It is almost possible, he accepted, for the human brain to understand how an animal the size of Apollo 'thought'. His brain was immense, fifteen times the size of the human brain. It was also a very good brain, with all the nerve endings and cells required for what humans regarded as sophisticated thought. But what did they think about? What were the imperatives, the values, the meanings of life in a world so different to the one that had shaped the human brain?

If you are the largest thing in the world and never known serious threat, did your brain have room for thoughts that have never been allowed the human race?

Acreman shuddered when he reflected on how much of the human thought process was taken up with questions of survival, power, fear, conquest, expansion—the whole inexorable anxiety of the territorial imperative. Apollo would not even know what these concepts meant.

And yet, like all the whales, his brain presented human scientists with a terrible enigma. *Our brains,* he thought, *have been developed and enlarged to accommodate the pressures of our expansion as a race.* Since man had moved from the forests, his brain had doubled in size.

But what had caused the whales and the dolphins to continue to develop their brains? It was known that the process had gone on for some fifty million years and was continuing, but in human terms there appeared to be no imperative, no reason. The cetaceans had not known any of the pressures that had caused the human brain to grow, and yet their brains had grown.

Acreman could not escape the thought that they were using their brains, needed their brains, for other thoughts. He was equally convinced these might be mental horizons that man might never see. His obsession with a device like the Janus machine had begun with this paradox.

So far, neither the machine nor the animals they had taught to use it had come close to resolving the paradox, but Acreman thought that this was part of the paradox itself. How do you explain something you do not understand? Barbara's belief that the dolphins knew no fear was a case in point.

Acreman reached out and stroked Apollo's head. His huge eye opened.

'You have a great deal to tell us, sir,' he said. 'I hope we have the right to ask.'

The huge circle of the holding net looked right. Its orange floats were forming a six-hundred-foot ring on the lee of the tanker, where the water was almost motionless. Acreman could see a gaggle of skimmers working around the outside of the ring as off-watch members of the tanker crew went out to get their first close-up look at the whale.

McSweeney called to him.

'How are we going to do this, boss?'

Acreman and Barbara changed places. Dave and Louise were already struggling into their wetsuits.

'Are we in contact with the *Eros*?'

'All the way. I've just been talking to the communications officer. He says your boss wants a word.'

'Okay,' Acreman said, putting on a set of headphones.

'Hello, *Eros*,' he said. 'This is Acreman. We need a few arrangements before we put this animal down.'

'Hello, Frank,' Harry's voice came back immediately. 'I want to pass on my official congratulations. What you've done is nothing less than historic.'

'Thanks, Harry. We're in good shape. But the animal hasn't eaten for twelve hours and I want food in that net before we let him down. It might also take his mind off other things. I don't know what to do about exercising him. He's a hell of a size, Harry, we've named him Apollo.'

'A case of sink or swim,' Harry said. 'I'd just get on with it, Frank. Sooner the better, probably. The food is no problem. I've got about ten tons of prime butterfish on ice in the ship's hold. We'll dump them in as soon as you say the word.'

'Put Morgan in,' Barbara called. 'And Doris and Macho with portable Janus gear. I think Morgan's big enough to help Apollo keep afloat while he's getting over the cramps. He could certainly push his tail about.'

Acreman looked startled. 'The dolphins maybe—but orcas have been known to attack big whales.'

'Oh, come on,' Barbara said. 'Morgan's not a wild killer whale. He's the only thing we've got that's anything near big enough. If Apollo gets cramp and sinks, that's it.'

'Is Morgan reliable enough?'

'With Doris around, certainly.'

'And Macho—does he get on all right with Morgan?'

'I think we might need Macho's ideas.'

'Okay. Harry, I want Morgan, Macho and Doris in the water. Fit the dolphins with portable Januses and plug me through when they're in the water. We'll stay here until that's been done.'

McSweeney was holding the airship fifty feet dead centre above the ring.

'Ready when you are,' he announced.

Acreman called his assistants around him.

'This question of cramp is the big one. So we'll put Apollo

154

down in his sling and just let him sit that way for a while. Then we'll dump some fish in and hope he goes after them. He did the last time and swimming in the sling will be good exercise. Then, well, then we just have to stand back and let it happen. We'll deflate the sling and simply let it sink. Harry will have a fit but it's the neatest and cleanest way of getting him clear of it. Any questions?'

'Do we go down before or after?' Dave asked.

'With him. We can't be much help anyway, but I think we should be in the water.'

Acreman started to get into his wetsuit, but stopped when he saw the pilot's mouth drop open.

'Say again,' McSweeney said breathlessly into the microphone. 'I think I got that wrong.

'I don't know what this is, boss,' McSweeney said. 'But there's a female robot wanting to talk to you. She just wished me a nice day.'

'Hello, Doris,' Acreman said, feeling good. 'Can you see what we have?' He looked through the window and, as expected, saw two silver arrows arc out of the water. A second or so later, Morgan performed a less spectacular leap.

'Who the hell is Doris, and why's she got such a funny voice?'

'Doris is a dolphin. They're speaking through a translation machine.'

'You telling me I've just exchanged the time of day with a dolphin, boss? The boys at Andrews just ain't gonna believe this!'

'Doris,' said Acreman. 'I'd like you to meet Mr. McSweeney. He's the man who works this big machine.'

'Hello, McSweeney. Are there two of the great ones?'

McSweeney looked helplessly at Acreman. 'That's a dolphin?'

Acreman nodded.

'Er … hello, you … dolphin. This is Lieutenant McSweeney. Oh, shee-it!'

'I already said, "Hello, McSweeney." Answer the question.'

'What's she talking about?' the pilot asked desperately. 'Man, this is weird!'

'Hello, Doris. Acreman. We do not understand the question.'

'We see one great one, Acreman. Or we see the tail. But what is that above it … another?'

'No, Doris, though I'll admit it looks like one. This is...' he paused at a loss for words. 'An air boat. It floats in the sky.'

'Another of your machines, Acreman.'

'Another, Doris.'

'It is better to look at than most.'

Acreman smiled. McSweeney reacted nervously a few seconds later when another staccato voice came through his headset.

'Hello, Acreman. You come back good. I not happy, Acreman. Barbara gone long time.'

'Who the hell's that?' McSweeney demanded, his face aglow with wonder. 'Is that a dolphin, too?'

'No, that's the orca.'

'What's an orca?'

'*Orcinus orca*—the killer whale.'

'You got one of those down there, too?'

'That's right. But he's very young, hence the simple language. Name's Morgan. Say hello.'

'Hello ... er ... Morgan. This is Lieutenant McSweeney, U.S. Air Force, calling. How are you?'

'I just told you I not happy, not not not happy. Where Barbara? Who McSweeney?'

'I'd better take over,' Acreman said. 'Take a look down.'

Twenty feet of black silk suddenly lifted from the waves and did an exuberant roll through the air.

McSweeney shouted, 'Sweet Jesus!'

Barbara took the microphone.

'Hi, baby. How you doing?'

'Not happy, Barbara.'

'You're okay, baby. We went to find you a friend.'

'The great one is for me?'

Acreman looked at her sharply.

'For all of us, Morgan. The great one is sick. Soon he come in water. You keep him up, okay?'

'Too big.'

'Try, Morgan, no more you talk. Macho. Come in Macho.'

'Hello, Barbara,' came instantly. 'I like your new machine. Can it come down here? I want to see inside.'

'It can't, Macho. It is an air machine. Anyway, are you fit?'

'Not very. It's been boring. We've been in the tank too long.'

'Well, that's over now, friend. How do you like the great one?'

'Is it trained? Can it speak?'

'No.'

'Then it will be like Morgan. Stupid.'

'Are you still bothering Morgan, mister?'

'No. Not much.'

'Well, we've got work for you now. Listen, Macho, and you, too, Doris. We are going to put the great one in the water soon. He has a name—Apollo. He has come a long way and has cramp. We want you to watch him and get Morgan to give him support if he has trouble keeping his blow hole above water. Have you got that?'

'Yes,' said Macho.

'Doris?'

'Yes, Barbara. Welcome back.'

'Thank you. Make sure Morgan understands. Doris, Morgan will not attack the great one, will he?'

'No, Barbara. Not now he is trained. His kind only play with the great ones sometimes. They like to eat their tongues.'

'Their tongues,' Barbara squealed. 'Why, Doris?'

'They taste good. Like you like ice cream, remember?'

Barbara, still a little sickened, realized abruptly that she also liked pressed tongue. 'I get you, Doris. Well, make sure Morgan doesn't do anything like that.'

'He won't. When is Apollo coming?'

Acreman was now fully dressed. He took the microphone from Barbara. 'Now,' he said. He looked at McSweeney and the pilot nodded. 'Thirty feet. Right, boss?'

The engines rose in pitch and McSweeney put the nose down.

Acreman and the other three jumped when McSweeney gave them a thumbs up.

They hit the water and, before they even had their masks clear, the two dolphins and the orca were under them and pushing for the surface. Acreman got his ride from Morgan, who, being over excited, went up too fast so that Acreman's ears popped painfully. He didn't think about it. It was just fantastic being back with them.

In a ring—four humans and three cetaceans—they waited while Apollo descended slowly towards them.

The cradle hit the water with hardly a splash. Apollo lifted his head, lowered it, moved his tail once so that his head dipped into the water and then blew a ten-foot spray of fine water particles.

Acreman, in the skimmer, watched with growing confidence. He spoke into the walkie-talkie and men on the tanker began to empty boxes of fish over the side. They floated out towards the whale. It took a lot to claim his attention, but, eventually, the huge mouth opened and he moved his tail as before, making enough way for the food to be swept into his gullet.

Eventually, Acreman decided it was time to lose the sling. He had a Janus receiver in the skimmer and he spoke to the animals.

'We're going to blow the sling in a minute. Is that okay?'

'Yes,' Doris said. 'We think he is okay.'

'How can you tell?'

'He is speaking and sonaring normally.'

'Speaking?'

'Not language speech,' Doris corrected. 'Just water sounds made by great ones.'

'But can you understand it?' Acreman demanded with great excitement.

'Enough. He is not concerned. He is just interested.'

'Can he understand you, Doris?'

'Yes. Some. He will be able to read my signals. And, given time, I will learn a lot of his sounds.'

'How much time, Doris?' The whole point of bringing Apollo here hung on her answer.

'I will be able to tell—if he will stay here—by tonight,' Doris replied. 'Is that what you want to know?'

Acreman grinned wryly.

'Well, that would certainly help.'

'If you let him go, Acreman, we can start. Morgan wants to know if he may eat any of this fish.'

'Sure. But he has to help first.'

Acreman looked around. Barbara, Dave and Louise were hanging on the ring of the big net. Apollo had now worked his way halfway across in the direction of the tanker.

He spoke into the walkie-talkie.

'Harry. If everything's okay on your end, we're going to lose the sling.'

'Good luck, dear boy. There seems very little I can do to help. He seems to be feeding.'

'This is it, Harry. It's his decision now.' He addressed the Janus microphone. 'Are you three ready?'

'Ready.'

Acreman pulled a lever on a box on the skimmer. Several small servos around the whale cradle snapped open and it began to deflate rapidly. In a matter of seconds, Apollo was in the water. Then the sling and its air bags vanished and the whale wallowed, lifting its head, rolling from side to side. He blew twice and Acreman felt a flash of panic.

'Morgan, I think he's sinking!'

There was a flurry of white water behind the great whale's tail and Acreman saw Morgan's black and sharklike dorsal cut through the water at high speed. Then it vanished and, for nearly three minutes, there was no sign of the young *Orca*. Apollo, however, was still on the surface. He was blowing more than he needed, but at least he was afloat. Then he seemed to settle again and Acreman saw Morgan's dorsal lift abruptly in front of his head as he surfaced for air.

'Doris!' Acreman snapped. 'What's happening?'

'We have to do something quickly, Acreman. Apollo is deciding not to live.'

'What!'

'He is breathing too slowly and sinking. Morgan has been under him but he cannot hold one of that size for very long.'

'What the hell do we do? Why won't he swim? We've seen that his tail's not cramped!'

The Janus speaker was silent for a moment.

'Let Morgan attack,' came a voice. From the clipped nature of the word-use, Acreman recognized Macho's style.

'What the hell are you saying, Macho?'

'Do it. Quickly. He will not use his teeth. We have to wake the great one up. His life is going to sleep.'

What options do I have? Acreman thought. He knew nothing. Macho seemed positive.

'Morgan. Listen. Did you hear, Macho?'

'Yes, Acreman.'

'Do you know what he is saying?'

'It was my thought, Acreman. He took it.'

'Never mind that, Morgan. Do you know what to do? You must not hurt him.'

'No, Acreman. I will play with him.'

'Okay, baby. Do it!'

Before he had finished speaking, the three cetaceans lifted from the water about three feet in front of Apollo's head, crashing down with a mighty splash. The orca turned almost on the spot and ran straight for Apollo's huge flank, ramming him with a thump that could be heard on the tanker.

Apollo blew and his tail flapped. He turned and began to move away from the attack, but Morgan had already turned and, from his speeding dorsal, Acreman saw that he was swimming straight at Apollo, at about twenty knots.

Again the great whale thrashed his tail and turned, but Morgan kept on coming, sideswiping his head with another loud slap. Apollo gave a loud, thin cry, his vast tail lifted out of the water and he vanished.

'Oh, Christ,' Acreman said to himself. 'That's it.'

He waited for several minutes.

'Doris ... for God's sake! Has he gone?'

'No, Acreman. He's fine. Look to port. Tell Barbara to look down and hold on.'

Acreman hardly had time to swing around. He yelled to Barbara but his words were drowned by the noise of Apollo attempting to clear the water. Almost thirty feet of him rose from the waves as though he was being drawn out by some mighty rope. The vast mass seemed to pause, then crashed down, throwing a ten-foot tide of water over the rim of the net. Barbara was washed away and Acreman studied the tossing water anxiously. A bright orange life jacket eventually broke the surface and Barbara held up her hand with an 'I'm okay' signal.

All of Acreman's speakers were now bleating for attention. Harry's plaintive voice was asking for an explanation of what he termed the 'berserk Leviathan', Morgan was punching a series of incoherent sentences through the Janus, and Dave was swimming frantically back to the skimmer, blind to the danger of Apollo, who was now swimming around the net ring at some speed, pursued by Morgan's gleaming black dorsal.

'Doris,' Acreman called urgently. 'I think that's enough.'

'I agree, Acreman. But Morgan is young and this is his first game with a great one.'

'Can't you stop him?'

'Yes, I can. But he won't like it.'

'Just stop him, Doris. If this goes on, Apollo's likely to breach the net.'

By now, Apollo had almost completed the circle and Morgan was still coming up behind him. But as Acreman watched, he saw the dorsals of the two dolphins cut between the great whale and the orca.

Morgan's dorsal turned abruptly and again there was a loud sound of bodies clashing. Doris lifted out of the water in a somersault, her tail slapping down across the orca's head.

'Morgan,' Acreman said. 'Speak to me.'

'Why, why, why, hit me? Why hit me, Doris?'

'Morgan, stop swimming. Come over here.'

There was no response for almost ten seconds, then, to Acreman's considerable relief, he saw Morgan's head lift above the water, look in the direction of the skimmer and then move slowly towards it. Acreman turned and signalled Barbara to join him.

'That young bastard tried to bite me,' said a voice in the Janus machine. Acreman grinned, feeling he was in control for the first time since Apollo had been set free. 'Who's been teaching you to swear, Macho?'

Barbara clambered aboard the skimmer and Acreman handed her the Janus mike. 'Calm Morgan down.' He turned to watch Apollo. He was now swimming slowly around the ring, making mewing sounds. Acreman noted that he was blowing about every five minutes, his normal rate. As he watched, the whale dived again, but surfaced a few moments later on the other side of the ring.

'Harry,' Acreman said into the walkie-talkie. 'I think we've managed it. Will you dump in another load of fish?'

Deck hands on the tanker began to pour barrels of small fish down the shute.

Apollo swam almost up against the tanker's side and started to feed. Acreman heard loud cheers from the watchers on the deck.

Looking down, he saw the silver heads of the two dolphins, the black blobs of the Janus transmitters attached just behind the blow holes, looking at him over the side of the skimmer.

'Thanks, Doris! And you, too, Macho. That was a great idea, even if it did get a little out of hand.' The two dolphins waggled their heads.

'Now,' Acreman said. 'It's really up to you. Try and make contact with Apollo. We have to see if he can read an image from you two, a sonar-shape. And then somehow we have to get him to go and look for that shape. Do you get that?'

'Yes, Acreman. What is the shape?'

'It's the memory of which we-spoke. We think there is one here and it lives very deep. Too deep for Apollo even. But he should be able to see it with his sonar if he goes down as far as he can go.'

'It will take time, Acreman.'

'But can you do it?'

'We know already we can read his sonar-shapes. We have already been doing it. So we do not need to speak with him. We will read his transmissions. But we have somehow to cause him to go and look for this other great one. That will be difficult as we do not know what interests Apollo.'

'Others of his kind interest him,' said Macho. 'And I think he can read our sonar-shapes. When the bastard was playing his games, I showed Apollo two more of Morgan's kind and he went very fast!'

Acreman reflected ruefully that that was probably what had caused Apollo to leap out of the water. One orca was trouble enough; the sonar suggestion from Macho that there were two others about could well have panicked him.

'You must be careful, Macho. He, too, is a young animal.'

Then Acreman remembered the reference to a mother and he asked Macho what he meant by that.

'That will interest him,' the young male dolphin replied. 'If we can show him the shape of a great one in the depths, perhaps he will think it is one of his kind and go look.'

'That's really an intriguing thought,' said Acreman. 'Can you do that?'

'We can try,' said Doris. 'But first we must see how well he accepts our images.'

Acreman looked at the submarine. 'We don't have a lot of time, Doris. Get going on it.'

The huge metal sling, four sections of carbon steel bar measuring almost a hundred feet, sank slowly into the Fracture, its deflated air bags acting like parachutes.

The young male Megalodon stirred uneasily in the cave as

162

the substantial alterations in current reacted in its head crypts. He moved slowly out and turned left, swimming north up the trench in the direction of this new target.

The sling gathered speed as it fell. The fabric of the air bags flattened and ripped as the rate of descent increased and soon the parachute braking was gone. The sling tilted forward and plunged down into the great emptiness of the Fracture.

The young male increased his speed but kept close to the bottom, causing a hurricane of fine sand and small rock. In the rock caves on his back hid tiny transparent crabs. The fish that lived and fed around the Megalodon could not maintain the animal's new pace and they fell back in a confused shoal.

Now the sling was descending with the speed of an arrow and the Megalodon had difficulty getting a clear bearing on it. It settled momentarily to allow the lateral line sensors to draw an attack line, but the sling hit the face and skidded wildly out into the void, so that the Megalodon had to swing his head sharply to keep focused. He beat his tail rapidly and his speed increased to nearly thirty knots. He shot along the northern face of the Fracture, scanning left and right as the sling careened off the face on its way to the bottom.

Natural caution for an object so alive returned to the Megalodon as he came close enough to the sling to see it. But he maintained his speed and, huge mouth open, teeth bared, turned on his side for an investigatory pass. But the huge mass of the sling, now under the full pull of gravity, shot past the Megalodon on into the deeps.

Puzzled, the Megalodon tilted downwards and chased the sling. But swim as he might, he could not catch it, and the sling eventually hit the bottom, burying half its length in the soft sand. Sections of rock torn free by the sling's contacts with the face fell in a storm of loose rock and sand and the water became so clouded, the Megalodon, left well behind, finally located it only by his sensing mechanisms.

He approached the free end of the sling slowly, mouthed a section of pipe and closed his teeth around it. Then he slewed its head sideways, trying to tear it open. But although the steel tubes bent, they did not tear, and no food flavours came to the Megalodon.

In a fury of frustration, he thrust hard with his tail and tore at the sling. One of his teeth broke and he felt a stab of pain.

The sling reared out of the sand like a living thing, but still there was no food flavour. Eventually, the Megalodon dropped the sling and lay next to it, confused. He could not believe that an object so large could not be food. He remembered the flavours that had come from the other objects as hard as this and decided to wait.

Suskin pounded up the deck to where he had left Asquith. He found Harry leaning over the side, chuckling with delight at the huge whale in the ring of floats. He was thumping the rail, crying, 'Bravo. Bravo!'

But Suskin did not hesitate to interrupt him.

'Professor ... Professor Asquith,' he cried. 'I'm sorry, Professor, but there is something you should see!'

Harry turned irritably. 'Not now, Suskin! Look at that beast. Come on, man, you'll never see a sight like that again.'

'Please, Professor. This is very important. I think you should also call Dr. Acreman aboard.'

'I can't possibly do that, Suskin. Look, I promise, as soon as this is over ...'

'Professor! My screens are showing activity on the bottom. Masses of it!'

Harry stood back from the rail and frowned.

'Really?' Then his face cleared. 'Oh, wait a minute, Suskin. I'd have told you if I'd known, but I didn't. They abandoned the big sling, the whale sling. Rather a waste, I admit, but that's the way Dr. Acreman decided to do it. That's your problem.'

'I don't think so,' Suskin said doggedly. 'In fact, I don't think so at all. The sling caused a lot of activity; rocks and stuff. But there's something else. I've got a clear outline on it now. I think you should come and look.'

'Does the other outline move?' Harry asked carefully.

'It's not moving at the moment, but it must have got there somehow. As you know, our problem is we can't tell much when things are moving about down there, but as soon as it settles ...'

Harry broke in.

'Look, old man, you've read the reports. Avalanches and all that. That was a very big bit of metal we dropped; a hundred feet long. That really could have caused an avalanche.'

'For Christ's sake, Professor! I've come to you because I thought you'd understand. I'm sick to my gut of people trying to explain this away with crap reasons. You're the expert, surely you'll at least look at what we have now!'

Harry was taken aback by the force of Suskin's outburst. 'All right, old man. Things seem to have quietened down out there, anyway.'

'And Dr. Acreman?'

'Why don't I have a peep first?' Harry said, starting down the deck. 'Acreman's going to be very busy for a little while.'

Suskin shrugged and started after him. He went down the stairs at such a pace Harry had trouble keeping up. In the communications room, a tense-looking operator immediately hurried across to Suskin.

'It's still there. And we keep getting a flurry of activity. The front moves and then the sand lifts up. But the big object is still there.'

For the first time, Harry felt a thread of genuine alarm. Suskin walked across to the big sonar screen and stared at it. Harry followed. The picture was quite clear. There were two wavy vertical faces that did not move. Then there was a thick blob of white with two thin lines extending from the front of it like the antennae of a dogfish.

As they watched, the forward part of the solid white blob moved, the thin lines waved and then the whole image milked out.

'Sand,' Suskin said tensely.

Harry looked at the white outline and knew, with a mixture of wonder and dread, that life and his future were about to take a bizarre turn.

He sat in a padded swivel chair before the screen and studied it closely. A strong sense of fate began to suffuse his brain. Could it be, he wondered—could it possibly be—that the electric mudfish of the Amazon basin were not to be his singular contribution to the great body of human knowledge? No, magically, something bigger might be possible. Something so much bigger it was making his mind spin. A completely new species, a living fossil to rival the coelacanth. But immensely more important. Harry shook his head.

But then, being Harry, he thought about the pragmatics. How could he keep his hands on it? How could he extricate it

165

from this military and political mess? He could think of nothing now but this hidden ace, nothing else that would keep him in the game. But he was in the wrong place to make contact with the National Ecology Trust. Every message from the *Eros* was logged and monitored and no one must know that the tip-off had come from him. It might save the Megalodons but it would blacklist Harry and the Institute for all time.

'Commander … who have you told about this?'

'No one, Professor. I told you because I needed your backup. But we don't have too much time. The *Poseidon*'s due to go down as soon as Dr. Acreman has the whale ready. In fact, we might not have *that* long. I attended the Day Briefing this morning and those Navy guys don't rate your whale. They'll be going down anyway unless Dr. Acreman has something positive to offer tomorrow.'

'Aren't you Navy, Commander?'

'Signals squadron, Professor,' Suskin grinned wryly. 'Those blue-water types think we're the soft end of the Service. Doesn't bother me normally, but now I need a lot more clout if I'm going to stop that sub from going down.' He stared hard at Asquith. 'As I think I should with that thing on the prowl.'

Harry made no reply for a long moment.

'You'll excuse me if I'm less than forthcoming, Commander, but as you'll have noticed, I'm not entirely my own master. What would you suggest "that thing" is?'

'I'm not even prepared to guess, Professor. But, amongst other things, it's killed two of my friends. I don't give a damn what security wraps you're under—I think it's your moral duty to tell me what you, the expert, think it is.'

Harry looked distinctly unhappy. 'Long time since I've heard that word used around here. All right, Commander, let's trust each other. It's beginning to look like a Megalodon shark.' He watched Suskin's face keenly and was rather impressed when he saw nothing but relief written there.

'That doesn't surprise you, Commander?'

'I don't surprise anymore, Professor. I don't think I will again until this is over. I don't pretend to know what Megadon …'

'Megalodon,' Harry corrected automatically. '*Carchardon Megalodon.*'

'… is,' Suskin finished firmly.

'Nothing very mysterious about it, Suskin. Just a big shark species. We just haven't come across one before, that's all.'

Suskin shook his head and whistled. 'I know a few people who might regard that as something of an understatement, Professor.'

'That's because we want to believe in monsters, Commander. Hasn't the motivation which causes people to pay to see films like *King Kong* ever intrigued you?'

'Not up to now, Professor,' Suskin said dryly. 'And, with respect, I can think of better times to discuss it.'

Harry, all set to launch into a much-loved lecture on the subject of the vicarious instinct and its relationship to perverse human sexuality (on which subject he had considerable practical experience), took the point.

'You're right, man. There's someone we have to tell about this right now. Can you find Dr. Acreman?'

'I'm the signals officer, Professor.'

'Good. Then you get him down here. But in the meantime—until we're sure—not a word to anyone.'

Acreman arrived, looking angry, about ten minutes later. He was still in his wetsuit, which dripped onto the steel floor.

'What the hell is this, Harry? I've got a million things to do!'

Harry nodded at the screen. 'I thought that might interest you.'

At that moment, the front of the white blob moved again.

'Bless you,' said Harry.

Acreman, his mouth open, leaned forward.

'Those thin white stripes—is that what I think it is?'

'It's the sling you dropped,' Suskin said. 'We followed it down. Interesting, Frank.'

'Interesting,' Acreman gasped. 'Harry, don't you see what this gives us? We can measure it!'

'Mmm, I've been doing the sums myself.'

'Jesus Christ!' said Suskin, realizing what they were talking about. 'Are you saying …?'

'The sling's one hundred and eight feet long,' Acreman cried. 'That makes the shark at least ninety feet, probably more!'

'Magnificent,' said Harry.

'A shark ninety feet long,' Suskin panted. 'How big are its fucking jaws?'

Acreman was fixed to the spot. He answered with his own question. 'How big are its parents?'

The Russian submarine captain heard the reports of his chief diving systems technician, the communications officer and the chief sonar and hydrophone technician, in silence.

'It all makes for a most difficult approach,' Markov said eventually. 'The underwater topography is like the Caucasus. If we descend into one of the deep valleys, as we should for security, it must point in the right direction for our surveillance equipment to be of any use. And there is no guarantee of that. Otherwise, we have to proceed in shallow water—sometimes very shallow. We know that the new American satellites are capable of heat and infrared detection down to thirty metres and, in some places, we would be shallower than that.

'Also, Litkin ...' He looked at the sonar and hydrophone technician. 'You hint at abnormal activity. Can you not be more specific?'

The sub's detection equipment man shook his head with frustration. 'It is purely hydrophone information, most of it more confusing than helpful. Our sonar is useless, you understand. We are still eighty kilometres in a straight line from the RV. I'm sorry, Captain. The best I can say is what I have said already. I am getting peculiar sounds from the hydrophones focused in the direction of the RV.'

'Try again, Petr,' Markov smiled. 'Commissar Beltyin is polishing his torpedos, it will not be on the record.' Litkin looked at the others, grinned and shrugged.

'Rumblings, growlings, even the odd *shriek*. Then some sounds that would normally cause me to think they have a squadron of submarines at that point—heavy movement vibration. It is hard to describe. But no engine noise other than those we know about; that of one submarine and small support craft. The big tanker does not use her engines at all. So what can I say? If there were really other craft there, my equipment would have their sound signatures by now. I am sorry, skipper. It is most unsatisfactory.'

'No, Petr. It is information upon which we must act. The best you have so far. I think we have no options. I am not prepared to risk detection by a shallow water approach. We will pick our way carefully along the deep valleys, keeping our eyes—or rather Petr's metal ears—open. It will take more time, but it is the only safe way.'

He pulled the flexible stem of his command microphone towards him.

'All hands, prepare to dive. I repeat, prepare to dive.' He looked at his chief diving systems technician. 'We will proceed as soon as you have located a valley pointing in the right direction.'

8

A sense of suppressed excitement spread to encompass the three men in the communications room of the *Eros*, each for their own reasons.

Acreman felt vindicated and was becoming aware of the magnitude of his discovery, the effect it would have on his career, the colossal boost it would have on funding for work with animals like Apollo.

Harry felt some of the same, but, aware of the political manifestations, he was thinking desperately. From the glow in Acreman's eye, he knew that Frank could not even conceive that other forces might not allow him to keep his find. Harry knew that he was facing the greatest test of his life—a coup of grand design and delicacy was required.

Suskin simply wanted the thing dead. Otherwise a kindly, humane man, he had reacted traditionally to the shark. It scared him. It would have scared him had it been of normal size. This one scared him mindless. But he also felt considerable satisfaction that he had found the answer to their problems. There could be no question of the *Poseidon* going down now.

Suskin broke the reverie.

'I want to call an emergency meeting of the Project Management, including the Navy reps,' he said. 'We've recorded everything on the screen for the past hour. We have the original sandstorm, the sling going down, activity in the storm and then this. It's moved about four times. I reckon that should be enough.'

'It well might not be,' Harry said.

'Come on, Harry,' Acreman insisted. 'This, on top of the other evidence!'

'You've got something else,' Suskin demanded angrily. 'Why wasn't I told?'

170

'What's your security status, Commander?' Harry asked gently.

'What do you think? I command this communications net.'

'That might not be quite good enough, either,' Harry said, almost to himself.

Suskin was red with fury. 'I don't give a damn, Professor. I'm sounding the alarm with you or without you. With the *Poseidon* ready to dive, I don't have any choice. We'll all look a lot less foolish if we stick together.'

'He's right, Harry,' Acreman said. 'We've our own team to think about as well. Can't you get it into your head that that thing is down there ... now? And there must almost certainly be others.'

Harry sighed. 'I'm very aware of that uncomfortable reality. But I've already suffered as much of a credibility gap as my reputation will stand. We have to be sure we can make it stick.'

'What else do we need?' Acreman demanded.

'A positive visual sighting,' said Harry. 'What we always needed.'

Suskin reached for a telephone. 'Get me Admiral Whitting.' He looked at the others. 'Nothing can get near that thing without a good chance of ending up dead.'

'The whale could,' said Harry.

'No, Harry,' Acreman said firmly. 'I'm not prepared to run that risk.'

'Since when was there a cetacean that couldn't outperform a shark? If we fitted Apollo with a motorized camera, remote-controlled, we could operate it as soon as he makes sonar contact.'

'He's completely untrained, Harry. And, for Christ's sake, this is no ordinary shark.'

'You're being pedantic, Frank. You know you are. What did you bring him for?'

Acreman avoided his eye.

'Are you telling me you've changed your mind now that there's positive evidence of a Megalodon?' Harry demanded.

'Perhaps.'

'Well, fortunately, it's not your decision,' Harry said.

'What does that mean?'

'I run the Institute, Frank. I decide what use our animals are put to.'

'Do you want my resignation?'

'No. And what purpose would it serve? If you want to look after Apollo, supervise his work.'

'You're determined to use him?'

'No. But I suspect we will come under irresistible pressure from the Project. Assuming that, I want to work out our best options—in the interests of the safety of the animals and our crew.'

'Which could mean sacrificing Apollo.'

'If you wish to see it that way. I think Apollo, of all of us, humans and dolphins alike, has the best chance of obtaining the confirmation we need without serious risk.'

'I can't agree,' Acreman said. 'That beast is a totally unknown quantity.'

'It's not a *beast*,' Harry said quietly. 'It is a large species of shark. And Apollo is a very large species of whale. You have no basis to assume that it is more of a threat to him than, say, a hammerhead is to a dolphin. And you know very well that dolphins can outswim hammerheads. They can also kill them with their beaks if they choose.'

Suskin broke in. 'If you two have finished, I have to tell you that Admiral Whitting has convened a full meeting of the Committee for 0930—that's thirty minutes from now. You're instructed to attend.'

'Did Admiral Whitting indicate the nature of the agenda?' Harry asked.

'He said we would be considering how our information affects his other options.'

'I see,' Harry said softly, and made his decision.

'Commander, could you possibly use one of these radios to have a sandwich delivered to my cabin. I can't talk on an empty stomach.' He waved to Acreman. 'Frank, I think it would be wise if we spent a few moments together, comparing notes.'

He said nothing more until they were settled in his cabin and Acreman had removed his wetsuit.

'Frank, I know you want action, but it's not something that exists naturally in nature. You have to put the right elements together if you want a spark.'

'I don't have time for a lecture on basic physics, Harry,' Acreman growled. 'Are you going to tell this meeting that we refuse to use Apollo in a proven, hazardous situation?'

172

'No … and before you shout me down, I'll tell you why. Because they won't listen. They have the power and all we can do is prevent their using it. All of science is exploited by the various funding agencies because of that power—if you want a truly appalling example, look at the Los Alamos Project—the development of the first American atomic bomb. Most of the leading scientists voiced objections to the implementation of their theoretical work, but they then found it was too late—it rolled on inexorably and they were just brushed aside.'

'What the fuck has all this got to do with us, Harry?'

Harry looked at his watch. 'We have exactly sixteen minutes to do something before we get brushed aside. Answer me one question, Frank. In an ideal world, what would you, the ecologist, like to do with this extraordinary thing you have found?'

'Oh hell, Harry. I don't know. I'm not even sure I know what you're talking about. To study it, obviously; declare this area a marine conservation reserve …'

Harry held up his hand. 'That's all I wanted to know. No, one more thing, Who can we spare from our team?'

'Louise, I suppose.'

'Get her down here on the double.' Harry started rummaging through his briefcase for an address book.

Louise came through the door a few moments later, carrying a sandwich on a tray.

'There was a steward outside your door with this. He nearly dropped it.' She stared at Asquith. 'I think he was listening at your door, Professor.'

Harry grinned. 'The plot thickens. Never mind, I presume he's gone now.'

'Yes, he positively scuttled off.'

'I want you to run an errand for me, my dear, and it must be done today. Get on the midday shuttle, using whatever guise is necessary. This evening, and not before, you will call this number and use these exact words: "Is that George?" If you get an affirmative, you say, "The game is on but I must leave it to you to find the course. My secretary will provide promising locations." '

Asquith made her repeat it.

'Don't I need to mention your name, Professor?'

'Just say you are calling from the Institute. I wouldn't like people to think I was putting play before work.'

Louise looked at Acreman for help. But he was just as puzzled.

'Off you go, Miss Putnam. Come along, Frank. We're due at that meeting.'

Harry wondered as he looked round the bridge conference room whether they were quite so badly out on a limb as he feared. Whitting, who usually displayed an air of authoritative boredom, seemed tense. And there were no absentees. Whitting was supported by his two civilian aides, Horning and Lawlock, who Harry knew reported directly to Washington, and there was a full complement of Navy brass including Lewis, who commanded the *Poseidon*. Acreman had arrived with Barbara, carrying a brown card file and a small cardboard box. Suskin had a large television set arranged on a sideboard with a VTR playback machine set up alongside it. Whitting coughed and called the meeting to order.

Suskin opened. Asquith listened with admiration as the communications man described the three attacks, illustrating each of them with a short sequence of tape showing the sonar plots. When he reached the sequence Harry had seen earlier, Suskin stood up and used a long pointer to show the sling descending like a tiny hairpin, the cloud of sand that seemed to roll along the bottom towards it and the solid shape of the looming Megalodon. Suskin had edited the four movements so that they appeared as a sequence, which Harry thought was cheating, but it was certainly a confident, unemotional presentation. Whitting had set his jaw firmly and everyone took their cue from him. Suskin looked angry, then depressed.

Whitting asked Harry if he had anything to add. Harry looked across at Lawlock, the Washington aide, and asked whether he was allowed to reveal evidence that had previously been for Washington's ears only.

Lawlock said, 'No.'

'In that case, I'll hand over to Dr. Acreman,' Harry said expansively. 'And reserve the right to summarize.'

Acreman opened the little cardboard box and, as Harry had suspected, extracted the tooth shard and passed it around the table. Harry wondered whether he was doing the right thing, letting Acreman do their presentation. This was certainly the wrong way to start. As he'd feared, the officers and civil servants fingered the shard with bewilderment and handed it on quickly, not wishing to display their ignorance.

But then Acreman became more professional. He took a small slide projector from his briefcase, called for the lights to be dimmed and, with nice theatrical timing, shocked the audience with a coloured picture of the biggest shark mouth Harry had ever seen. Even though he knew what was coming, he could not resist a gasp of horror. The effect on the others was traumatic.

'What the hell is that?' Whitting demanded loudly. 'Lights! Turn on the lights. I want a discussion on this.' The lights came on but Acreman left the image on the wall, like some ghostly nemesis.

'Dr. Acreman!' Whitting said angrily. 'This is not a cheap cinema for horror movies. I want this committee to make up its mind coolly and calmly and we've already heard that the species you're supposed to be describing is extinct, damn it! You can't possibly have an actual photograph of a what-the-hell-do-you-call-it, Megadeath!'

Harry giggled.

'Megalodon,' Acreman said calmly. He turned to the image. The mouth was about ten feet high with the huge, six-inch teeth gleaming faintly. A man could easily have stood inside it. On the outer edge of the frame, the great pallid eyes, still as death, mesmerised everyone in the room.

'This is a projection,' he said calmly. 'It was made by zoologists at the San Diego Sea World. They took fossilized Megalodon teeth, which are far from rare, and set them in a model head of the correct ratio. That display now stands in the foyer of their new Shark Chamber. Half the kids in California have seen it.'

'I've examined it myself,' he continued. 'So has Professor Asquith. We concur that it is accurate so far as it goes, with one reservation. We think the head you are looking at is very small. They have erred in favour of moderation.'

'Even so,' said Whitting angrily, 'it's still a fantasy.'

'Yes,' said Acreman, picking up the tooth shard. 'But this isn't. And this is not fossilized, it's living tooth material and it was embedded in the bow section of the *Jules Verne*. I removed it myself. I would like the committee's permission to show my own projection of a head based on this tooth.'

Whitting agreed with evident reluctance.

Acreman slipped another slide into the projector, leaving the other one in place. This provoked another rustle of horrified amazement. It was more than twice the size of the original. Acreman called for the lights to be switched on again and he clicked off the projector.

'All right, gentlemen. I don't propose to show any more visual evidence because we are now entering the realm of true hypothesis. But there is one further fact we do have to take into account. One of the best methods of establishing the age of wild animals is by their teeth. There are growth lines on teeth very similar to the rings one can use to date trees. I have to tell you that the projection you have just seen based on the growth lines from its tooth, is, in fact, a young animal, not yet fully grown. And, as sharks do not procreate themselves, we have to face up to the fact that this one must have parents. Those animals could be twice as large as the projection. I appreciate that this is all very hard to accept but I must add that I believe the evidence, especially in the light of Commander Suskin's sonar pictures, to be incontrovertible.'

He sat down and stared stolidly at Whitting. The admiral's eyes flickered to the wall and then slowly travelled around the sombre faces of the committee members.

The silence was broken by Captain Lewis, skipper of the *Poseidon*.

'Was any of this evidence available before the dives made by my predecessors?'

Whitting flushed.

'I can tell you, sir, that it was not.'

'But Dr. Acreman has said that he removed this chunk of tooth from the *Jules Verne!*'

Whitting was thumbing madly through some papers.

'I have here,' he said hurriedly, 'an abstract of a report made to the Project office on the tooth shard. It says categorically that Professor Asquith expressed the opinion that any conclusion to be drawn from it was hypothetical.'

'I presume you've inserted "categorically",' Harry said mildly. 'I never used that word.'

Whitting did a double take. 'Yes, that's right. I merely wished to emphasize that your report, Professor, did not regard the evidence of the tooth as relevant. It was, as I have already attempted to show this meeting, hypothetical.'

'Any conclusions the committee draws from my reports are their own,' Harry insisted. 'I must make that point.'

Lewis turned slowly in his chair to look directly at Whitting.

'I'm kind of getting the impression, Jack, that you really don't want to believe in this thing.'

'Not at all, not at all,' Whitting said, distinctly flustered. 'I just can't be expected to run an operation of this size other than on the basis of facts. And I say again that, in spite of today's new evidence, we still don't have any facts. What's more, we're not the final arbiters. If there's any recommendation to come from this committee, it's got to be soundly based. That's all I'm saying.'

'The committee's your problem,' Lewis said sharply. 'Mine's my ship and my crew.'

Whitting straightened.

'It seems to me we're being blown somewhat off course. This meeting is really to decide how we coordinate the *Poseidon*'s dive with the increased surveillance facilities now provided by the Cetacean Search Unit. Professor Asquith, can I ask you to brief us on that.'

'But what about the Megalodon?' Harry asked. 'Surely, you don't intend to gloss over that.'

'I understand that your new whale was designed to assist with that. We've heard the evidence of bottom activity, a Megalodon if you like, and it will certainly come into our logistics when we've heard all the evidence. For the moment, I would like everyone to consider it in the same way as we would consider any other natural hazard. It has to be planned for. And the whale comes into that. Right, Professor?'

'We intend to use the whale, which has very deep diving capability, to give us a more definitive sounding on the Megalodon possibility,' said Harry carefully. 'But the whale has to be trained and that will take time.'

Whitting shook his head.

'I'm afraid we don't have that time. I have a security report from Washington indicating that our activities here have started to attract international attention. We must have the *Poseidon* on station as soon as possible. That is a prime imperative!' Whitting turned to Lewis. 'You know that too. Right, Cy?'

'I know I'm under orders to make my descent this time

tomorrow morning,' Lewis agreed. 'But it seems someone left a few things out of my briefing.'

Whitting turned to Acreman. 'I took the liberty of asking one of your trainers, Mr. Spurling, whether contact with the whale was sufficient for us to keep to that schedule. He advised me, less than an hour ago, that progress had been remarkable and that your dolphins were already reading the whale's sonar. Is that right, Dr. Acreman?'

Damn, Harry thought.

'So far as it goes, yes,' said Acreman. 'But you seem to be forgetting the welfare of those animals. I'm not sure we have the right to put the whale down into what is now an area of definite hazard.'

Whitting looked aghast. 'Dr. Acreman, have you any idea how much this Project is costing! Surely, you can appreciate that our purpose is primary!'

'I don't know what your purpose is at all, Admiral. I don't have that kind of security clearance. But I'm not launching that animal into the jaws of a Megalodon.'

Lewis spoke.

'Can it protect my ship, mister?'

'No. He might give you some warning.'

'Is it able to do that now?' Lewis asked.

'Yes,' said Acreman.

Lewis turned to Whitting.

'I want clearance to arm my hardware. That's for starters.'

'Not the nuclear hardware, Cy. I have a specific veto on that.'

'Chemical, then. But all the tubes. We take out the nukes and refit with high explosive.'

He turned to Acreman, speaking firmly, but reluctantly.

'Doctor. I *do* know what's behind all this and I can tell you you're wasting your breath. We go down tomorrow with or without you even if King Kong and Godzilla are both waiting for us. I know something about whales. I like them. You seem to know a lot more. I want any help I can get and if your whale can scout the perimeter, my crew and I will be deeply in your debt.'

Whitting, looking pale with tension but immensely relieved, turned to Harry.

'You reserve the right to reply, Professor.'

'I have nothing to add,' said Harry.

Harry spoke urgently to Acreman as they hurried down the long corridors, firing questions and brushing aside Acreman's own queries and objections.

'Was Whitting right? Do you have a good contact?'

'No, it's very basic. The dolphins can read Apollo's sonar images.'

'Does the whale react to their images?'

'Yes. Well, he certainly reacted when Macho sent images of killer whales.'

'Explain this to me. What do you mean by images?'

'It's a sound impression. We think that the reason the cetaceans have such large brains is to accommodate massive memory. It fits—if you live in an environment that can be as dark and as murky as the sea, the information they get from their sonar could be more important than sight. We think they remember the sound-shapes of things and can transmit, and understand, those sound-shapes from other animals. We know the dolphins do that and, according to Doris, she can read the images from the echoes Apollo puts out.'

'Good, very good. And, as I understand it, your plan is to send Morgan down to his maximum depth, then have him transmit a sound-image of the Megalodon in the hope that Apollo will get interested and go down to investigate?'

'Something like that. Macho has suggested that Apollo might be more interested if Morgan transmits a sound-image of a large whale. It doesn't matter what image we use so long as we can get Apollo to dive. Once he's down deep, he'll pick up the Megalodon for sure and the other animals will get that image and tell us about it.'

'Accurately?'

'Very—that signal will have a lot more than just shape. Remember the work Doris was doing with aero-engines. The Megalodon image will contain information about mass, speed of movement and an exact measurement. The dolphins, particularly Macho and Doris, are perfectly capable of verbalizing that information through the Janus.'

Asquith stopped and rubbed his temples.

'It's all too good to waste, Frank.'

'You've lost me again.'

'We have to stop Whitting from ruining it for us—for the time being, anyway.'

'Well, you have, Harry. Louise left an hour ago. Isn't she going for help?'

'Yes.'

'You don't sound too sure.'

'I can't get that man Lewis out of my mind—the sub captain. He knows what's going on. I think he took us seriously. But he's still going down and taking sixty-odd men with him.'

'In a way, that's why I'm glad we don't seem to have much of a choice.'

'What do you mean?'

'The sixty-plus men. You were right about Apollo's ability. I don't know that he could outfight the Megalodon—but he could certainly outrun it. And, on the information we have already, Apollo's no fool.'

'If only it was as simple as that,' Harry sighed.

'Isn't it?'

'You're a cetologist, Frank, and a damned good one, but you don't know that much about sharks.'

'I admit that. I don't understand why you are suddenly so worried.'

'My fear is we're in for the biggest battle in the history of the sea—total bloody carnage!'

Acreman felt the deep intensity of this outburst like a physical blow.

'But I've just said I think Apollo would have the sense to run ...'

'It's got nothing to do with Apollo. Have you ever seen sharks in a feeding frenzy? One drop of blood—just one drop and ...'

Acreman never got to hear the end of the sentence. The public address system called Harry's name.

'Priority announcement for Professor Asquith. Mr. Vance requests Professor Asquith to proceed immediately, as a matter of urgency, to his cabin.'

'What's that about?'

Harry started to lumber in the direction of his cabin. 'If it's got anything to do with Vance, it's trouble.'

Harry entered his cabin rather too quickly, stumbling over the high sill. Vance stood facing him, looking calm, even expectant. Louise, very close to tears, was sitting on the bunk *in handcuffs*. Harry collected himself, considered the scene very carefully and spoke abruptly to Acreman.

'Get out of here, Frank. Apollo's your priority now.'

'What's this all about, Vance?' he said briskly.

'I intercepted this woman trying to get aboard the noon shuttle and it's been established that she was trying to contact a subversive organization.'

'Really,' said Harry mildly. 'I was under the impression she was going to confirm a golf date for me.'

Vance shook his head. 'It won't wash, Professor. We've checked the number you gave her to call. George Burlington.' He paused, a note of contempt creeping in. 'President of the National Ecology Trust.'

Harry stared at Vance. 'I know you're under some pressure, so I want you to consider the answer to my next question very seriously, bearing in mind it will be in front of a witness. The Trust you have just mentioned was created following an initiative by a president of the United States. Do you regard it as a subversive organization?'

'You are not in a position, Professor, to tell us who our enemies are and who they are not.'

Harry picked up a phone.

'This is a ship-to-shore call from Professor Asquith. I want an urgent connection with Mr. George Burlington at this number ... '

Vance snatched the phone. 'Vance ... Security. Cancel that call.'

'In any reasonable court,' Harry said, 'that would constitute assault. I'll give you one more chance to get yourself off the hook, Vance. I'm going to tell you openly, and I invite you to check it, that I've been playing golf with George Burlington for nearly ten years.'

'I'm not on any hook, Asquith. You are!'

'You're on a loser,' Harry snapped. 'I have a very good memory and I can remember word for word the message I gave Miss Putnam.'

Vance's mouth tightened as he reviewed his evidence. A nerve twitched above the left corner of his tightly clamped mouth. He had arranged this set-up convinced that a confrontation would cause Asquith to crack.

There was a knock on the door and a mess steward strode in. 'Got to get the dishes,' the steward said, picking up Harry's sandwich tray.

'Get the hell out of here,' Vance roared, venting his frustration on the steward. 'Okay, Professor. You want to take sides, that's fine by me. But you hear this. I'm placing this person under cabin arrest until I get orders as to what's to happen to her and I'm issuing a general security order, restricting any of your group from leaving this ship.' He turned to leave.

'Vance,' said Harry sweetly, nodding at Louise's wrists, 'you forgot your thumbscrews.'

With an angry twist which brought a gasp of pain, Vance freed Louise and walked out. Harry put his arms round her shoulders.

'Never mind, my dear. We can't win them all.'

Louise Putnam's place on the midday shuttle was taken by the mess steward who, in a hurry, had arranged for a twenty-four-hour pass when he returned Harry Asquith's tray to the galley.

The adult pair of Megalodons had not been totally unaware of their offspring's activity.

The protein-rich bonanza on which they had gorged themselves was now a week in the past. The need for another meal was stirring in them and they had read the changes caused by the descent of the sling. But their hunger was not yet such as to cause them to return to the cool open waters of the Fracture. Further, they were aware that the young male had left the cave to hunt and that the food target that had attracted him would no longer be available to them.

Instead of lying comatose on the warm cave floor, tremors of movement began to stir in the vast forms of the adult pair, a general state of restlessness preparatory to the hunt.

The gargantuan meal that had descended into the trench so unexpectedly had also caused a fractional change in the gentle metabolism of the Megalodons. Totally conditioned to a poor diet, bulked mainly with cellulose, the pair now had a memory of the richest fare.

Normally, they would have been content with their traditional diet. But now they, like the surface sharks who find themselves swimming along beaches populated by humans, had been excited by a new taste.

More simply, the Megalodons had been tempted—they were now man-eaters.

Their brains, though huge, were not sufficiently sophisticated to record this change of appetite specifically. They knew only that there were tastier diets to be had. And they were at least capable of realizing that this tastier diet might require more aggressive hunting. Whereas they would normally have moved out of the cave and satisfied themselves from the Fracture's normal harvest, they now knew that a more diligent search could produce more satisfying food rewards.

By the end of the day, both adult animals had moved to the mouth of the cave and were focusing their lateral pits in hope of those rich food targets.

Apart from the activity at the edge of their range, which they knew to be the young male, nothing disturbed the pattern of those black waters. Until something did, they would harbour their energy, stimulating their cold-blooded bodies from the heat of the cave floor. They were ready to hunt. But as yet, they had no target.

On the other hand, the young male was now ravenous. Titillated by the *XT-4* unit and disappointed by the hard, inorganic metal of the sling, he had now been seriously undernourished for two days.

He needed more food than his parents because he was still growing. He had no control over his appetite, and his brain was not good enough to rationalize the pangs. He was anxious and suffering severe hunger pains and the adrenalin that had flooded through his already mighty form in the course of the attack on the sling now burned like an uncontrollable fire of desperation for food.

He had also, because of the time lost hunting non-food objects, gone beyond the point where his hunger could be satisfied by the traditional wastes of the Fracture. To stay alive on that fare required a continuous steady intake, and the young male had not bothered to maintain it.

He needed a lot of food quickly, before he could return to his natural feeding pattern. Yet he would not accept that the sling would not produce food flavours. Nothing that large that was not food had ever come down before. So he tore at the sling until it was reduced to a misshapen ball like a tangle of wire.

And the young Megalodon's hunger and anger pushed him towards the threshold of madness.

Mess Steward Sam Kaimu was what intelligence jargon called a ferret. A native Hawaiian, he had been recruited when his personal efforts to stem the growth of plastic grass and American holiday hotels over the islands had proved no match for the millions of dollars fertilizing this particular exercise in neocolonialism.

He had travelled to Cuba and learned a great number of tricks that turned his gentle Polynesian stomach but had since been required to use only two innocuous ones—skilled eavesdropping and simple radio operating.

His masters were aware of his essentially placid nature and did not rate him particularly highly. From the beginning they had known virtually all there was to know about the *Eros* and its submarine extensions. In a group of islands containing some of the most advanced U. S. military facilities on the planet, a marine mining experiment was hardly worth moving a trained operator from the wealth of other work. Thus Sam Kaimu had only joined the *Eros* from the NASA training station at Kaena when word reached his organization of the accident to the *Jules Verne*.

Since then his reports had been bland. He knew nothing of the hopes of the Project Management Committee, for these were protected by mainland security. His only source of information was the day-to-day interflow of conversation aboard the tanker, and, as the *Eros* and the submarines had so far been unable to proceed with their mission, Sam Kaimu had had nothing to report of any significance.

Not that this disturbed him. He actually enjoyed his work as a waiter and the few occasions when he had unearthed something of importance, it had made him very nervous.

On the short flight to Hopkins field, he had done his best to hide the extreme apprehension he was feeling now. It was compounded by the fact that, while he had nothing material to report, his instincts were telling him he should talk to his masters.

He was listened to with less ridicule than he had anticipated.

'As we understand it, you are actually suggesting that there is a degree of abnormal activity aboard the ship, but you don't know why?'

'Yes. Except that there is this talk of something in the sea that might be dangerous.'

'Has anything happened at all to indicate that the *Eros* and these submarines might be involved in anything other than a mining experiment?'

'Nothing whatsoever. On the contrary, the problems they are having are openly discussed. They can't do the geophysical survey until the lasers in the submarine are correctly positioned.'

'Our other sources support what you say,' Kaimu was told.

'There is this large whale that has been brought in.'

'We know all about that as well. You will agree they could hardly have kept that a secret. We know what they are doing with dolphins. It is interesting but irrelevant. Our own people have a system which offers much more effective control, using surgically implanted electrodes.'

'Then I think, perhaps, I have wasted your time. I apologize, but after overhearing the several heated exchanges between Professor Asquith and his team, especially the last, involving the security agent, in which there was mention of subversive organizations, I felt obliged to seek your guidance.'

'Not at all. Your concern reflects our own.'

'You have some other information?'

'No, nothing specific. But there is an aspect of this affair which has stopped making sense. We cannot believe that the Americans would put three of their most expensive nuclear submarines at risk, if the purpose of the *Eros'* mission is as innocent as they would like us to believe. At first, we were pleased that these accidents were keeping the submarines out of commission. Now, well, their persistence is exceeding what is credible.'

Kaimu nodded. 'Unfortunately, I do not see how I can find out much more. If indeed there is another purpose, it is an extremely well-kept secret. Perhaps I should have some assistance.'

'That will not be necessary. Continue as you have been. We will make a secondary investigation of the Zone.'

'Am I to be told what that is?'

'There is no need. But we will now expect you to communicate more fully. Report anything which you judge to be out of context.'

Acreman returned to his cabin and, in spite of Barbara's aspersions about the decayed state of their sex life, insisted on getting some sleep.

He slept badly, troubled by dreams of giant fish. At a sub-conscious level, Acreman was afraid of sharks. Once, when conducting an underwater study of barracuda, a dangerous fish itself, Acreman had been forced to ascend in front of a hammerhead shark. The barracuda were all around him, maintaining a distance that never varied, no matter where Acreman swam. So, to take his pictures, he had simply allowed himself to sink, causing the barracuda to remain calm and be perfectly focused.

When the roll of film was finished, Acreman had looked down and found that he was less than twenty feet off the bottom and, directly beneath him, covering the sand like a blanket, was a giant manta ray, its poison spike raised in anticipation.

He had panicked and inflated his life jacket. The barracuda had scattered.

But, with the barracuda gone, he had seen, circling slowly above him, a twelve-foot hammerhead shark. His choice had been the manta or the hammerhead. In an icy sweat, he had forced himself to examine the options and realized he had none. There was very little air left in his bottle.

Of all the sharks, hammerheads are the most ugly. The flat planes of bone that protrude out on either side of their heads are a gross peculiarity of evolution. As he lifted towards the shark, it turned, showing its gill flaps, the inward crescent of its mouth, sharp teeth overlapping the skin, and one baleful eye.

Acreman had been sick into his mouthpiece.

This emergency had kept him busy for what had seemed like several minutes. He had gagged for air, swallowed the vomit and eventually managed to clear his air supply. By the time he was breathing normally, he discovered he had lifted well past the big grey shark. It had showed no further interest in him, continuing to swim lazily, scanning the water in search of a more suitable food target.

Acreman had never spoken of the incident but it returned with embarrassing frequency in his dreams.

He awoke, thrashing the blankets off him, his body slick with sweat. Barbara grabbed him and held on hard. When he was fully awake, he lay staring at the steel ceiling. He told Barbara he had dreamed of the adult Megalodon and she scoffed and stroked his hair.

'Come on, love. Stick to the reality, that's nightmarish enough.'

Acreman knew he would not get any more sleep that night and, after half an hour, he slipped out of the bunk and dressed. Barbara stirred and asked him what he was doing. He told her to go back to sleep, he was only going for a walk. She nodded and turned over.

Acreman climbed to the deck and looked out across the big netted holding pool. Arc lights had been rigged to illuminate it and he could see Apollo, cruising slowly, followed by Morgan and, silver in the light, the two fins of the dolphins. Acreman had instructed them to work continuously on contacting the whale and they were following his instructions. He envied the cetaceans their ability to snatch rest. He went below to the Search Unit's communications room, to find Louise sitting at the radio panel, sipping coffee.

'You should be getting some sleep,' he told her.

'I couldn't. Would you like some coffee? I brewed a pot.'

'Yes. Have you been talking to the animals?'

She shook her head defensively. 'No, I wasn't sure I should. I've just been sitting here, listening to them.'

'Are they talking much?'

'Not English ... except for Macho, who keeps coming out with the odd line.'

She brought him a brimming mug of coffee. Acreman sipped it gratefully and turned up the Janus amplifiers. As well as a direct radio link to the interpretation synthesizer, the radio packs worn by the animals had an open microphone that transmitted their sonar signals and calls.

Acreman was also able to detect, faintly, the low-frequency sonar clicking from Apollo. He was calling regularly but, as he did not have a transmitter, his high notes sounded remote and ghostly.

He picked up a microphone linked to the Janus machine. 'Doris? Acreman. How is it going?'

'Very well, Acreman. Apollo is quicker than we expected. No, that is not right. We did not know how quick he would be. He is quick.'

'You're not suggesting we should fit him with a Janus pack?'

'No, not yet. He could not shape his sounds to it. And his frequencies are different. You would only hear random nonsense.'

'Has Macho had any luck projecting an image that might interest him?'

'No, but Morgan has. Macho does not like that very much.'

'How did Morgan manage it, Doris?'

'It was an accident. Macho had been sending him sonar images of other great ones but he did not seem interested. Then Morgan sent an image of his father—he was very nervous at that.'

'Be careful, Doris.'

'I stopped him. Now I have explained that he must send big images and that he is doing. Apollo is searching for them. I think Morgan's frequencies are better for Apollo than ours, perhaps because Morgan is closer to him in size.'

'So what are you doing now?'

'Apollo is practising on Morgan. He is going down to his deepest level—about eighteen hundred feet and Apollo is tracking him with his sonar. He has no difficulties, and we are reading his sonar responses, also with no difficulties.'

'That sounds great, Doris. But how will you get him to do a really deep dive into the Fracture tomorrow?'

'As Macho suggested. Once Morgan has perfected his projection of a great one, we think Apollo will go down to investigate. If Morgan then leaves and Apollo sees a real great one, he will follow it. He likes to dive and he likes the game.'

'The game?'

'We *play*, Acreman. Remember?'

'Okay, Doris, I'm not going to lay my Protestant work ethic on you. It sounds like a good scheme. Will Morgan have got his image-making together by morning?'

'I'm sure he will.'

The following morning, Acreman discovered ruefully that

half the work the dolphins and the orca had busied themselves with during the night was unnecessary.

The *Poseidon* had commenced her dive at 0900 exactly.

Five minutes later, Apollo lifted his huge tail and vanished below the surface.

Acreman, at the Janus mike, called urgently to Doris.

'What's going on? Did somebody transmit an image? It's too soon. He won't have enough air.'

There was a long pause. Eventually, Doris responded.

'He's following the submarine, Acreman. We should have thought of that. We don't have to project an artificial image —he has the submarine.'

'Where is he now?'

'Coming up. Don't worry, Acreman. This is better. We can encourage him to dive on the sub. It is easier. He can keep going down to it. And if he finds something else, we will be able to see the difference and tell him to pursue that.'

'Okay. That's fine. But just don't send him off after anything but the sub without informing me first.'

'Okay, Acreman.'

Aboard the *Red Ensign,* Sonar and Hydrophone Technician Litkin glanced once at the phasing neon pulses of his master sonar repeater and turned to his captain with a shout of excitement.

'Captain ... I've just received a clear reading! There must be a connecting strata with an open view through to the RV!'

Markov glanced towards the officer on duty at the bridge plotting table where a chart of Hawaiian waters was trapped under glass. The electronic tracer arm of the ship's Inertial Navigation System was crabbing slowly across the chart and the navigator was nodding confirmation.

'We've just passed the main spur of the Molokai Fracture itself. That's very deep water in a trench all the way to the RV. It's not an approach I'd recommend, Captain. The trench is notorious for its bottom currents.'

Litkin spoke up. 'Captain, I can also clear up those mysterious hydrophone traces we discussed before. It's a whale. A big one, I would say a sperm from the sonar outline. It must have been attracted by the submarine. She is now diving on a very slow descent.'

'I know about that,' Markov said, his relief obvious. 'Part of the work the Americans are doing is with cetaceans. Our people are not very interested. We had a signal yesterday that they had brought in a whale.'

'It sounds *very* interesting,' Litkin commented.

'We do as we are told,' Markov said. '*I* am interested in that Fracture. You say it will give us a clear sonar view, all the way to the RV, Navigator?'

'Yes, sir. But the currents will reduce our speed substantially and make steering difficult. You risk colliding with the rock face.'

Markov ordered a change of course. 'Let us see whether she can do what they claim she can do,' he said, slapping the steel shaft of the retracted conning tower. 'Secure the ship for maximum depth.'

Aboard the *Poseidon,* Captain Lewis implemented a decision he had made the night before and called his crew over the intercom system.

'Now hear this, this is the captain speaking. We've commenced our dive, and as you can all tell, we're going down real slow. You also know that this is a hazardous mission, hence your volunteer status and your special pay. From here on down, we'll be at full emergency stations and I'm shortly ordering the closing of all our watertight doors.

'Before we go to that status, and we have a little time yet, I want you all to know why I'm doing this.

'Two Ohios of our squadron have tried this dive before. You may take it that we wouldn't be trying where they have failed were it not a mission of prime importance to our country.

'I guess you probably also know that both our predecessors suffered casualties, severe in the first instance, serious in the second. But neither of those subs knew what we know and, certainly in the case of the second sub, there probably wouldn't have been casualties if they'd been buttoned up like we will be.

'Also, we're well prepared in other ways. As of now, this vessel is on an active service mission. All our tubes are primed and we have armed our warheads with chemical charges. We have no nuclear capability, but we don't need it.

'Now, you will be wondering what all this fuss is about and that I *can't* tell you. I'm not being evasive. It's our job to go down and find out what's caused the trouble in the past. What is known I'm going to give to you straight.

'The experts topside reckon that the undersea wall that our predecessors went down is unstable and they got busted by rockfalls. So we're not going the same way. We'll stay well clear of the wall until we get to the shelf we're aiming for.

'Another possibility is that there's volcanic activity on the bottom. Now, if we get any sign of that, we'll come straight up and I can lift this boat a damned sight faster than any gas bubble. It won't be comfortable, but it won't hurt anybody.

'Then lastly, and no doubt the gravevine's ... I mean *grapevine*'s hard at work on this one, there's a remote possibility that an unknown species of animal life exists down there. This place is one of the deepest ocean trenches in the world and we frankly don't know all that much about the creatures that live in the very deep ocean.

'Now I for one don't rate this possibility too highly, but I must tell you that there are others who do. So we've taken precautions against that. Firstly, there's this boat's fighting capability. We have enough fire power to blast half a dozen battleships to scrap metal. I think we can more than handle anything Mother Nature might have dreamed up. And we also have an underwater scout. You all must have wondered what that big whale was doing swimming around in the net. Well, that's a very special whale. It's been trained to guard this vessel and it's out there now. It weighs sixty tons and it's the largest living thing on the earth. It's capable of seeing—with sonar—much better than we are.

'Okay, that's it. Nobody ever took this much trouble with any submarine before, so I want you all to rest easy, stay alert and do the job you've been trained for. Number One, close all watertight doors, and go to *silent running*.'

Lewis turned away from the intercom microphone.

Martin, the first officer, gave the necessary orders for sealing the boat into separate compartments and the stillness of *silent running* descended all around them. Radio operators, others charged with the boat's engines and her trim and the three sonar watchers hunched over their screens, all began to exchange their information in hushed voices.

Martin found his captain studying a detailed chart of the Fracture bottom and a geological stratification of the face.

'That was a really good idea, sir,' Martin said. 'I've had more men asking me about this mission than any other I've been on.'

'Did you hear my slip?' Lewis asked. 'Gravevine, for Christ's sake! Is that what they call a Freudian slip, Number One?'

'I don't think it matters.'

'Well, we will know this time tomorrow.'

Lewis walked across to the sonar screens. They held the now familiar outlines of the bottom. Lewis must have studied it a hundred times. Far out on the right-hand edge there was the big rock that Suskin thought was a monster. Lewis stared at it and thought it looked like a rock. It was all of three miles away from the *Poseidon*'s descent path and it was as still as a rock. A blob of white suddenly traversed the screens.

'Is that our scout?'

One of the operators nodded.

'It's coming past about once every nine minutes.'

'Not too close, I hope.'

'Well, quite close, sir. But we don't seem to be getting any turbulence.'

Lewis had asked the civilian scientist, Acreman, about the whale affecting the *Poseidon*'s trim and had been told that it wasn't a problem. Whales had apparently developed methods for overcoming drag and turbulence.

Their hydrodynamic design was such, Acreman had said, that the water went up behind their fins instead of straight along the body. And there was something special about their skin. Acreman said it was being shed all the time so that friction and drag were left working on shed skin.

'Are you suggesting they swim out of their own skins and leave the water working on the shed skin?' Lewis had asked with considerable scepticism.

Acreman had simply replied, 'Yes.' Lewis had not pursued the matter, having come to the conclusion that Acreman had ceased to find any aspect of the cetaceans particularly amazing.

Lewis watched the white shape of the whale skid past again. Initially he had been very cynical, almost scornful, of the proposal that they share this mission with a whale. Now he found the animal's presence comforting. It was like going for a walk with his dog.

'Keep one eye glued on that rock there,' Lewis instructed the operator. 'I want to hear from you, even if it twitches.'

He turned to his first officer.

'Secure to dive, Number One?'

'All secure, sir.'

'Take her down real slow.'

Harry, Acreman and Suskin were on watch in the tanker's main communications control room. Acreman wanted to be near the big sonar screens. He had left Barbara in charge of the Cetacean Search Unit's radio and the Janus transmitters had been patched through to repeat on one of Suskin's channels.

Each man held his silence, obsessed by markedly different considerations.

Suskin was concerned with a growing sense of helplessness. He had been through this too many times before. He knew what it felt like to sit here when things began to go wrong. His entire mind was taken up with a sense of dread as to how he would react when the urgent voices began and he could do nothing but sit and watch.

Acreman was concerned with Apollo, Doris, Macho and Morgan and his own conscience. He felt slightly high, all his faculties peaking as though his blood had been drained and replaced with pure adrenalin. He, too, was aware of his inadequacies. What could any human do now? The cetacean part of this operation was now entirely in the hands of the animals. Animals? He could no longer think of them as that.

Earlier Acreman had asked Doris whether she wanted to go on with the mission. It was the first time he had ever asked a dolphin for a value judgment.

Possibly because it was the first time, Doris appeared to have trouble answering him. But when she eventually responded, Acreman realized it was not the values that were being questioned, but the question itself.

'We are just doing it, Acreman.'

'I know, Doris, but you don't have to.'

'What is "have to" in that context, Acreman?'

'If you don't like this, you could do something else.'

'What?'

'Anything you like.'

'This is interesting, Acreman, playing with a great one.'

'It is not just a game. There is danger in the deep water.'

'There is another great one in the deep water, you said.'

'But it is not like Apollo. It will be very stupid. It will kill.'

'Like Morgan,' said Macho.

'Worse than Morgan's wild kind. It will kill without thinking.'

'Don't worry, Acreman. Nothing can kill us.'

'I could kill you, Macho,' said Acreman coldly.

'Not without thinking,' said Macho. 'And anyway, you are land beasts. This is a sea beast. Nothing in the sea can kill us.'

'Doris, are you listening?' Acreman called, needful of her wiser counsel. Macho was not so named by accident.

'Macho is right, Acreman. We are different. We cannot be killed here.'

'What the hell's so different, Doris? Dolphins are killed by sharks, sometimes.'

'Only when they have quit life, Acreman. When they have sickness.' Acreman knew that, when Doris spoke of sickness, she was describing not just physical illness but that peculiar mental malaise that sometimes caused dolphins to commit suicide.

'You're saying that because you're alert and watchful and alive, it can't touch you. No matter how big or how quick or how angry it might be?'

'Yes, Acreman.'

'I wish I had your confidence.'

'You can't Acreman,' Macho said. 'You are terrible in the sea. It would get you!'

'Thank you! So it's okay to go on then, Doris?'

'I have nothing else I wish to do, Acreman.'

But in spite of the exchange, Acreman still felt guilty. Perhaps it was all right for the quicksilver dolphins and the mighty Morgan. But was it all right for Apollo? The great whales had often been described as the world's last innocents; inhabitants of an Eden that had never known a snake. Acreman felt a little like the snake, with ten tons of butterfish replacing the famous apple. It was small consolation that according to Doris, Apollo was enjoying himself. Acreman wondered how the sub skipper, Lewis, would feel if he knew that his mighty vessel, the most advanced example of human ingenuity, was no more than a stick in a big game of fetch.

Harry, who had awakened in a sweat at three a.m., was scribbling shorthand notes in an old school notebook. He was trying to get the chronology right for his first address on the subject of Megalodon.

It was Harry's way of getting his mind off other things, but it wasn't working now. All his life Harry had toyed with the dream of standing alone before the hushed ranks of the Royal Zoological Society, armed with a paper containing totally original, utterly unique revelations. It was a vision more distracting than any sexual fantasy.

But since the incident with Vance, Harry had suffered a mounting sense of claustrophobia. There was no way he could get off the ship, no way to avoid involvement in what was about to happen. Harry was scared witless.

The young male was finally forced to avail itself of the Fracture's natural food supply.

He tore at the mangled sling one last time, turning awkwardly between the narrow walls, and slowly worked his way back towards the cave. He swam with his huge mouth slightly open, scooping up the floating deposits of tarry weed, remains of old wooden crates and meat and vegetable scraps from passing ships and, in the main, from the *Eros*.

To make even a minute difference to his raging hunger, the young male needed to take in several tons of this sparse fare, and there was never that much in the Fracture on any one day. He ate all there was but remained in an agony of need.

Aboard the *Poseidon* and in the tanker's communications room, the sandstorm created by the young male was spotted. Everybody noticed the sudden flurry at the head of what they had now all come to call 'The Rock'. Then both sets of sonar screens blanked to a milky whiteness as the young male began its slow return to the cave, a sequence which disturbed a great deal of sand and obscured 'The Rock'.

Suskin, who had seen it so many times before, reacted automatically, coolly.

'Control to *Poseidon*. Bottom activity!'

Lewis's response was equally controlled.

'*Poseidon*. We copy.'

195

'Control. Suggest you hold your present position while we analyze.'

'*Poseidon*. Holding. We will wait for you.'

Suskin turned to Acreman.

'Any thoughts?'

He shook his head.

'The sub's less than a thousand feet down. Apollo's still diving to her but he won't go beyond the sub. It has to lead him down much deeper. Apollo won't be getting very much more than we're seeing.'

Suskin looked depressed. 'What the hell do I advise?'

'Hold them there for a moment,' Acreman said. 'I'll have a word with Doris.' He spoke rapidly into the Janus mike. Suskin watched him, wishing Acreman had given his chief dolphin a less nutty name. It was almost impossible for Suskin to really believe in the dolphins anyway, totally impossible to seriously run this kind of operation on the advice of a| 'Doris'.

Acreman sat back, waiting. 'She's sending Morgan down to his maximum—about two thousand feet. He knows what we're looking for.'

Four minutes later, there was a crackle from the Janus loudspeaker.

'Big thing moving, Acreman.'

'We know, Morgan. What is it?'

'Too deep, Acreman. Just big moving.'

Acreman shrugged at Suskin.

Suskin reluctantly opened a channel to the sub.

'Control to *Poseidon*. Regret target too deep for proper identification.'

'*Poseidon* to Control. What says the scout?'

'Control. Scout seems in love with you. You will need to be much deeper for her to be drawn to target.'

'*Poseidon*. Our screens indicate no substantial content in the misting. Initially, yes; now, no. Do you confirm?'

Suskin was aware that the sonar operator aboard the *Poseidon* had been specially picked for the job, leaving a teaching post at the Sacramento Communications School to join the sub. Suskin had more experience but the *Poseidon*'s new man was considered almost psychic in his ability to interpret the fine nuances of the images.

'*Poseidon*—wait.'

Suskin looked at his own screens and saw that the misting was already thinning. He waited, expecting 'The Rock's' sharper outline to cut through the fading sandmist. It did not.

'Here we go again,' he said unhappily to Acreman. 'Can you get me another report from the orca?'

Acreman nodded and instructed Morgan to go down again. This time, they had to wait a little longer. No one was exactly sure how deep a killer whale could dive in safety. The Navy's own Deep Ops programme, conducted off Hawaii several years before, had used two killers and a pilot whale. The killers eventually got bored with the programme and quit, but before that they had been monitored to depths well in excess of fifteen hundred feet. Morgan was also a young, fit animal and very keen. Acreman assumed the long wait was Morgan pushing his luck.

'Gone, Acreman. Big movement gone.'

'Christ,' said Suskin. 'What the hell do we do now?'

'There has to be some kind of overhang down there that it shelters under,' Acreman said. 'It can't bury itself in the sand, I don't think.'

'You don't think!' Suskin said harshly. 'For Christ's sake, mister. We have to be more definite than that. Are there sharks that bury themselves in the sand?'

'One or two,' Acreman admitted. 'I still think there's got to be a cave or something.'

Suskin remembered his own conjecturing about what had happened to the *XT-4*, but he was still far from happy. He wanted to be able to tell the *Poseidon* something definite.

'*Poseidon* to Control. You guys taking a coffee break?'

'Control. Sorry. We copy absence of target. We think there's a cave or a big rock overhang.'

Lewis heard this aboard the sub and his mouth set a little more grimly. During the long silence from the surface he had ordered his torpedoes to be primed and his crew to 'stay alert'. But it was one thing to have a target, even if it only turned out to be a big rock, quite another an enemy that was working from a bunker. Torpedoes had one real limitation. They could not turn corners.

'Mr. Simpson,' he said to the grey-haired man seated before the sonar screens, 'they can't seem to help us out too much. What's your assessment?'

'I've been reading the reports on the previous trys,' Simpson replied, 'and I'm still most inclined to the rock-fall theory. What we just witnessed exactly duplicated the image you would see if a large rock—admittedly a very large one—had rolled down the bottom.'

'I'm rather more interested in what's happened to it now,' Lewis said.

'If it is a rock and has settled into a natural depression, which is, after all, the kind of thing that would stop it rolling, we won't see it. It's become part of the bottom, undetectable.'

'And what would have started something that size rolling?' Lewis asked.

Simpson frowned. 'I can't answer that. It's not my field. But the reports mention possible seismic activity.'

'Guessing,' Lewis said.

'We're all guessing at this range, I'm afraid.'

'Okay, so we will go a bit closer. But we'll keep our guessing pessimistic. We'll continue to assume that rock can bite. What's the state of the wall, Mr. Simpson?'

'Steady as a rock,' Simpson grinned.

'*Poseidon* to Control. Unless you can come up with something different, we're recommencing our dive.'

'Control,' Suskin said. 'We don't have anything. Good luck.'

In the cave, the young male settled alongside his parents and tried to digest as much as he could of his unsatisfactory meal.

Much of what he had eaten was almost totally inedible and, over the next few hours, the young male regurgitated glass, metal and a large quantity of rock and sand. Although he had removed all the nourishment from the waste, it still presented a familiar appearance to the older animals and they began to stir uneasily, their own latent hunger triggered.

The adult male moved forward a few feet and took the *XT-4* unit into its huge mouth. It had seen the young male chewing it and some of the flavours it had once contained had come to the adult male in the water. It bit down and the bell flattened and split, inch-thick steel peeling back like the lid of a sardine can.

A head and several limbs, all bleached white and tinged with pockets of gray putrescence and the green scale of gangrene, floated from the wreckage and hung, as if on wires, in the murky water. With a flick of its tail, the adult male aligned its mouth to allow this macabre, disjointed spectre to dance inside. The adult male waited expectantly but these scraps had no flavour so he settled again to the warm floor.

He and his mate would need to feed that day. But the young male had already cleansed the Fracture of its daily ration.

'I thought you said the Fracture would give us a clear run to the RV,' Markov growled as, for the third time, his helmsman was forced to make a radical and dramatic course change to avoid the rock face.

The navigator replied tersely, 'No, Captain. When I made that observation, you were at a depth of about one thousand metres. We are now at seventy-two hundred metres—at the bottom of a great rock "V". It will widen and narrow constantly and we will have to zigzag. Exactly as you would do if you were walking along a dry river bed.'

Markov said, 'And those walls are also giving us an intermittent sonar view, correct?'

The navigator agreed. Litkin nodded confirmation.

'How many whales did your signal say the Americans were using?' Litkin asked.

'Just one,' Markov snapped. 'Litkin, please attend to the immediate problem. If we hit a rock face at this depth, the pressure hull will rupture.'

'It is just ... ' Litkin started to say and then, 'Hard aport, Captain!'

Markov repeated the order, then cursed.

'If it narrows any more, Litkin, let me know immediately and we will have to take her up. But, for the time being, we will stay here. I doubt that I need to remind you all,' he stared deliberately at Commissar Beltyin at the Weapons System State board, 'that we are on the fringe of American territorial waters and it is an Ohio-class ballistic missile submarine that we are approaching.'

'If only for the record,' Litkin said, 'I think you should know that they seem to be using more than one large whale. There are certainly signs of two.'

'I have told you already that we are not interested in the whales,' Markov said. 'Confine yourself to the American submarine, and, more to the point, the way immediately ahead.'

9

For several hours, there had been a great deal of activity in the huge cave. The young male was swimming in wide circles, disturbing the centuries of waste that had built up on the floor. The disturbed sand and weed irritated the huge eyeballs of the adults and they lifted to the roof to try and escape it.

Suddenly, the faint throb of changed current swept in among them. The young male shot to the mouth of the cave, tested the acidity and turned to see what his parents were doing.

They, too, had tested the water and were now manoeuvring towards the mouth of the cave. Any knowledge of a relationship that might have existed among the three animals now ceased. They were no longer mother, father and son—simply three hungry sharks anxious to reach the food target first. But the cave mouth was too small for them all to leave at once and they thrashed and fought to be the first to get out.

The adult male was twice as powerful as the others and he brushed them aside and slid slowly out into the trench, his enormous head scanning side to side to get a bearing on the food target. His mate emerged a few seconds later and the young male behind her. They turned as one in the direction of the source and moved slowly up the Fracture in a wedge formation that caused the side-swinging tails of the female and the young male to brush against the face, releasing great quantities of loose rock in a maelstrom of confusion.

Suskin thought his equipment had failed. All three screens, each responsible for a mile of the Fracture under *Poseidon*, milked over.

He shouted to a technician to check the power supply and called the sub.

Acreman was also on his feet, calling urgently to Doris. The

Poseidon was almost nine thousand feet down, less than two hundred feet above the shelf and, for the past nine hours, the only hazard they had faced had been boredom.

'Control to *Poseidon*. How are your screens?'

'*Poseidon* to Control. Milked out. And we're getting massive vibration off the bottom through our hydrophones. It sounds like there really is an avalanche in progress down there. We can hear rocks falling, no question about it.'

Suskin's technician reported that power supplies were functioning normally. One of the operators called out that he thought the screens were okay, too. It was a massive disturbance on the bottom.

Suskin stood back and studied the screens with icy objectivity. The milking was not static. It was distinctly thicker in places and there appeared to be a kind of wave formation running through it. Then he realized that the wave had a path—it was heading north up the Fracture towards the *Poseidon*.

'Control to *Poseidon*. Hold your descent. Ignore the bottom. We'll watch that. Refocus all your shipboard monitors to look due south. I say again, south.'

He turned to Acreman. 'Okay, mister. I think this has got to be it. Get that whale down fast.'

'But no one animal could cause that amount of disturbance,' Acreman protested. 'You saw how much there was before.'

'I don't give a fuck what's causing it!' Suskin bellowed. 'Get looking!'

And then Acreman knew what was happening. No *one* animal! More than one. A shoal. A pack. All of them!

'Acreman,' the Janus machine chirped. 'Apollo is going down past the sub. There must be another great one.'

'Doris. Morgan. Go down with him as far as you can, please. Don't leave him alone. I must have his images as soon as you get anything. Anything.'

'Diving, Acreman. But he is well outside our range—already. We cannot even see his shape anymore.'

Only the young male had the courage and the experience to leave the bottom. He alone had visited the hurtful light zones recently and knew that the risk was bearable, the rewards great. And his hunger was now a savage, raging need that would override the pain of the light.

While his parents continued their swift progress along the floor of the trench, inclining their snouts in the direction of the target, the young male soared—striking an angle that would bring it directly to the source. And then he paused.

There were now two large targets!

The brain of the young Megalodon had never had to encompass two targets. He was thrown into an agony of confusion. The sensations tingling in his lateral pits were strong but useless. He could not see and, for a moment, he did not know which way to swim. Still invisible to the surface watchers, he lay still, stabilizing fins and dorsal tail beating fine patterns as he flicked his huge head from side to side, trying to make something he had never made before—a decision.

And then one of the targets separated and became clear. It was slightly smaller than the big mass that had first excited his senses, but still very large and the young male had no difficulty following it, especially as it was leaving the zone of light and apparently coming down towards him. He flicked his tail turned his snout towards the surface and began to turn slowly on his side as the target continued to come down rapidly.

The young male opened his mouth.

'Acreman!'

'Yes, Doris.'

'Apollo has found it. We have continuous images. Morgan is holding at his deepest point and relaying to me. Acreman, it is *not* a great one.'

'What is it, Doris?'

'A shark, Acreman.'

'Here we go!' Suskin cried. 'Control to *Poseidon*. Stand by your armament. Cetacean Search confirms alien animal presence. Our screens indicate possible attack from the south.'

'Doris,' Acreman called anxiously, 'how big is it? How big in relation to Apollo?'

'The same, Acreman. A little larger!'

'That has to be a young one,' Acreman called to Suskin. 'Tell them to hold their fire. I want Apollo up. Doris, did you hear? Signal Apollo up.'

'I can't tell them not to defend themselves,' Suskin growled. 'There's sixty-eight men involved. The whale will have to look after himself.'

'Don't be a fool,' Acreman cried. 'It's not just Apollo. They're going to need every torpedo they've got in a minute. There are more of them down there and the others will be much bigger.'

'Acreman,' the Janus called. 'Acreman, we cannot contact Apollo. He has had to swim fast. The thing is making an attack.'

Suskin spoke rapidly to the sub.

'Control to *Poseidon*. This is a command order. Circumstances dictate you hold your fire unless your own screens dictate no option. Make an emergency ascent. I say again, make an emergency ascent.'

The battle came to the three small cetaceans as three-dimensional sonar pictures. They were all hanging at their maximum depths, breathing anaerobically from air stored in muscle and bone tissue. Apollo was pumping sonar pulses at rates up to nine hundred a second and the Megalodon was tracked in fine detail as it made what seemed a slow, lazy sweep in towards Apollo. The big whale was now swimming at high speed, directly towards the dark outline of the speeding Megalodon and the bounced reflections of sound were getting stronger.

Morgan, deeper than the dolphins, was listening to the reflected sound and constructing his own image, which in the cetacean brain was as clear as a visual sighting. He was pulsing copies of this image to Doris and Macho hanging in their own ceilings a thousand feet above him. It was this copy signal, and now Morgan's report of Apollo's seemingly suicidal curiosity, that Doris had interpreted for Acreman.

Doris had no way of telling Apollo what to do now. They would all come up when they needed to breathe and, in Apollo's case, that could be up to ten minutes later.

With traditional caution, the young Megalodon made a close observational pass.

His mouth flashed open and he sped past the whale, no more than a hundred feet away.

He was faster than Apollo, but the cetacean could manoeuvre better.

The whale moved. As the Megalodon passed, Apollo's powerful horizontally-working tail flicked and he turned in on the Megalodon, disturbing his pass. The Megalodon could have attacked but that was not in his mind. His tail flicked vertically and he rolled off-balance for a few seconds, slowed and then turned.

Apollo faced the shark, presenting the Megalodon with the smallest possible target. The huge jaws opened again and the Megalodon set himself an angled attack course, swimming up and over the whale to bring his teeth to bear in a raking slash across the widest part of Apollo's body.

But the whale, intrigued, worked its flippers rapidly, flagged his tail up and down and shot across the rear of the shark so that the attacking animal lost sight of him.

Doris and Macho, familiar with the sounds Apollo made, picked up a faint pulse of amusement.

The Megalodon turned again, furious, towards the target. This time, he had the ceiling and he swept down on Apollo in a long dive that allowed him to sense the whale no matter which way it moved. He opened his glistening jaws again and inclined his head in preparation for the ripping bite that must follow.

The whale realized quickly that it had made a bad mistake allowing the shark to get above it. It jerked left and right and dived but it could feel the gathering vibrations as the shark stayed on its tail and the distance between them closed.

Apollo was beginning to feel the effect of air shortage. He used the only facility the shark did not possess. Standing on his tail, he flexed a reverse thrust, slid onto his back and dived at the approaching shark, backwards, from below

The impact was heard clearly over the *Poseidon*'s hydrophone. It sounded like a loud underwater explosion.

And Apollo was lucky. At almost twenty-five knots, his solid bony melon struck the belly of the Megalodon directly between its lower fins. It was one of the few places on the shark where the animal was not thickly accreted with an armour-plating layer of molluscs and other ragged calcifications that would have ripped the skin off Apollo's head.

The Megalodon had never suffered an attack before! The pain suffused his simple brain and he spun sideways, totally out of control. His free-floating stomach ballooned from his mouth like a pink parachute, as though it was exploding. In fact, he had suffered no real injury and he regorged the blood-suffused skin and tried to reorientate himself. The battle had lifted him closer to the surface and he became aware of pain behind his eyes. He could also no longer find the fast-moving target. There was still the acid trickle of sensation in his pits and he knew that the larger target was there, but that the subject of his attack had gone.

Confused, unable to accept the light-pain any longer, he sank into the depths to join his parents who were still quartering the lower reaches of the Fracture, unwilling to rise into the light zone until the target came closer.

Acreman, kept posted throughout the battle by the dolphins and Morgan, raced up the stairs to the deck, in time to see Apollo surface with enough speed to lift three-quarters of his huge body out of the water. He was preceded by the other three, leaping jubilantly.

It was a few moments before Acreman became aware of Harry's hunched figure standing a few feet away against the rails.

'Harry! Where the hell have you been? We've found them. They're down there. Several of them. Apollo had a go at the smallest one. But, Harry, we have to put a stop to it! Can't you do anything?'

'What would you suggest, dear boy?'

'Oh, come on, Harry. We have to try and conserve them. Surely, you can make an official protest or something?'

Harry stared at the sea. 'I think it is now up to them, Frank.'

Suskin watched the young Megalodon dive back into the Fracture, or more accurately, into the swirling fog that filled the bottom two-thirds of his screen. He had seen the battle as a blurred phasing of little white dots, the two animals manoeuvring too quickly for the equipment. He had heard the impact clearly over the radio from the *Poseidon*. Now he called the sub.

'Control. Did any of that lot affect you?'

'*Poseidon*. We suffered some buffeting but nothing serious. We have no casualties. What happens now?'

'Control. *Poseidon*—wait.' He turned to Whitting who, with the two civilian aides, had come down to the communications room when news of the battle reached them.

'Abort, sir?'

'Wait, Mr. Suskin. Gentlemen?'

'The whale would appear to have successfully deflected the attack,' Lawlock said. 'We might just go on.'

'Give it one more try if the skipper's willing,' Whitting nodded. 'He still has his entire armament intact.'

Suskin was appalled. 'You can't be serious!'

'Put Lewis on,' Whitting said tersely. 'It's his decision in the final analysis.'

'*Poseidon*, this is Admiral Whitting. You are very near your station and your scout appears to have successfully deterred the alien animal. Do you have any basis not to continue?'

'Control, Captain Lewis. Where is that beast?'

'Returned to the bottom, Skipper.'

'Alive or dead?'

'We think injured.'

'We have no confirmation of that,' Suskin cried vehemently.

'Control. We'll talk it over here.'

'What do we do?' Lewis asked his first officer. 'I'm a submariner, not a zoo keeper.'

'We've proved that this animal can be stopped, sir. And we've eliminated other possibilities, like rock-falls.'

'You want to go on?'

'We're in pretty good shape, Skipper.'

'You do realize how big that thing is?'

'Well ... yes. Frankly, I haven't got my imagination to accept it yet.'

'Neither had I. Not until I heard that thump.'

They lapsed into silence. Lewis found it difficult weighing the odds. He found it very hard to accept that an animal, even a monstrous shark, could wreck the *Poseidon*. And yet it had taken out the *Jules Verne* without difficulty.

'What about the *Jules Verne?*'

'They had no idea what they were up against. I understand they were not armed. We are.'

Lewis nodded and picked up the microphone.

'*Poseidon* to Control. We think we're in shape to have another go. Is the whale still with us?'

Acreman, with Harry in tow, had returned to the communications room in time to hear this announcement.

'No,' he said. 'He's exhausted and has some lacerations. I

very much doubt he could be induced to go down there again.'

Suskin spoke into his microphone.

'The whale's out, *Poseidon*. You'll be on your own.'

'Okay. Here's what we do. We have one more go. I'm going down slower than you've ever seen. I don't want that thing to even notice I'm moving. But, if it shows again, or that milk storm down there gets any worse, we come up. Is that understood?'

Whitting nodded to Suskin.

'We understand, *Poseidon*,' Suskin said reluctantly. Acreman stepped forward to the Janus microphone.

'Doris, Macho, Morgan. The submarine is trying another dive. Will you monitor?'

'Yes, Acreman. What about Apollo?'

'Let him do whatever he wants.'

'He's going to dive again.'

'What?'

'If the sub dives, he will go down. He's intrigued by it.'

'Isn't he afraid of the shark?'

'You are using that word again, Acreman.'

Acreman stepped back and shook his head.

'I don't believe this.' He turned to Suskin. 'You had better tell them they still have their scout.'

The message was passed.

'*Poseidon* to Control. Commencing to dive. Rest the scout for a while if you like. Our ETA is four hours.'

Like any child frightened by a new and unknown experience, the young male sought his parents' company when he returned to the depths. He had suffered no real injury but his simple mind was awash with confusion. No food target had ever attempted to evade him before and none had caused him injury. More confusing still, none had engaged in these strange activities and then vanished.

In place of the nagging ache of hunger, the young male now suffered the real pain of internal bruising, and he swam swiftly, circling his parents in a series of sweeps that caused the sand cloud to lift and become totally opaque.

Blood oozed from the young male's tight-clamped mouth as he made a pass close to his father.

The effect of this minute quantity of food plasma on the

adult male was immediate and electrifying. It spun its entire two-hundred-foot body in a tight arc and made for the blood. To the source of that blood it was totally indifferent. To the Megalodons, as with all their kind, there were two simple kinds of food target: objects of a suitable size for their jaws and objects spilling blood. Had the blood spilled from the rock, the Megalodon would still have attacked it with unthinking ferocity.

Some essential nerve endings in the young male's reeling brain worked instinctively as the adult Megalodon commenced its attack. Quicker, infinitely more agile than its one-hundred-year-old parents, the young male turned at the last moment and the power thrust of his father missed by inches. Unable to turn in time, the adult Megalodon collided with the face, bringing down a forty-foot section of the gold-streaked quartz across his broad back. For a brief moment, a moment long enough for the young male to swim several hundred yards, the adult male was trapped. But three mighty sweeps of his enormous tail produced momentum enough for him to roll free. He rose listlessly. The event had wiped his mind clear of the blood memory. The young male was now swimming at a careful distance and the few ruptured blood vessels in his stomach wall had already been healed by the salt water in his system.

All three animals continued their restless circling, aware that this day was one of new events, aware of hunger, aware of the need to strike. Only the young male was particularly interested in the target that was again entering their horizon and he could still feel the pain of the attack. But that pain was ebbing slowly and, with his limited memory, the young male would soon cease to be aware that it had ever happened.

Markov ordered all engines to stop when the ship's forward hydrophone picked up the noise of the landslide, or as the listening crew interpreted it, the underwater explosion.

'A depth charge?' Markov queried of Litkin. 'The noise went on longer than from a depth charge, at least from any I have ever heard.'

'What, then?'

'I think something more natural, Captain. Perhaps the Americans are firing charges as part of their mining.'

Markov went to the chart table and stared at it long and carefully. He knew exactly where he was, but needed to hide the fact that he was no longer sure what he should do next. He carefully considered the capabilities of his ship.

The *Red Ensign* was capable of diving very deep. Her designers had recognized that American submarine detection equipment was considerably in advance of anything Soviet scientists had developed, as indeed was true of their space programme. They had therefore come to the simple but effective expedient of building the Delta-class vessels twice as strong as the Americans specified for their submarines of similar firepower. If the Deltas could not avoid the American submarine spy satellites and the sophisticated electronics aboard their destroyers, they could at least descend to depths where no American torpedo could reach them. The deep diving capability also gave her considerable immunity against depth charges. No such charge could be accurately dropped on a vessel fifteen thousand feet down.

And so Markov had been pleased when he discovered that his target was in a deep ocean trench, whereas his counterpart aboard the *Poseidon* had viewed the prospect with considerable caution.

When the *Red Ensign*'s forward hydrophones picked up the noises of the rock-fall, she was at her maximum depth, moving slowly up the Fracture on her secondary electric engines, virtually invisible to American surface surveillance.

But she was also vulnerable.

She could hide in the deep depths, but she could not fight in them. All her missile systems, including ship-to-air and ship-to-shore defence missiles, could not be fired until she was much closer to the surface.

Markov decided that this should not concern him. He was there to watch and wait. His orders had contained no details, simply that he should proceed at high speed to the target bearing and there report on what the Americans were doing. His missiles were armed, but that was standard procedure. He considered it the most remote of possibilities that he would be called upon to use them.

'Slow ahead forward. Complete crew silence. Full radio silence,' he ordered.

Two wide valleys of submerged rock separated the *Red*

Ensign from the slowly circling Megalodon pack. They were swimming at a depth of roughly nine thousand feet.

The *Red Ensign* was moving directly into their mouths.

Suskin saw the increased activity on the bottom and reported urgently to the *Poseidon*. But by now everyone involved in the operation had blunted nerves, and white clouds on sonar screens gave no new information nor did they change any of the imperatives.

'Let me know if anything new happens,' Lewis had answered sternly. 'Otherwise, I'm taking every precaution open to me.'

Privately, Lewis was coming to the conclusion that they might be facing a combination of problems. His expert sonar consultant, Simpson, had reported definitely that this latest bang was a rock slide. Lewis did not know what the giant shark was up to down there, but he was reasonably convinced that the *Poseidon*'s creeping descent could not be disturbing it. Maybe there was some seismic activity on the bottom, as well as the Megalodon. If it was a shark, it wouldn't like its home being disturbed by heaving rocks. Lewis kept his ship moving and prayed that the other activity, whatever it was, would keep the Megalodon busy.

'Skipper?'

Lewis turned to see Simpson waving to him.

He walked the few paces to the *Poseidon*'s sonar screens.

'I thought I'd use the time to have a little look around,' Simpson said. 'We've had all our screens set forward since that last attack warning. I've just taken a glance aft. What do you make of that?'

'You'd better tell me, Mr. Simpson. We've got so many foreign bodies down in this hole that I wouldn't bet on anything.'

The blip was quite small, but it had a definite elongated shape. They were not getting a continuous image: the blip was constantly interrupted by the blanking effect of the Fracture walls.

'Could it be the whale?'

'No, it's out front.'

'The shark, then?'

'Well, Skipper, I've been assuming that's down below.'

'Another one!' Lewis said unhappily. 'That guy who runs the

Cetacean Search Unit said something about there being more than one.'

Simpson made no immediate response. He reached up to a shelf of red-covered books and started thumbing through them. Simpson shook his head.

'What is it?' Lewis demanded.

'I don't know, or let's say I'm getting confused. But if I was projecting images for identification to my class back home, I'd flunk anyone who didn't recognize that as a Russian Delta.'

'Coming for us!'

'And exactly as they do it, given their deep diving capability,' Simpson said.

'Sweet Jesus,' Lewis said, 'that's all I need.'

'Maybe I'm wrong, Skipper. We don't know what a Megalodon looks like, anyway.'

'That's a hell of a choice,' Lewis grunted reaching for a microphone. 'A Russian nuke sub or a second Megalodon.'

Harry was slumped next to Acreman in the communications room of the *Eros* when Lewis reported his suspicions about the new blip on his screens. All morning he had been trying to work out ways of getting off the ship. The news of the Russian submarine snapped him back to instant alertness. Acreman saw the effect of the news on his boss and wondered what was going on.

But he had a much more immediate priority.

Suskin was resetting his own sonar projectors and calling to the hydrophone crew to refocus aft. They waited.

Maxwell was working at his computer, feeding in the new readings. He looked startled and shouted to Suskin.

'Confirmation, Commander—it is a Delta!'

'What the hell are they doing here?' Suskin said. He turned to the Marine messenger and ordered him to call Whitting.

Acreman stood up.

'We must warn them,' he said urgently. 'They're coming up the Fracture right under the Megalodons.'

Suskin shook his head.

'There's not a damned thing we can do. We don't know their radio frequencies and, even if we did, there's nothing that can send a radio signal down that deep. That's why they go down there.'

'There must be some way.'

'You want to try a note in a bottle?' Suskin suggested sarcastically. 'They'll know what they're in for soon enough. It might even sort out our other problems.'

Acreman turned desperately to Harry. To his complete surprise, Harry, who for the whole of that morning had been sloping around like a corpse, was upright in his chair, smiling, alert.

'For God's sake, Harry. I won't have my animals in the middle of a nuclear confrontation. Surely, you can get that through to these idiots. This whole project's dissolving into a farce.'

Harry nodded, grinning. 'I agree, dear boy.'

'Then do something.'

'No, Frank.' Harry said. 'Don't tempt fate!'

Whitting hurried into the communications room.

'Clear this room,' he called to the Marine captain guarding the door. 'I want a clear line to Washington. Nobody stays who isn't required to man the equipment.'

'Delighted,' said Harry. 'Come on, Frank.'

Outside, Acreman took Harry by the arm.

'I don't know what you're up to this time, Harry. But for pity's sake, get a warning to those people. They have less than half an hour before they hit the Megalodons.'

'You heard what the man said,' Harry replied urbanely. 'They're too deep. Games of war, and all that.'

'You make it sound as though it serves them right.'

'Is that how it sounds? I'm rather hoping it will serve us ... *right*. If they don't get the *Poseidon* up now, they need their heads examined.'

The radio-telephone on Hope Ward's golf cart bleeped halfway through the swing of his wedge shot to the 18th green. Leaving the iron impaled in a not inconsiderable sand dune, the general returned reluctantly to the cart and bellowed: 'Hope Ward. This had better be real important!'

A minute or so later, he called to his partner.

'I'm out, Mike. Could you call the club and get my aide out here on the double?' He set the cart in motion in the direction of the clubhouse, where he was met by Lockwood, a Marine captain who had come directly from the Pentagon. The went into conference in the Francis Drake Lounge. The mural on one wall was an impression of the last fight of the *Revenge*, an energetic maelstrom of stormy seas and fiery cannonballs. Hope Ward looked at it and winced.

'It's out,' he grunted. 'Whitting just called from the Zone and is wetting himself. It's all happening at once. They've stirred up those big sharks the prof was bleating about and that heat trace we got a week or so back from observer nine *was* heading for the *Eros*. It's a Delta.'

'Probably the *Red Ensign*,' the Marine captain said soberly. 'Big vessel, with lots of muscle.'

'Whitting wants to call it off. For the time being, anyway.'

'The Committee would find that very unacceptable, sir. The President's standing with Congress is waning daily and, if we don't get that bill through in the very near future, he just may not be able to command the votes.'

'I know that, damn it!'

'With respect, sir, Admiral Whitting's forte is administration.'

'You mean he has never been under fire?'

'Well, yes.'

'You suggesting he's cracked up?'

'Were you able to establish the exact status of things? Has the *Poseidon* been attacked? I'd be very surprised if that Russian captain pushed too close. The fact he's there at all must indicate they know we have a counter.'

'Nothing's happened yet,' said Hope Ward. 'Well, it hadn't five minutes ago. But the way Whitting was talking, all hell was about to break loose.'

'As I've said, sir, Admiral Whitting is essentially an administrator. Reviewing our status totally objectively, it seems our priority is to protect the secrecy of the project.'

'Enlarge on that.'

'The Russian submarine cannot take offence or gather any relevant information from a single U. S. craft manoeuvring in international waters.'

'They could well smell a rat if they find she's working with massive surface support.'

'I agree. If anything has to be moved, it is the *Eros*. Her presence is contradictory. Now, the shark problem. Do I understand that, although these beasts have been disturbed, they have not actually attacked our sub?'

'I reckon not. Whitting would have said if they had.'

'Well, sir, surely that is positive information. An attack by those sharks has always been a presumption. Isn't the fact that there has been no attack, even though they have been disturbed, an indication that they might not attack?'

'You know I don't rate the shark problem that high, anyway,' said Hope Ward. 'The *Poseidon* is armed.'

'We must, of course, avoid any use of that armament,' Lockwood warned. 'That could cause a confrontation with the *Red Ensign*.'

'So your suggestion is we move the *Eros* and let the *Poseidon* go about her business.'

'If she can. If not, she can return to Pearl until our visitors have lost interest and then take up her station again. We might lose a few days at most.'

Hope Ward ruminated for a while.

'Whitting gabbled something about them getting a measurement on one of the sharks. The line wasn't that good on the cart, but I think he said two hundred feet. Is that possible?'

'Of course not.' Lockwood frowned. 'Whoever heard of a thing like that? And if we have to tell the Committee we've pulled out for a shark, no matter how big, I'd just as soon not attend that session.'

'Me neither. Get me Whitting.'

Anyone of authority aboard the *Eros* had now returned to the communications room. There was an instinctive awareness in these men that things were coming to crisis point, even among those who knew very little. They gathered closest to the source of the information.

Harry Asquith was among them. He sat in a corner, attempting invisibility. He was probably the only one there who was looking forward to Whitting's announcement. Harry had played a great deal of cards in his youth and fancied he had applied his skills to the game of life. But this was the first time he had seen five aces all turn up at once.

Whitting had called this emergency briefing over the intercom and it took time for the various heads of sections to assemble. Watching them gather, observing the various stages of nervous reaction that were being displayed according to how much they knew, Harry also thought that perhaps he was

214

less of a coward than he had always considered himself to be.

With a choice of a Megalodon attack, an undersea conflict between two of the most lethal machines ever fabricated by the insane side of human ingenuity, and even the chance that the Russian submarine might use one of its missiles to remove the *Eros*, he, Harry Asquith, a practising sidestepper on all matters hazardous, was feeling more contented than he had in weeks.

Whitting tappped the metal top of the plot table with a steel ruler.

'Everyone here is, I think, aware of recent developments. We are now at a Status Red alert, I have no need to outline what that involves, security-wise.

'There have been discussions at the highest level about our continuation and I'm pleased to be able to tell you a positive approach has been decided on.'

Harry sat up and for the first time started to listen. This could mean one of two things. Either he had won or, alternatively, he was about to witness a manifestation of group madness. To Harry's absolute horror, Whitting quickly confirmed the latter.

' ... and so Captain Lewis has been instructed to increase the rate of his dive, while this ship makes ready for sea. In summary, gentlemen, it's all or nothing.'

There was a hubbub of reaction from all corners of the room. Both Suskin and Acreman were on their feet, shouting questions.

'That takes no account of the Russian submarine,' Suskin insisted. 'Are you suggesting they won't spot the *Poseidon*? Do you think they're here by accident? We must assume they've got word of the Project—that surely could result in an attack on the *Poseidon*.'

Acreman spoke before Whitting had a chance to answer.

'This course of action must be reversed,' he said icily. 'You seem to have forgotten one thing. We have a large whale in our charge. The dolphins and the orca we can bring aboard, but not the whale. I insist that the animal be returned to its natural habitat and that's going to take considerable time.'

Harry looked at both of them and they knew they were wasting their time.

Whitting confirmed his fears.

'Dr. Acreman, under normal circumstances an animal that

had exceeded its usefulness would be dealt with summarily. You have a much easier option. When the *Eros* sails, let your whale go. Now, gentlemen, we must give all our attention to the *Poseidon*.'

Acreman was about to protest further, but Harry waved him out.

'Harry, this is unbelievable!' Acreman said. 'What chance will Apollo have, alone, this far south?'

'Slightly better than ours, Frank.'

'But they don't realize they've lost out. There's simply no point to any of this.'

Harry smiled sourly. 'You're becoming a good zoologist, Frank. Be objective. It would make an interesting paper on ape behaviour.'

'What would?'

'The big sharks eating the little sharks.'

'Oh, come on, Harry. Your feeling self-righteous isn't going to help us out of this one. We have to try and warn those people in the submarines!'

'Do you mean the Russians?' Harry said scornfully. 'Those Commies? The Red Peril? Just remember, you're under U.S. Navy discipline here, my boy. God help us all. In any case,' he added, studying Acreman's face and discovering, somewhat to his surprise, that the anguish was genuine, 'I don't think it's possible. You heard what Suskin said about reaching them, and he's a signals expert.'

Acreman took Harry by the shoulder and started to haul him in the direction of the communications room. 'I just don't believe that, Harry. They can't go down there in those things and lose total contact with the rest of the world.'

'All right,' Harry said, shrugging free. 'I'll come quietly. But you'd do well to learn that we are not members of a rational race.'

A strange silence prevailed in the communications room. Suskin and his technicians were all there, but no one spoke. In fact, when Acreman and Harry burst in, heads turned but there were no greetings.

'What is this, a wake?' Harry demanded.

Suskin winced and waved at his main sonar repeater.

'Give or take fifteen minutes,' he said holding a long pointer towards a sausage-shaped blip on the bottom left-hand side of the circular screen. 'That's the Russian Delta coming on, inexorably, as they say.'

'What about *Poseidon*?'

'Holding her station,' said Suskin glumly. 'Until this is ... over.'

'With warheads primed, no doubt,' Harry said.

Suskin looked up at him sharply. 'You never know what the Russians might do when the Megalodons spot them.'

'They're not going to do anything,' Acreman said harshly. 'They're just going to die!'

Harry spoke softly, 'My young friend here doesn't believe you couldn't reach them with all this sophisticated equipment.'

Suskin looked at Acreman without blinking. 'This close to a U.S. military installation, which is now what we are so far as they are concerned, every signal they get will be scrambled, and in code, via their own satellites. They operate like that—as we do—so that they can't be talked out of winning the next world war by us. Now it's just possible, if you get on to the President of the United States, that he might agree to ring up their Big Cheese and advise them that one of their nuke subs is about to be eaten by a shark. But I think you might just be wasting your time. I think it could take longer than you've got.'

'But try!' Acreman roared. 'Goddamn it, you have to try. Even if they ignore it. Hell, if I could think of a way of getting one of my animals to swim over there with a message, I'd try. But they don't have Janus equipment and ... '

'And you've now got about eight minutes,' said Suskin, standing up abruptly. 'On the other hand, you're right, although it'll probably cost me my pension.' He spoke into a microphone. 'Cy, this is Eugene. I'd like your opinion on something unofficial.'

'Go ahead, Eugene,' Captain Lewis replied.

'Cy, I'm swimming well out of my depth now and my only excuse is that things are a little confused up here at the moment. Also, I want you to know that this is totally my initiative and mine alone ... '

'Get to the point, Eugene, or do you just want me to loan you some money?'

'There's a group of us here thinks it might be friendly to tip that Delta about what's up ahead.'

There was a long pause.

'Eugene, it might also make good sense. We've been sitting here debating what could happen to us if there's any messy shooting. And if I was in command of that ship, I'd start shooting the moment one of those things came at me. Problem is, Eugene, they won't hear plain speech. But I presume you've worked that one out already.'

'Right. I'm wondering, what would happen if you put out a straightforward SOS, Cy?'

'Brilliant!' Harry said. 'Congratulations, Commander.'

'Eugene, I think we'd both get court martialed.'

'You can bet on it, Cy.'

There was a pause of no more than a few seconds. Then the staccato pulsing of the international distress signal was heard through the speakers linked to the *Poseidon*.

Suskin leaned back in his chair.

'Now all that Russian captain has to do is to put his own job on the line,' said Suskin wearily. 'What a crazy fucking world.'

'Never mind,' Acreman said jubilantly. 'You tried. We're not at war. They must respond to a SOS and then ... '

He never completed the sentence. He and some fifty crewmen were thrown about the ship like rag dolls, when a torpedo armed with a conventional warhead exploded less than two hundred feet below the *Eros*' keel.

It must be said in its defence that the young male was now insane.

Dazed from the whale attack, he had settled briefly to the bottom and was then required to survive a genuine killer attack by his father. Lifting out of range, he swam too high and was further stunned by light-pain. And, all the time, he continued to search desperately for something to assuage the raging hunger that was now all-consuming. Alone, these imperatives would have pushed the young male's tiny brain to the edge of its limited rationality.

When, through this storm of pain, need and confusion, his sensing pits abruptly presented it with *three* huge food targets—the *Poseidon*, the *Red Ensign* and the deep-diving Apollo—the young male went berserk.

A thing of gross instinct, he projected his one-hundred-and-fifty-ton mass through the dark sea at thirty knots towards the nearest of those targets, the *Red Ensign*.

The Russian submarine had just circumnavigated the last of the tall rock bluffs between itself and the circling Megalodon pack, and was so placed the young male simply had to dive down on it; a manoeuvre which greatly increased its speed and the impact of its huge teeth. It did not bother with an investigatory pass.

Aboard the *Red Ensign*, the speeding shape of the Megalodon swamped their sonar screens just minutes before the attack was joined. Captain Markov had believed that he was ready for anything; his crew were at their battle stations and his armament was primed. All the sonar screens were focused forward, as were her hydrophones and a pair of extreme low-light TV cameras.

Markov thus became the first human being to see a live Megalodon and he was a man of sufficient nerve to look at the great shark right through its final attack. Rigid with shock, he saw the distinctive shape of a fin and recognized it, even though it was so grossly enlarged. And through the weed coat now flattened by the Megalodon's swift approach, he saw the flashing tail as large as a ship's sail. He saw the tremendous open tooth-lined mouth and he had almost thirty seconds to wonder how such extraordinary weapons could have evolved in a beast of nature.

'Fire one and two,' he said flatly to the stunned crew on the bridge. He even saw the first torpedo strike home and explode.

But then he and every man aboard the *Red Ensign* were engulfed in a bright sea of red blood to which their own was soon added. The enraged Megalodon, with the top half of his head blown away, struck through twelve feet of the bow of the *Red Ensign*, unleashing knife-sharp jets of water, pressurised four tons to the square inch, on the bodies of the crew.

The second torpedo missed completely. It sped on for nearly half a mile until its homing computer acknowledged the miss and it self-destructed, two hundred feet beneath the vulnerable bow of the *Eros*.

There was no one left alive aboard the *Red Ensign* to hear that explosion, any more than they had been able to respond to the SOS signal that immediately preceded it.

Acreman pulled himself and Harry to their feet. He raced for the steps leading up to the deck as the communications room began to fill with noises that had last been heard on earth before the Ice Age. Holding to the deck rails, they looked out on a scene that was like nothing any man had ever seen before.

There was no longer any sea; instead a curdling lake of bright crimson. As they stared, the lake deepened its colour and strange currents churned the surface, as though a giant hand was at work beneath the waves.

Abruptly, the waters parted and a grotesque object, whistling and screaming in obvious agony, rose towards them.

At first sight, it was a nightmare of butchery; thirty feet of raw flesh from which the huge disc of an eyeball hung on a thick, twitching cord across an open, dripping maw lined by foot-long, blood-caked teeth.

The two stunned humans shrank back from the deck rail as this obscene parody of nature rose even higher towards them. A giant black-grey dorsal cleared the crimson waves. Almost at eye level they saw what looked like an island of shell-fish coral, fringed with long slivers of weed ending in a vast but distinctively triangular tail. They watched the tail lash fitfully at the red sea, a dying thing still working to the reflexes of its former life. And then, slowly, it subsided. The shattered head turned. The undamaged part, with the fixed white eye, presented itself to the two watchers, and the mouth opened, oozed redly and seemed to smile at them. A hose-spray of blood from a severed artery in the vast head painted the side of the ship, and the two watchers, with a flood of viscous, foul-smelling plasma.

Acreman fought for control of his heaving stomach, lost it and vomited green into the red sea.

Aboard the *Poseidon,* the explosion of both *Red Ensign* torpedoes was picked up instantly by sensitive hydrophones engineered for that purpose alone.

'Now hear this,' Lewis roared into his command microphone. 'We are not under attack. I say again, we are not being attacked. Now, all hands go to your stations and prepare for emergency ascent. Torpedo room, arm one through five and stand by. You will act only on my personal command.' He spun to address his weapons systems officer. 'Get down there, Mr. Gray. I don't want any mistakes, not a one!'

'Number One, stand by to take her up. Let the log show this mission is terminated, by order of the captain. Blow all main and trim tanks ... planes to hard arise.'

'All tanks blown, sir,' Martin repeated, his eyes on his flooding and pumping gauges, flow meters and ballast tank readings. 'Fore and aft planes to hard arise.'

Simpson called sharply. *'Contact.* Range three thousand yards. *No engine. No sound signature!'*

Lewis, watching his rate of rise meters, answered Simpson without turning.

'Heading our way?'

Simpson held up his hand.

'Second contact ... AND ANOTHER ... range two thousand yards. No sound signature. No engine. Speed ... approximately thirty knots, heading one-seventy-five ... We're running straight for them, sir!'

'Helm to hard aport. Mr. Simpson ... report.'

'Range now three thousand yards and passing.'

'Steady as she goes ... where's the rock face?'

'Well clear.'

'Tell me when I have open water, mister.'

'You have it now. Contacts receding ... the two large ones appear to be attacking the smaller. Range now four thousand yards!'

'Let's get the hell out of here!' Lewis said. 'Engines full ahead, both.'

There is no loyalty or family love in the life of the shark, be it very small or very large. The adult pair had followed the young male, reading the same signals, ready to make their own attack runs now they had a target at their own level. They watched the young male attack and then their thinking minds dissolved. They sensed and smelled the abundance of blood from the injured young male and the plasma spilling from the destroyed target. Cutting like huge knives through this sublime redness, they drank, tasted, bit in a paroxysm of mindless elation that desiccated the *Red Ensign* and the freed bodies of its crew that were large enough to eat.

Then, turning, they followed at speed the blood slick as the dying young male, no longer concerned with light-pain, shot up into the hurtful sky.

But even their feeding frenzy could not overcome their conditioning against the light. They waited.

Eventually, however, the body of the young one, deliciously open, perfectly defenceless, came down to them and they went about its destruction with great energy and commitment until the severed pieces floated up out of their reach.

Hanging over the rail, wracked with nausea, Acreman watched the sea below him boil, this time with immense power and energy. A great whirlpool formed round the *Eros*, with currents so strong she began slowly to twist on her immense anchor cables. The blood of the dying Megalodon appeared to be sucked into this vortex, causing pink surface ripples and wavelets like the spume from a lung wound.

From the sea beneath there came a series of high whistles and screams and the distinct sounds of tearing. And then the sea itself vomited.

Sections of twisted metal, imploded human body fragments and great bleeding pieces of the young Megalodon lifted through the eye of the watery cone to swirl lazily in the red water.

'Feeding frenzy,' Harry shouted. 'Don't look, Frank. Don't look any more!'

Acreman, ochre-red from head to toe, the drying blood caking his eyes and nostrils, fought against hysteria. Harry grabbed him, swung him away from the red maelstrom and pushed him through a doorway. They started to stumble down a flight of stairs.

All over the ship, sirens were screaming and urgent orders spilling from the public address system. Harry heard Whitting's voice command the ship to hear him and he caught Acreman by the shoulders and held him still.

'Now hear this, all crew! This mission is aborted. I say again, aborted. All submarine support personnel will go immediately to their stations and implement emergency surfacing drills. Medical and surgical, prepare for possible rapid-ascent casualties in one hour. Yellow Watch, stand by to move the ship. Section heads, go to the bridge for briefing in fifteen minutes.'

'Come on, Frank,' Harry said gleefully. 'Let's get you cleaned up.'

Coming up the steps, Barbara found them. She took hold of Acreman and held him to her, moistening her fingers with saliva to clear the caked blood from his eyes. When he had stopped shaking, she stood back and addressed him urgently.

'Frank! Listen to me. You must come below. We have trouble with the dolphins!'

Remembrance of his charges struck through the haze that was blurring Acreman's brain—a veil of hatred of all human predators, a primal fear of all animal predators, a deep, sickening disgust of a species conflict as old and as essential as time itself.

'Take me down,' he said. 'I can't see very well.' He turned appealingly to Harry. The older man simply nodded.

'You'll be all right, Frank. Just follow Barbara.'

In their control room, words were spilling from the Janus speakers in a babble of incoherence. Louise, white and scared, was pleading into the microphone.

'Please, please don't all speak at once ... somebody just tell me whether any of you are hurt. We can't help unless you do.'

Acreman stood still, shook his head several times and took the microphone from her hand.

'Acreman,' he croaked. 'Doris. I want Doris to speak. No one else.'

Thinly, but clearly, the response came.

'Yes, Acreman?'

'Doris. Are any of you hurt?' He cast a glance at Dave Spurling, who was fiddling with the Janus controls. 'Get me more volume. They sound miles away.'

'You've got it,' Dave grunted. 'They *are* miles away.'

Then the Janus responded again.

'None of us are hurt in our bodies, Acreman.'

'Then where are you, Doris? What's going on?'

'Acreman, we are taking Apollo home.'

'Doris,' Acreman cried, 'that's not a good idea. He may survive. You won't. It's many, many miles!'

'Perhaps, Acreman. But we will see him most of the way and Morgan the rest. Apollo is too young to survive loneliness.'

'But do you two really have to go? Couldn't Morgan do it alone?'

There was a long pause.

'We have no wish to stay, Acreman. Have you seen the sea?'

Acreman slumped into a chair.

'If we waited, Doris,' he said brokenly, 'could you find your way back?'

'Yes, Acreman. But don't wait.'

In the silence that descended on the room, he heard Louise sobbing. A few moments later, a hand touched his shoulder and he turned to find Harry standing close behind, looking sober and in control.

'They'll be back, Frank. Or others of their kind. It has to be, now it's started. When you get to my age, you'll learn to recognize the inevitable. Take the Megalodons—those that are left will stay alive now.'

'Will they?' said Acreman bitterly. 'How?'

'They have to explain what happened to the Russian submarine. It is the Megalodons or World War Three. Take the word of an old campaigner. They'll be back.'